# The Fishermen and the Dragon

# The
# *Fishermen*
## and the
# *Dragon*

FEAR, GREED, AND
A FIGHT FOR JUSTICE
ON THE GULF COAST

## Kirk Wallace Johnson

VIKING

VIKING
An imprint of Penguin Random House LLC
penguinrandomhouse.com

Photo credits may be found on page 319.

LIBRARY OF CONGRESS CATALOGING-IN-PUBLICATION DATA
Names: Johnson, Kirk W., author.
Title: The fishermen and the dragon : fear, greed, and a fight
for justice on the gulf coast / Kirk Wallace Johnson.
Description: [New York] : Viking, [2022] | Includes bibliographical references and index.
Identifiers: LCCN 2021060150 (print) | LCCN 2021060151 (ebook) |
ISBN 9781984880123 (hardcover) | ISBN 9781984880130 (ebook)
Subjects: LCSH: Ku Klux Klan (1915– )—Texas—History—20th century. |
Refugees—Texas—Social conditions—20th century. | Vietnamese—Crimes against—
Texas—History—20th century. | Fisheries—Texas—History—20th century.
Classification: LCC HS2330.K63 J63 2022 (print) | LCC HS2330.K63 (ebook) |
DDC 322.4/209764—dc23/eng/20220105
LC record available at https://lccn.loc.gov/2021060150
LC ebook record available at https://lccn.loc.gov/2021060151

Printed in the United States of America
1st Printing

Book design by Daniel Lagin

*For Marie-Josée,*

*August,*

*and Isidora*

# Contents

## ACT III: 90 DAYS

## ACT IV: POISONED WATER

# Author's Note

THIS IS A BOOK ABOUT A RACIST BACKLASH AGAINST REFUGEES fleeing a ruinous war. As you can imagine, the Ku Klux Klan and their allies used racist and vile language in the pursuit of their goal to drive newly resettled Vietnamese refugees out of the fishing industry along the Gulf Coast.

Precision and truth are the lodestars of any nonfiction author, but, sensitive to the toxic legacy of this language, I have no interest in tearing at old wounds or inflicting fresh ones. In presenting this account, I wrestled with how to treat the incendiary words that appeared routinely in documentary footage, print coverage, and my own interviews with many of the individuals behind this campaign. I have subjected each instance in the book to a test of essentiality ("Why is this important to include?"), in the belief that you don't need to be subjected to the fortieth time the Grand Dragon of the Klan or his supporters used the N-word or G-word.

At the same time, I didn't feel morally correct cleaning up their language in order to avoid troubling my readers, for two reasons. First, the Vietnamese on the receiving end of these epithets enjoyed no such luxury. Second, this is a book about racism and the Klan; it struck me as impossible to write in a way that doesn't trouble. Deleting language from the past doesn't undo the hideousness of what those deploying it sought to achieve. Accordingly, the only instances of these slurs appear in direct quotations.

The house style of Penguin Random House is to capitalize the *B* in Black when referring to a person. I have similarly capitalized the *W* in White, persuaded by professor Kwame Anthony Appiah's argument in favor of it in an essay for *The Atlantic*. I have not altered these descriptors when using quotations from contemporaneous accounts.

Along the Texas Gulf Coast, White interviewees routinely used the word "Anglo" to refer to a White person and "Mexican" to refer to someone of Latin American descent, even if they were longtime American citizens (or their ancestors lived there prior to Texas becoming a republic or its annexation as a state). First-generation Vietnamese interviewees regularly used the word "American" to refer to a White person. For reasons of clarity and consistency, I have opted not to use such terminology.

After discussing it with author and professor Viet Thanh Nguyen, I have also eschewed the term "boat people"—used for a generation to describe the mass exodus of Vietnamese refugees in the mid-to-late 1970s—for the principal reason that it reduces them to their experience as victims, stripping them of personal agency. To Nguyen, the term is "objectifying and dehumanizing, and masked by pity . . . people without control over their own stories."

In a similar vein, I have minimized use of the term "refugee," especially after the Vietnamese arrived in the United States. These were men, women, children, fathers, mothers, siblings, and grandparents who heroically stood their ground against a campaign of hate and exclusion to assert their rights—both moral and constitutional—to pursue life, liberty, and happiness in America.

Nhất phá sơn lâm, nhì đâm hà bá

Slash the forests, destroy the waters

—VIETNAMESE PROVERB

*The Fishermen and the Dragon*

# Prologue

THE NAVY-GRAY PAINT OF THE TRAWLER WAS FADED AND CHIPPED, spattered with the excrement of gulls that jostled and shrieked overhead when the catch was still good. The *Cherry Betty*'s engine was ancient, coughing up black diesel fumes as the boat motored slowly down the channel toward the dark water of Galveston Bay. Blue, rainless sky that March morning. A perfect day for a ride.

On the southern side of the narrow channel, which separated the fishing towns of Seabrook and Kemah, a Vietnamese fisherman was sitting in his living room with a friend, making plans for the upcoming season of shrimping. Their conversation was interrupted by the sight of a trawler, overloaded with passengers, growling past.

They shot to their feet and ran to the window. Most of those on board were dressed in white robes, with rifles slung over their shoulders.

There was a cannon on the stern.

Something was hanging from one of the outriggers.

"What is that?" the Vietnamese fisherman asked his friend nervously. "Is that a sack of shrimp?"

———

DAVID COLLINS GRINNED AS HE PILOTED THE *CHERRY BETTY* AHEAD. Earlier that morning, soon after the Grand Dragon of the Texas Knights of the Ku Klux Klan had given them the go-ahead, the boat was swarming with passengers, some in hoods, others in army fatigues and black KU KLUX KLAN—REALM OF TEXAS T-shirts. The Confederate flag hanging from the boat's mast whipped in the wind as they passed the boatyard that White fishermen of Galveston Bay had come to refer to as "Saigon Harbor."

The drawbridge connecting Seabrook and Kemah lowered, blocking their forward progress. Collins threw the engine in neutral and the boat drifted alongside the Kemah boardwalk, which was thronged with tourists and locals. John Van Beekum, a photojournalist for the *Houston Chronicle*, was on his day off, tucking into a shrimp sandwich, when he caught sight of the Klan boat. He sprinted to his car, praying he had enough film in his camera and that he could get back before it disappeared.

Members of the Texas Knights of the Ku Klux Klan patrol Galveston Bay, menacing Vietnamese fishermen.

Off on the horizon, a massive oil tanker churned through the heart of the bay toward one of the refineries clotting the bay with smokestacks, chemical tanks, and hundreds of miles of underwater pipeline. It was only recently that the latest tanker collision, which had spilled millions of gallons of crude to the seabed and caused a months-long fire that turned the sky over Galveston Bay black, was finally extinguished with a foamy soup of chemicals.

Word was spreading quickly. The owner of "Saigon Harbor," a White transplant from Illinois, was storming the docks, shouting at Vietnamese fishermen to get off their boats and go hide at home. Some wanted to stay, with guns, to protect their trawlers.

WHEN THE DRAWBRIDGE RAISED, COLLINS SHIFTED INTO GEAR and the *Cherry Betty* resumed its trip. The Klansmen standing along the bow, their arms folded below the blood drop cross symbol on their robes, were making it difficult to see, but he knew the channel well—he and his brother had been shrimping here ever since they moved from Florida as teenagers.

Van Beekum raced back to the boardwalk with his camera just in time to snap dozens of pictures. As those on board flashed Sieg Heil salutes and mugged for the camera, most on the boardwalk seemed amused.

Just then, another young man, who once fought for the South Vietnamese navy, was about to fire up the engine of the beat-up shrimp boat he'd just bought. Ever since arriving in Texas as a refugee five years earlier, after the collapse of his country, he had been saving every penny he'd earned assembling car radios in Houston in order to break into fishing. He was in a triumphant mood, about to take it out for the first time, when the *Cherry Betty* skulked past.

He looked up, wide-eyed. It looked as though there was a body hanging from a noose off the outrigger, its boots swaying four feet above the deck.

When Collins cleared the channel, he steered the *Cherry Betty* north, hugging close to the shoreline. As someone loaded a shell into the cannon, the Klan boat approached the dock jutting out from the home of the man who had become the greatest obstacle to their plans.

He was a highly decorated South Vietnamese colonel who'd spent the past two decades in battle. Ever since arriving in Texas, he'd become the leader of the Vietnamese shrimpers of Galveston Bay.

If the Klan could drive him from the coast, the rest might follow suit, and the White fishermen would have the waters to themselves again.

## Act I

Blood
in the
Water

Murder in a fishing town is like the day before a hurricane hits. Everybody knows it's going to be a terrible tragedy, but they can't help feeling excited.

—DIANE WILSON

# I

# The Deformed Crab

FIVE YEARS BEFORE A PAIR OF BULLETS TORE THROUGH HIS gut and heart, Billy Joe Aplin reached over the silt-smeared water of the tidal flats with a boat hook to snare a small buoy bobbing near the grassy shoreline. As he pulled it toward his skiff, the rope gathered in soggy coils by his white rubber boots.

Billy Joe was a bear of a man, six feet with broad shoulders, strong nose, square jaw, and jet-black hair. His palms were callused from the thousands of times he'd hauled in these ropes, hand over hand as the trap emerged, water streaming out its chicken-wire sides until its quarry of blue crabs came into view, stunned by sunlight and sea breeze. Above him, a big dome of sky, humid and swarming with gulls impatient for a crack at his catch.

Their skiff drifted calmly at the mouth of the Guadalupe River in San Antonio Bay, their favorite spot to lay traps. His wife, Judy, lit a cigarette and took a long drag in the Texas heat. His ten-year-old daughter, Beth, was already perched on her culling stool, ready to sort the catch. Billy Joe Jr. and Cheryl Ann, only five and four, huddled close to their mom. Superstitious fishermen thought it was bad luck to bring a woman on a boat, but by 1975, Billy Joe had endured such a streak of bum luck that he couldn't afford not to bring his family out with him: they were his deckhands.

He'd met Judy in 1964 when she was sixteen, a ninth-grade dropout picking crabs up the coast at a plant in Port Lavaca. They were pregnant a few months later. Billy Joe was in his senior year then, but figured providing for her and their newborn daughter, Beth, was more important than trigonometry, so he dropped out, bought a decrepit crabbing boat and a heap of rusty traps, and got to work.

Each morning, they'd wake before sunrise and motor through the cold morning fog to run their traps in the bayous. But in the economic hierarchy of Texas fishing, crabbing was near the bottom, just above oystering, barely enough to feed a family. The real money was in bay and gulf shrimping or working as a captain on the party boats, so Billy Joe went to night school and earned his mariner's license. Before long, he was taking wealthy Houstonians deep-sea fishing for red snapper out of Galveston, dropping Beth off in the mornings with a family friend, Captain Jack Gunn, while Judy helped on the boat . . . until Beth whispered to a classmate during a sleepover that Jack had molested her. Judy talked Billy Joe out of killing Captain Gunn, but it was enough for them to pull up stakes. Every six months, it seemed, they were packing their things, chasing the catch and a lucky break. Beth hated saying goodbye to new friends, and was turning inward.

Billy Joe knew they needed something more stable, but his ambitions had a habit of getting snagged and torn up along the unforgiving coastline. An engine could kick out or explode. A hurricane could scatter the catch or disappear a boat. Rising fuel prices ate into his slim margins—plenty of days he only earned enough to cover gas. By the late 1960s, though, after a few good seasons, he had finally saved enough to graduate to shrimping. They bought their first trawler, which he named *Judy's Pride*, and for a brief spell, the future seemed brighter.

But one fateful morning in July 1969, his luck began to curdle. After dropping Beth off with a relative, Billy Joe and Judy went dragging for shrimp in high spirits: in her purse was a wad of cash—the final bank payment before they owned *Judy's Pride* outright. But something quickly went wrong. Almost as soon as their ninety-by-thirty-foot nets drifted to the bottom of the bay, the trawler lurched and began listing; *Judy's Pride* was snagged upon something on the floor of the bay. The bays were filled with debris, boulders, oil pipeline, shipwrecks—the Texas Parks and Wildlife Department once dumped hundreds of junked cars to build artificial reefs for game fish, switching to concrete pipes only after the tide swept the cars away.

Whatever had seized their nets caused *Judy's Pride* to circle her tether

Billy Joe Aplin.

and quickly take on water. The moment before it capsized, Billy Joe and Judy dove into the gulf, treading water as the boat began its descent into darkness. Judy remembered her purse and started screaming. Billy Joe dove down to search for it, again and again, but came up empty-handed. A fellow shrimper by the name of John Collins came to their rescue on a salvage boat, winching up the wreckage and Judy's purse. Beth, then four, ironed the waterlogged cash while her dad sulked in the living room, watching the Apollo 11 moon landing.

Neil Armstrong and Buzz Aldrin lived near the Manned Spacecraft Center, in El Lago, right next to the Galveston Bay shrimping towns of Kemah and Seabrook, where Billy Joe frequently docked. In that moment, it was hard not to be embittered by how small his life seemed in comparison. The next morning, he made his final bank payment on a wrecked boat and was knocked back down to crabbing and oystering.

He seemed to tempt misfortune. He soon indulged in an affair that nearly destroyed his marriage. After getting caught up in a gun deal gone bad with some mobsters in Galveston involving a dozen Lugers with Nazi insignia, he fled with his family to Alaska to work as a dive boat captain for divers repairing oil pipelines.

By the mid-1970s, though, things had cooled down enough for the

Aplins to return to Texas, with enough savings for a down payment on their first home, a small redbrick two-story on the outskirts of Seadrift, a speck of a fishing town halfway down the Texas Gulf Coast to Mexico. His folks and several siblings had recently moved there; his brother Doc ran a fish house in town, buying the daily catch of shrimp, crabs, and oysters.

Seadrift was barely half a square mile, with one main street that ran right down to the docks and boat launch. There were a few bars, a run-down motel, churches, and a clutch of ramshackle fish houses—where the daily catch was sorted, weighed, and iced. A café for diesel-strength coffee before shoving off into the bays. A two-man police force, volunteer firefighters, and not a stoplight in sight. A cemetery strung with barbed wire to keep the wild hogs out, sited far enough inland to keep hurricanes and floods from disinterring the dead.

Fewer than a thousand people lived in town, which was sealed off from just about everything. There weren't any civil rights marches or antiwar rallies in a town like Seadrift. When the draft board came knocking, some of the boys went off to fight and die in Vietnam; others hopped buses to dodge the draft in Canada. To Billy Joe, who received an exemption owing to a bum leg, the war was someone else's problem in another country, far removed from his own life.

Their house was just a couple hundred yards from the water's edge. Judy planted a row of red canna lilies along one side of the home, a rosebush under the back window, and wisteria out front. Live oak dotted the backyard, which opened onto chocolate-colored fields of cotton. Beth was overjoyed to finally unpack her bags for good and decorate the walls of her own room. Billy Joe bought an *Encyclopædia Britannica* for the family on an installment plan, plucked at his guitar after dinner, and dreamed of the day that he could return to shrimping.

AS THE SUN CLIMBED OVER SAN ANTONIO BAY, HE EMPTIED THE first trap out onto the deck and Beth got to work, swiftly culling the sooks and jimmies and she-crabs into a steel drum, tossing back the hardheads, the stone crabs, and the sponge crabs laden with eggs, sending the gulls into a squawking, dive-bombing frenzy. After Judy rebaited the first trap with a fistful of foul-smelling chicken necks, Billy Joe heaved it back into the water and motored on to the next buoy, his prop churning up muddy clouds in his wake.

Coaxing things up from these bays was all Billy Joe had ever learned to do, and he was more hard-pressed than ever to make it work, now that they had a mortgage and three mouths to feed. But there was reason to cling to hope: thanks to the explosion of Red Lobster franchises in the 1970s, American bellies were swelling with seafood, making the crabs skittering into his traps more valuable with each passing day. If he could just stitch together a few good years, a shrimp trawler was within reach.

They only had a couple of traps left to run before they could call it a day. But as Billy Joe shook the next trap out, his eyes immediately fixed on something wrong. Amid the junk fish flopping around was a large blue crab with a bizarrely misshapen shell clacking sluggishly along the hull.

He was agitated. The fishermen in town were trading strange stories of zombie fish in the bays, rolling along the surface. Dolphins dying off. Freak shrimp turning up without eyes.

He was used to the vicissitudes of nature: a late-winter freeze might delay the mating season or a drought could leave the water in the bays too salty for crustaceans to thrive. But as best as he could tell, nothing in the natural world produced mutated crabs or zombie fish.

The deformed crab twitched in his hands. As the CB radio crackled with the chatter of bored shrimpers, Billy Joe flung the crab overboard with a scowl and gunned the engine.

He had an inkling of what was behind it all, but if he was right, it was a frightening road ahead.

Back in town, as she mended a net in one of the dilapidated fish houses, a woman, a fourth-generation shrimper and native Seadrifter, quietly nursed the same dark suspicions.

## 2

# The Lone Fisherwoman of Seadrift

WHEN DIANE WILSON WAS LITTLE, THE ROADS OF SEADRIFT were paved with oyster shells. In front of her grandmother's house was a three-story mountain of shells that she and her siblings would sled down like Colorado snowpack. The dust from the ground-up shells was so fine that when the wind kicked it up, it would coat every poison oak and dewberry vine for miles.

The oysters were dredged from the bays that her family had been shrimping and crabbing since the 1890s. Seadrift was officially founded in 1848 by German settlers, but only after a centuries-long extermination of the Karankawas, a group of Native American tribes who worked the land and bays, by French, Spanish, and early Texan colonists. Two decades after a Texas militia massacred dozens of Karankawas at the mouth of the Colorado River by Lavaca Bay, turning the water red with blood, White settlers registered the stolen land with the state, laying out the town's dozen streets in the shape of a sail.

Diane's grandpa, who went by "Chief" on account of the Cherokee ancestry of his father, opened a fish house in the early 1900s, around the time a rail line and an ice factory were put in to trundle freshly caught fish, oysters, and crabs up to Houston. For $300, White settlers could buy a five-acre plot of fertile land that churned out just about any fruit or vegetable anyone tried, and before long, boats filled with sweet potatoes and watermelon departed daily from Seadrift for towns up the coast. The fertility of the soil and the bounty of its bays was such a draw that the town's population swelled to nearly two thousand. Hotels, banks, and churches popped up, and a newspaper, the *Seadrift Success*, was published.

Seadrift was a boomtown until June 28, 1919, when a massive hurricane rolled in and rendered it a wasteland of timber and mangled steel, dragging much of the town into the gulf when the floodwaters receded. As surviving residents fled, the train service was canceled, the hotels went under, and the newspaper was shuttered. Within a few years, only a few hundred Seadrifters remained.

No hurricane was going to scatter Diane's family, though. They cleared the wreckage, rebuilt the docks, mended their boats and nets, and returned to the bays. Diane, who was born in 1947, took her first job in the business as a five-year-old, helping her grandma pinch heads off shrimp in a rank-smelling fish house for two cents a pound. They called it "women's work," but she hated being indoors and used any excuse she could to scamper down to the waterfront, peering through the cracks of the docks as crabs scuffled with catfish over discarded shrimp heads.

After she stole a leaky skiff as a six-year-old, shoving off with a mayo sandwich and a jar of pickles that she used to bail water, Chief decided that she was better suited out on the bays. She became a deckhand, helping her dad and grandpa drag for shrimp in the bays and run the crab traps in the lagoons as the wind whipping over the waterfront tangled her mop of black hair into a thousand knots. Most mornings, her grandpa would wake at dawn and head down to the wharf with a jelly jar full of coffee to take in a deep breath of the water's heavy smell, knowing in a matter of seconds whether it was worth heading out that day.

Superstitions about where the shrimp might be found ran so deep that Diane's dad once pledged he'd join her mom at church—something he'd resisted for years—if he ever pulled up two thousand pounds of shrimp in a single drag. When it happened a few days later, he found

God, beaming as the winch groaned beneath the bulging nets. From then on, they were fixtures at the local Pentecostal church, which met at night in a foggy riverbank clearing surrounded by willows. As the congregation gathered in rusted-out trucks filled with chains and tattered shrimp nets amid hordes of mosquitoes, the Reverend "Brother Dynamite" led them in services that lasted hours, speaking in tongues and wrestling with the rattlesnakes and copperheads he kept in cages by his pulpit.

Diane felt that nothing much good ever happened on land, especially when men started preaching. She felt her own mystical connection to the water, which she saw as an old woman, capable of being harmed, deserving of protection. Whenever she went down to the waterfront, she sensed that the gray lady in her dress of seaweed was happy to see her.

She was a good deckhand; she never minded plunging her hands in mud or complained when a jellyfish burned her arm or a hardhead catfish pricked her palms. She was quiet, but her mind pulsed with wonder at what was hidden in the watery depths. When they worked the Lavaca River, she'd crane her neck over the gunwale, looking for glints of the cannons and chests full of gold allegedly abandoned there by the pirate Jean Lafitte before his flight to Mexico 150 years earlier.

Her older brother was an attack pilot who earned the Distinguished Flying Cross and twenty-four air medals in Vietnam. He returned to Seadrift the most highly decorated veteran in a seven-county radius and could've worked anywhere but he was done taking orders, so he got himself a shrimp boat.

Her younger brother ran a fish house by the docks called Froggie's. Her cousins were in the business. Her sister was married to a shrimper. It seemed that everyone she knew made their living out on the water, but in her late teens, Wilson thought she would buck tradition and try something else. After reading a *Life* magazine article in 1970 about helicopter medics in Vietnam, she was inspired to enlist. By then, though, the country had fully soured on the war; her recruiter thought she was joking about serving there. She worked as a medic for injured veterans at Fort Sam Houston, where the air was so thick with marijuana smoke that it seemed like fog. Soldiers expressed their appreciation by dropping little baggies of weed in her pockets as she worked her way through the ward. She was warned never to leave a needle behind because there were so many soldiers struggling with addiction to stronger substances.

Confronted with horrifically disfigured soldiers in the burn ward, she realized the *Life* article that had sent her on this path hadn't presented the full picture. She became so revolted by the war and what it had done to these ghostlike men that she bolted from the base, sold her blood for cash, and bought a one-way bus ticket to Toronto. When she eventually returned, she turned herself in, received a dishonorable discharge, and returned to Seadrift to do what everyone else in her family did.

She was in a similar bind as Billy Joe: until she could afford to buy a shrimp boat, she was stuck crabbing. Her first boat was a small skiff, "brown as a turd," with an engine forever on the brink of exploding. In her midtwenties, she was running about 120 crab traps and only just scraping by, making a few thousand dollars a year. There were no feminists in Seadrift to celebrate the first female to work the bays, but plenty

Diane Wilson mending a trawl net.

of men griped about it over their CBs. There wasn't much daylight between fishermen's superstitions and misogyny: they once blamed a streak
of bad days on a hen that hitched a ride on the fender of a shrimper's
truck and hopped aboard his trawler when he wasn't looking. She wondered whether they'd have been so upset had it been a rooster.

She married a part-time shrimper, a Vietnam veteran struggling
with post-traumatic stress. She called him Baby, because he didn't like to
lift a finger to do anything, a trait that only grew as the pressures on the
household intensified. In a fit of exasperation after their first daughter
was born, in 1973, she offered to pay him ten dollars an hour to watch
his own child, but her proposed salary wasn't high enough, so she bicy-
cled her baby to her mom's first thing every morning before heading out
to run her traps. To make ends meet, she trucked live crabs from Seadrift's fish houses three hours away to the San Antonio airport, where
they were flown out to restaurants on the East Coast. It was an exhausting run that she did several times a week, and not without risks: she once
lost control of an overloaded truck in Cuero, where it flipped on its side
and sent live crabs scuttling all over Route 87.

Her folks were worried her skiff would explode or sink. The cemetery had plenty of headstones marking those who had drowned in the
bays—whenever a fisherman went missing, all the shrimpers of Seadrift
would gather in their trawlers and drag the bays until one of their nets
scooped up the body. She often wondered how many men's gravestones
would read BLOWN UP BY GAS ENGINE if their widows and children
weren't so embarrassed to admit it. Her own family urged her to find a
job on solid ground, if only for her baby's sake.

In the mid-1970s, Wilson knew that plenty of shrimpers were aug-
menting their earnings by running drugs up from Mexico—one ring of
Seadrift fishermen was busted with bricks of heroin concealed in their
trawlers. Any shrimper who took a three-day trip to Mesquite Bay was
suspect; she once came upon a massive bale of marijuana wrapped in a
black garbage bag and duct tape while beachcombing Matagorda Island.

She wasn't about to start running drugs, though, so her remaining
options were limited. On the northern fringe of town, tucked in the

corner of a vacant lot of milkweed and flatsedge, was a small crab-picking plant set up in 1976 by Verlon Davis, a local fish house owner hoping to capitalize on the growing demand for crabmeat. His plant was backed by a Baltimore restaurateur in need of fresh crabs during the off-season, when Chesapeake Bay was closed to crabbing, but his grandiose plans soon dashed up against a basic problem: he had barrels of crab but nobody willing to do the work. Lacerated fingers, aching knuckle joints, foul odor, and poverty-line wages. The best he could pay was 85 cents a pound; any higher and his buyers would just order from Mexico, where pickers were paid a third of that to process crabs from the same gulf. Good pickers, standing on their feet for ten hours a day, might pull seven pounds an hour for a daily take-home of $60. Verlon couldn't find anyone willing to do the job for more than a few days before quitting. He ran job announcements in the local paper for months before hopping in his truck and driving off in search of people desperate enough to take the job.

But after her unhappy days heading shrimp as a tyke, Wilson didn't want to spend her days in a crab plant. Until she could afford her own shrimp trawler, there was only one other option in town.

And so it was that she drove across town in late 1976, when she was twenty-nine, pulling into the sprawling compound of one of the biggest employers in the county, a massive petrochemical plant looming over Seadrift that specialized in manufacturing plastic.

# 3

# A Hurricane Warning

I N 1901, OIL PROSPECTORS PROBING AROUND THE SULFUR
springs of Spindletop Hill two hundred miles up the Texas coast in
Beaumont uncorked a hundred-foot-tall geyser of slick crude. Overnight,
Spindletop became the largest gusher in the world, spraying more oil into
the air in just nine days than had been extracted in Texas in all of the
previous year. Refineries the size of cities grew along the coast. Pipelines
were laid along land and upon the seabed. Massive storage facilities
sprung from the ground. Then the petrochemical plants came, producing a soup of chemicals like benzene, propylene, ethylene, and isoprene.
As more drills punctured the Gulf Coast, workers flooded into the oil
boomtowns. By midcentury, two hundred plants loomed over the bays
of Texas.

It wasn't long before the industry came to Seadrift, eyeing its rivers
and deep-channel bays. "I see no reason why this shouldn't be a very good
industrial center," the president of Alcoa (Aluminum Company of America) mused in 1950 at the opening of a new smelting plant in Point Comfort, on the eastern shore of nearby Lavaca Bay. During a tour of the bay
arranged by the local chamber of commerce, he marveled over the beauty
of the water. A reception was thrown in his honor at the Shellfish Café,

where boosters gave him an ornate belt buckle and thanked him for all the jobs his plant would bring to town.

By the early 1960s, the plant had seventeen hundred employees. Every few years, a ground-breaking ceremony would announce the start of a new operation. At the opening of a new plant to produce coal tar pitch for manufacturing electrodes, an Alcoa executive praised all the tax abatements that the town had granted the company: "We cannot come into a community and do what we have done without the community's help that you have given," he said, promising a "very pleasant relationship" in the years ahead. The plant manager told assembled bigwigs and journalists that this was "just the beginning" of development planned for the area, and drove a gold-plated shovel into the soil along the waterfront.

Nearby, a DuPont plant manufacturing nylon sprawled over a 1,725-acre compound. Union Carbide broke ground on its 2,700-acre petrochemical complex after securing a permit from the Texas Board of Water Engineers to divert 41 billion gallons of water each year from the Guadalupe River to make plastic resin for milk jugs and grocery bags. Farmers and ranchers voiced concerns that the diversion of water would allow salt water to creep upstream and foul up irrigation, but their misgivings were swatted away by a corporate vice president: other than being twenty degrees warmer, the water would be returned to the bays "virtually unchanged."

WILSON HAD GROWN UP ALONGSIDE THE PLANTS BUT NEVER ONCE considered working for them; she belonged out on the water. But her family was growing quickly—a new mouth to feed every year, it seemed—and the petrochemical plants offered something no crabber or shrimper ever had: a steady paycheck and health insurance. In 1976, she drove her truck up to the Union Carbide plant and applied for a job. When the man interviewing her realized she was a crabber, he hired her on the spot, exclaiming, "A fisherwoman is *bound* to know how to work hard!" They offered her a desk job, but she hated being trapped indoors, opting instead for a job outside with the men, changing pistons on giant compressors.

The air around the plant was so foul that she wrapped a bandanna over her nostrils while she worked. It was a noisy, busy place, black smoke and fireballs burping from towers while plastic-filled trains groaned by and hungry barges eased up the canal to be loaded. At the end of each day on the job, she came home and climbed into a bath, and the water would turn canary yellow.

She quit after three weeks.

WITH HER HUSBAND WORKING ONLY SPORADICALLY, WILSON TOOK a job at Froggie's, her younger brother's fish house in town, making just a few hundred dollars a month. If she could string together a few good years without anyone in her family getting sick or injured, she might be able to save enough for a deposit on a shrimp trawler, which could bump her up to a livable income. While waiting for shrimpers to return with their catch in the afternoon, she sat on the road out front mending massive shrimp nets under a muggy sun while her kids played in the small mountain of ice in the vault. She mended in bare feet, her skin forever tanned, her callused hands expertly weaving the shuttle stitching up tears and holes until her wrists were sore. Her best friend Donna Sue also worked at Froggie's; every couple of days, the two loaded heavy blue bins containing thousands of pounds of iced shrimp into the refrigerator truck that trundled it up to Houston.

It was hard, monotonous work, but every now and then things turned up in the daily catch that hinted at some dark mystery spreading through the bays. Mutated shrimp. Misshapen crabs. A friend trotlining for black drum up at the mouth of the Guadalupe River near the Union Carbide plant came in and told her he'd seen alligators rolling ghostlike beneath the surface; he laid the mutated fish he'd caught on her rickety desk with a searching look.

When mysterious brown algae bloomed in the bay and crept into the harbor, Wilson stepped outside the fish house and watched suffocating fish break the surface to gasp for air before dying. Shrimpers struggled to pull in nets heavy with algae: most fanned their nets out in their yards in faint hopes that the sun would somehow rid them of the algae, but nothing worked. One exasperated shrimper tied a net to the back of his truck and sped down the oystershell roads at eighty miles per hour, trying to beat the algae off, until a bewildered cop pulled him over.

Wilson wasn't sure exactly why, but she had an instinct that these little monstrosities needed to be preserved. Each time a fisherman brought something strange into Froggie's, she tucked it into a plastic bag in the back of her freezer, assembling a menagerie of mutations.

After her brief stint at Union Carbide, she had her suspicions about the connection between the plants and the health of the bays, but she wasn't a biologist or chemist. Something else might have caused these problems. Whatever it was lay far beyond her reach. She was a young mother drifting at the poverty line, after all—what could she do? Sue the plants, where half of her family worked? She didn't know a single lawyer.

IT WAS AROUND THIS TIME, IN THE MID-1970s, THAT BILLY JOE Aplin pulled up a mutated crab from the depths of Lavaca Bay. Aplin didn't know any lawyers, either, but a plan began to form in his mind. Late one night, he sat down at his typewriter and began writing a letter: NOTICE TO FISHERMEN.

"My name is Billy Aplin," he began. "I am a commercial fisherman and, as such, an independent businessman. The reason I write this is to EXPOSE the dangers presently threatening commercial fishing, which threaten the family security of individuals like myself whose livelihood depends on harvesting seafood. . . ."

He took a breath and bashed out the letters spelling out what he suspected was behind the strange things happening in the bays: A-L-C-O-A.

ALCOA'S OPERATIONS AT POINT COMFORT ON LAVACA BAY HAD grown so much that the county dredged a deeper shipping channel so that larger ships could access the plant. The dredgers cut through the estuary and dumped the sediment on what was once an oyster reef, five hundred feet offshore from the plant.

An island formed, and everyone called it Dredge Island.

As far as any locals knew, Dredge Island was just a 420-acre scoop of the seabed dried out in the sun. But in 1966, after the plant began manufacturing chlorine and sodium hydroxide, Alcoa executives decided to put Dredge Island to use, dumping millions of gallons of mercury-laden wastewater to settle in a lagoon on the island. Bit by bit, the overflow was dumped into Lavaca Bay through two large drains.

As the wastewater entered the bay, bacteria converted the mercury into methylmercury, which began to accumulate in algae. Algae-feeding fish were gobbled up by larger fish, which were hooked and netted by humans—a process known as biomagnification. The concentration of mercury in spotted sea trout and black drum were upward of one million times the concentration of the water in which they fed.

The mercury wasn't just affecting finfish. These were estuarine waters, where newly hatched shrimp fed alongside young crabs that absorbed nutrients from the seawater and fed on plankton in seagrass beds now laden with mercury.

BILLY JOE POUNDED AWAY AT HIS TYPEWRITER ABOUT SURVIVAL and corporate greed and the death of the bays. "I . . . am a victim of industrial pollution. The WATERS I fish have been POISONED. My ability to make a living, to feed, clothe and educate my children, has been RUINED by toxic wastes and biproducts of aluminum manufacture being released into Texas coast waters."

He wasn't pushing a conspiracy; he'd done his research. In 1970, the Texas Water Quality Board, acting on tips about mercury contamination in Lavaca Bay, initiated an investigation, sampling fish, crabs, and oysters. An emergency order was issued to Alcoa to limit mercury dumping, but the damage was already done: conservative estimates pegged the amount at 67 pounds of mercury sloshing into the water every day for nearly a half decade, tens of thousands of pounds that eventually settled over a 64-square-mile splotch on the floor of Lavaca Bay. Another 60 to 90 pounds were dispersed each day into the skies over Calhoun County. The only consequence came in the form of large signs posted around Dredge Island, warning people not to eat anything caught there.

But Billy Joe didn't know about Wilson or her freezer of oddities. Seadrift was a small town, but there was a stark divide between the natives and the newcomers: Wilson's clan had more than a hundred years there. Billy Joe had only just arrived a couple of years earlier. To her, the Aplins would always be the "Floridoneans."

And so he expected he'd be fighting a lonely battle. Plenty of his fellow fishermen worked at the Alcoa plant in the off-season or had relatives or wives who worked there year-round. But "for a fisherman who makes his living from the waters," he wrote, "to be indifferent to this threat is like ignoring a hurricane warning."

He laid out his proposal: if enough of his fellow fishermen joined the fight against Alcoa by contributing to a legal action fund, they might be able to save the bays. He had never done anything like this before, but he was angry. Unlike Wilson, he was ready to act. He wanted to file a class-action lawsuit against Alcoa to force them to stop poisoning the water. He wanted arrests. He wanted criminal prosecution.

# 4

# One Day in June, 1979

BILLY JOE'S CALL TO ARMS CIRCULATED AMONG THE SHRIMP-ers and crabbers in town, but his earnest attempt at political mobilization collided with a fundamental reality: these men were fishermen because they were stubbornly independent. They didn't want bosses, or even coworkers, if they could avoid it. For decades, outsiders had tried to organize them into cooperatives to pool their resources and their catch so that they wouldn't be at the mercy of the fish houses or their buyers, who played them off each other to drive prices down, but the conservative fishermen always bristled at the idea: a "co-op" sounded dangerously close to communism. And so they worked alone, competing with one another.

Wilson had once participated in a town hall with fishermen who'd gathered to confront a different problem: the shrimp coming in each day were much too small. After hemming and hawing, they collectively voted to abstain from going out for two weeks to give the shrimp time to grow. But before the meeting ended, one of the fish house owners was on the phone with his best shrimper urging him to sneak out and drag the bays that night. Most of the others followed suit.

So when Billy Joe tried to rally them against Alcoa and the other plants in town, all he achieved was a bitter recognition of just how powerless he was. Beyond the fact that they had people from nearly every family in town on their payrolls, the plants had so effectively insinuated themselves into Seadrift through goodwill gifts—coloring books for kindergartners, a defibrillator for the ambulance, a new computer system for the county sheriff—that when Alcoa's plant manager announced that the "oysters had cleansed themselves" just four months after the dumping on Dredge Island ended, it was enough for Seadrifters to look the other way.

Billy Joe was only a crabber—a newcomer to Seadrift, no less—whose words carried little weight compared with the speeches of those who wielded power in the county. "Every man, woman and child . . . have a better life directly or indirectly because" of the plants, a state representative crowed on the occasion of Union Carbide's twenty-fifth anniversary of operations in Seadrift in early 1979. "There is no question that without the combined effort of Union Carbide, DuPont and Alcoa, the standard of living and growth potential . . . would be much less than it is today." A county judge said he was "tickled to death" that the plants were there. US congressman Joe Wyatt hailed the plants for displaying "all the marks of exemplary citizenship . . . from employing as many local citizens as possible to care for our environment."

No fishermen joined Billy Joe's cause. He didn't raise a red cent for his legal fund.

IN THE SUMMER OF 1979, AS HE APPROACHED HIS THIRTY-FIFTH birthday, Billy Joe felt set upon from every direction. The plants kept expanding, adding smokestacks, sucking up more freshwater from the rivers, and receiving permits from the state to dump hazardous chemicals into the bays. The Iranian Revolution at the start of the year had led to an oil crisis, massive queues at gas stations, and quadrupled fuel costs that made it impossible to break even out on the water. After years of crabbing, he was hoping to return to shrimping by converting his boat into a simple trawler, but between hurricanes and flooding, the year was already turning out to be historically awful for shrimpers.

Making matters worse, a Galveston Bay research laboratory run by the Department of the Interior's Bureau of Commercial Fisheries had recently made great strides in developing the techniques to farm shrimp. Dow Chemical poached one of the lab's chief scientists to run one of the first commercial shrimp farms in America at its petrochemical plant—one of the largest in the world—just up the coast in Freeport. Union Carbide opened a shrimp-farming operation in India in 1978. Throughout the 1970s, the US Agency for International Development sent mariculturists to Vietnam, Thailand, and Indonesia to promote the "Galveston method" of shrimp farming; each year, more and more imported shrimp entered the US market, depressing the value of wild-caught shrimp from the Gulf of Mexico. Americans ate their shrimp so heavily breaded and fried they didn't seem to notice the difference, and at the rate things were going, imported farmed shrimp would soon dominate the market, driving shrimpers all along the coast out of business.

And then a new front opened up.

ON THE MORNING OF JUNE 3, 1979, A DRILLING RIG OPERATED BY Pemex, the Mexican state-owned oil company, was boring a deep-sea oil well called Ixtoc I in the Bay of Campeche, a thousand miles down the coast from Seadrift, when something went terribly wrong.

The bit was two miles below the seafloor when the drilling mud, which stabilizes the process, stopped circulating, sending oil and natural gas shooting up to the surface. Upon coming into contact with the rig's pump motors, it exploded, sinking the rig and kicking off what would become, for several decades at least, the largest peacetime oil spill in world history.

Thirty thousand barrels' worth gushed from the well each day. Pemex workers sprayed a chemical dispersant over the slick, breaking the oil into tiny droplets that then sank beneath the surface, out of sight. One

The Ixtoc I oil spill in the Bay of Campeche, Gulf of Mexico—the largest peacetime oil spill in history until the Deepwater Horizon blowout in 2010.

hundred thousand steel, iron, and lead balls were pumped into the well, but experts suggested it would be months before a relief well could be drilled to stop the spill. Five days into the crisis, a Pemex spokesman assured the public that "there is not very much danger to the ecology . . . if it *were* out of control," he continued, "there would be a danger to the ecology . . . but as you can see, it is under control."

Forty-eight hours later, the oil slick was already sixty miles long. Local Mexican fishermen were given rubber boots and spades to gather oil in plastic bags. Fish caught shortly after the spill had red, bulging eyes. A population of sea turtles was nearly extirpated. Shrimp and fish were eventually infested with tumors.

As the oil continued to gush, the slick expanded to the size of Manhattan and began drifting north into US waters toward the Texas Gulf Coast at a clip of nine miles a day. The US Coast Guard mobilized strike teams and strung fifteen-thousand-pound floating booms along the coastline, but conceded there would be too much oil for it to be wholly contained. US Fish and Wildlife Service teams were readied to clean oil-soaked birds. Researchers tested the toxicity of the spill by placing shrimp and fish in samples of oil and brine ladled from the slick—eggs and newly hatched fish died in the toxic broth.

Guy Pete, a veteran shrimper, was worried about the sun-blocking sheen of oil: "Every dollar I've ever made has come out of that gulf . . . I'm not a biologist, but the sunlight is just as vital to the sea as it is to a farm." The spill was "the biggest threat I can remember that we've ever had here."

The slick was days away from Texas waters when Billy Joe heard Cheryl Ann screaming in the backyard. He raced out to find his daughter fleeing from the neighbor's dog, which had recently dragged a man off his bicycle and chased kids on their tricycles. At long last, a problem he could solve. He grabbed his pistol, strode over to the dog, and shot it in the head. The neighbor's young daughter was in the backyard and witnessed the whole thing. The police came, and within a few weeks he was defending himself before a jury on animal cruelty charges.

On June 29, two days after Billy Joe received a not-guilty verdict, the whole family piled into their twenty-one-foot skiff at the crack of dawn to run their traps near the mouth of the Guadalupe River in San Antonio Bay. Beth was fourteen, Cheryl Ann was nine, and Billy Joe Jr. was eight.

As they drew close to their first set of buoys, Billy Joe's face clouded over. Someone had dropped a bunch of traps right between his. Even worse, it seemed that some of his traps were missing. He exploded, furiously yanking up each trap intruding upon what he considered his turf. He stacked them on the bow until there were about thirty traps in a teetering pile, and sped off in search of the culprit.

Within moments, they came upon a teenager, just a few years older than Beth, drifting in a beat-up crabbing skiff. Billy Joe started yelling at him about the rules of the bay, telling him to drop his traps somewhere else.

"No speak English," the young man replied. He seemed calm, unbothered by Billy Joe's anger.

Billy Joe flew into a rage, grabbing a trap from the stack and stomping on it until it was an unrecognizable mass of chicken wire.

"I'll bet you understand *that!*" he shouted, hurling it into the water.

Then, to Beth's surprise, her dad shoved the entire stack of traps from their boat into the bay. They sped off, leaving the shocked young crabber in a strong wake.

His name was Thảo. He was eighteen, and he had spent much of the past four years in a state of flight. The country from which he fled—the Republic of Vietnam—no longer existed.

Moments later, a close friend of his named Sáu Văn Nguyễn, who was crabbing on the opposite side of the river and had witnessed the incident, motored over.

The two had only recently arrived in Seadrift. Unsure of what to do, they fired up their engines and went off in search of the friend who had brought them there.

# 5

# Newcomers

WHEN BẰNG "CHERRY" NGUYỄN ARRIVED IN SEADRIFT IN 1976, the town was about 90 percent White and 10 percent Hispanic. There was a grand total of three Black residents. Nobody had ever seen a "Vietmanese" in town before. Bằng sure as hell hadn't seen a Seadrifter before.

Bằng hailed from Phan Thiết, a fishing port halfway between Saigon and Cam Ranh Bay, where he worked with his father on his family's sixty-foot fishing boat in the bays and the Gulf of Tonkin. When he was fourteen, they were out fishing late into the night when a boat roared through the darkness and clipped theirs, killing his father instantly. Bằng dropped out of school to provide for his family.

Bằng was nineteen in the spring of 1975, when South Vietnam's defenses melted away. Huddled close to the radio, he listened to reports of one city after another falling to the North, until the sounds of the approaching forces outside his windows drowned out the broadcast itself.

Their priest had told them to head into open waters to search for the Seventh Fleet of the US Navy, so Bằng and his seven brothers and sisters packed what they could and raced with their mother down to the family boat. For the first two nights they stayed at the docks, ready to escape but hoping the radio reports citing the imminent collapse of South Vietnam would prove to be premature. As the fighting intensified, aunts and uncles and cousins from both sides of the family fleeing villages up and down the coast raced down the planks of the docks and squeezed on board.

When the North Vietnamese forces finally came into view, Bằng fired up the engine and churned out into the bay. There were eighty-two members of his family in the fishing boat.

The coastline disappeared, and for most of that first day they searched in mounting desperation for the Americans. That night, a storm set in, forcing them back to their homeland to drop anchor just off the coast. As soon as they returned, though, a large-caliber gun fired upon their boat from the shoreline, the shells bursting in the water alongside them. Bằng didn't have time to hoist the anchor, so he cut it loose and steered back into the roiling waves of the storm and darkness.

When he eventually found an American destroyer, the family climbed aboard and were evacuated to Guam, where they were processed as refugees and flown to America. There were no Statue of Liberty sentiments or outstretched arms: even though a million South Vietnamese had been sent to North Vietnamese "reeducation camps," and hundreds of thousands of others were fleeing by boat, many of them drowning, a Gallup poll taken shortly after the fall of Saigon showed only 36 percent of Americans believed refugees fleeing the calamitous war of their country's own making deserved resettlement. President Gerald Ford ignored the polls, though, telling the nation that it would help those fleeing South Vietnam, for "to do less would have added moral shame to humiliation." Bằng and his family were among the first wave of 130,000 resettled within months of Saigon's fall.

When resettlement officials learned that Bằng was a fisherman, they sent him with his family to Lafayette, Louisiana, to work for a local restaurateur who owned a crab-picking plant in town. Until then, the owner had had an impossible time finding Americans willing to do the work: he'd once even hired seven "trusties"—inmates in the county jail permitted to work while awaiting trial—but after a few days, they all revolted and said they'd rather spend their days behind bars than pick crabs. But Bằng and several other Vietnamese families were willing to work the feverish hours at low wages, and word soon spread among other plant owners along the Gulf Coast.

Ever since opening his own crab-picking plant in Seadrift, Verlon Davis had been roaming the coast in his own desperate search for workers willing to move to Seadrift to get it up and running. As soon as he heard about the success of the Lafayette operation, he drove up and begged Bằng and his family to move to Texas.

BEFORE MOVING HIS ENTIRE FAMILY DOWN, BẰNG DECIDED TO check out the town first. When he arrived, he checked into a room at the barebones Seadrifter Inn overlooking the waterfront. He was all of five feet, handsome and compact, with a cigarette perpetually dangling from his lips. For the first few months, he worked at Verlon Davis's fish house at the docks, unloading White crabbers' boats, lugging traps, and weighing the catch. Each morning, he looked up a new English word in his dictionary and tried it out with the first White person he saw. More often than not, he was met with confused stares, but whenever a word landed, his confidence grew.

He borrowed money from Verlon to buy a simple boat and two hundred traps, and started working the bayous, becoming the first Vietnamese crabber in Seadrift. He worked from seven until seven, and often slept for only a few hours before heading back out to run his traps at night.

After a few months, he set his traps in a channel and drove up to spend Christmas with his family in Louisiana. But when he returned, all his traps were gone. In the shallow waters where he'd left them, he found a box cutter.

Despite the setback, Bằng decided to stay. He'd fallen in love with a Hispanic woman; they were already talking about marriage. He liked

Verlon and his wife, Georgia Ann, who treated him like a son, and decided that his own family could make a good life for themselves in Seadrift. When they arrived, in 1977, they moved into trailers that Verlon had set up in the field next to the plant. Rent was $150 a month. Given the large size of Vietnamese families, a single trailer often had ten or more people.

As the plant began processing crabs, more and more Vietnamese friends and relatives of Bằng's began moving to town. Within a year of Bằng's arrival, Seadrift's population of one thousand had grown by 150, all of them Vietnamese. Verlon kept adding trailers to the field outside the plant, which the White townspeople began referring to by various names: Trailer City, Saigon City, Chink City, Gook City.

VERLON SAW VIETNAMESE MEN FOLLOWING THE SAME PATH AS the White men in the area. They saw crab picking as women's work, and didn't want to be cooped up with their wives or sisters in a foul-smelling processing plant all day. Like Bằng, they began looking to the bay. Better to catch the crabs than pick them.

Unlike a shrimp boat, which required a costly, fuel-guzzling motor at a time of rising costs, pricey nets, and permits with time-consuming applications, a shallow-draft boat with a cheap engine and rudimentary crab traps fashioned out of chicken-wire or mesh was all a crabber needed; all together, the price of entry was about $5,000. There were no permits required for crabbing. For many of the Vietnamese men, crabbing was their first chance at a kind of independence: no boss, no punching the clock, and, crucially, no fluency in English required. Although some had crabbed or fished back home, many of the younger men in the community who grew up in the war had known only fighting and flight.

Unlike White Seadrifters who had access to bank loans, the Vietnamese, many of whom struggled to speak English or make sense of the paperwork, were effectively sealed off from the usual sources of capital. What they had to their advantage, though, was a centuries-old system known as hui, which functioned as a private loan club. All members of the club contributed their earnings to a pool, which was then distributed to a single family each month on a rotating basis. No paperwork or lawyers were required; the system was bound by trust and intense stigma if a member failed to pay his share on time.

Through the hui, a Vietnamese family could get enough money overnight to put a down payment on a boat or buy it outright, to the bewilderment of the Whites selling them the boats, often at an exorbitant markup. Where were the Vietnamese, crammed into trailers and working for peanuts at the plant, getting all this money? Rumors started to spread among White fishermen about a secret government program giving refugees interest-free loans. They were increasingly convinced that the government, which existed to them in the form of Parks and Wildlife agents inspecting their boats and catch—oftentimes writing tickets—was out to get them: perhaps the resettlement of Vietnamese refugees was part of some deeper plot.

By 1978, two years after Bằng's arrival, twenty-three of the twenty-nine crabbers operating out of Seadrift were Vietnamese. Unlike most of their White counterparts, they went out in any kind of weather, and returned with mountains of crabs: some two million pounds of crabs were landed in Seadrift that year, 1.3 million of which were brought in by the Vietnamese. Verlon was flying so much crabmeat to restaurants on the East Coast that he had to dispatch crab-filled trucks to both San Antonio and Houston airports to keep from exceeding the airlines' limit of five thousand pounds per flight.

One of the newest arrivals to town was an old friend of Bằng's from another fishing family in Phan Thiết. He'd been conscripted into the South Vietnamese marines in the final months of the war, and even though he'd never seen combat, his father was terrified that the North Vietnamese would kill him for having worn a uniform. After a perilous escape with his brother and twenty-four family members across the South China Sea, he was resettled to the United States and found his way to Texas, where he began to learn the basics of crabbing from Bằng.

His name was Sáu Văn Nguyễn.

———

**BẰNG WAS RUNNING HIS TRAPS WHEN HE HEARD A BOAT APPROACH-**
ing at full throttle from around a bend in the channel. "I got a problem!"
Thảo shouted as Sáu bobbed in his wake. "This guy, as soon as I put my
traps in the water, he picked mine up and stomped them, every one of
them!"

Bằng was pissed. His friends were just getting started, and he knew
from bitter experience what it meant to lose traps. In the beginning,
when Bằng didn't know any better and dropped traps too close to those
set by White crabbers, he got an earful. But even when he went out early
and laid them in places where there weren't any, White fishermen still
yelled at him for working in "their" territory. His experience wasn't
unique—several other Vietnamese crabbers had gone to the police about
stolen traps: one Vietnamese family was missing 86 of their 150 traps;
another crabber showed up at the docks to find that someone had
smashed the controls of his boat with a hammer.

There was a lot of talk about the "unwritten rules of the bay," but
Bằng couldn't help feeling that the White men simply didn't want the
Vietnamese around, no matter where they fished.

"Wait right here!" he told Sáu and Thảo, tearing off in search of
another Vietnamese friend of his. When they returned, the boats sped
off in search of the man who had destroyed their traps.

**BETH APLIN SAT IN THE BACK OF THE BOAT WITH HER DAD, TIRED**
and bored. They'd been running traps all morning, and the sun was already high and unforgiving. She took a bite of her bologna sandwich
while gulls hovered expectantly. Billy Joe killed the engine to save fuel
while they ate, and as the boat drifted in the quiet, she could tell he was
still fuming over the confrontation with the Vietnamese crabber.

She thought of the Vietnamese girl with long black hair who had
recently joined her class. She'd heard whispers among her classmates
that the Vietnamese had sewn gold into their hems before fleeing, but

the girl wore T-shirts and jeans like the rest of them. Other junior-highers called them slurs, but she'd never heard her parents say a bad word about them. She heard many had come from fishing families back home, and she felt a kind of kinship with them.

She was lost in her thoughts when she heard a buzzing sound off in the distance. It sounded like more than one boat, and it was getting louder. When the boats appeared, far on the horizon, she could tell they were coming fast because of the spray they kicked up as they careened toward them.

Billy Joe nervously tried to start the engine but it was temperamental.

As the boats drew near, Beth was terrified by the sight of several Vietnamese crabbers, who were waving knives. They surrounded the boat and were drifting within reach when Billy Joe's engine finally started.

Billy Joe drew his knife and started waving it. "Oh yeah?! I've got a knife, too!" he shouted, and stabbed at their boats. Terrified, Judy screamed at the kids to crouch down. The Aplins owned guns but never kept them in the boat; they didn't know if the same held for the Vietnamese. Junior and Cheryl Ann were balled up in a little covered area under the bow of the boat, but Beth was too scared to hide; she grabbed hold of the back railing, crying hysterically.

Hemmed in by the Vietnamese, Billy Joe throttled forward and reverse, churning up waves that pushed their boats back. When there was enough of an opening, he rammed through, his bow grinding alongside the Vietnamese boats.

Beth watched in terror as the Vietnamese men pursued them, but Billy Joe pushed ahead, the engine screaming. When the docks of Seadrift came into view, the Vietnamese boats fanned out in different directions and disappeared.

# 6

# Collision Course

**B**ACK ON DRY LAND, BILLY JOE SENT JUDY TO WAIT WITH THE kids in the truck while he spoke to the police. As she watched him through the windshield, she thought back to the day they met, when she was only sixteen and waiting at a bus stop right up the road in Port Lavaca. Billy Joe wandered past just as a boy from her former high school started shouting at her for spurning him. He didn't know her, but within seconds he was raining blows upon her harasser.

Judy was rattled. She was used to fishermen hollering at each other, and she knew the White fishermen were suspicious about the Vietnamese— she had even driven around their part of town with Billy Joe at night, slowly rolling down unlit roads to see whether the Vietnamese were building crab traps or more boats. But she never sensed that any of this would put their lives in danger.

WHEN BẰNG RETURNED TO SHORE, HE CALLED THE GAME WARDEN to report what Billy Joe had done to their traps. He said he was just trying to talk to Billy Joe about why he'd destroyed them, but that when his boat got too close, Aplin started chopping at it with a knife. He admitted to circling their boat, but that when he saw a girl crying in the back of the boat, he felt bad so they peeled off and went home.

Bằng and Sáu were taken into custody, but Billy Joe decided against pressing charges; he didn't think the small fine they'd get was worth the hassle in court.

But nothing was the same with him after that; a switch had been flipped.

The next morning, Billy Joe didn't rise early to go crabbing; he was done with it. He dry-docked his boat and began the process of converting it into a simple shrimp trawler. He'd have fewer encounters with the Vietnamese, he figured, since they hadn't yet broken into shrimping.

Over the course of the next few weeks, he made his fury at the Vietnamese known. When a Vietnamese crabber pulled up for fuel, leaving the engine running while he went inside the fish house, Billy Joe hacked off the tie ropes and threw the boat into gear, leaving it to drift into the harbor and spin in circles.

On another occasion, he was at his brother Doc's fish house when Sáu pulled up in his boat. Billy Joe barked at him to come up for a "talk," but Sáu, who was only five-foot-five and a hundred pounds lighter, remained in his boat, nervous. When Billy Joe raised a rifle and aimed it at him, Sáu threw the engine into reverse and fled.

Sáu was confused and angry. Why was Aplin so fixated on him? After all, it was his friend Thảo who had inadvertently set Billy Joe off in the first place by dropping his traps close by. The two had a similar build and haircut—maybe Billy Joe was confusing them?

The next day, Sáu and several Vietnamese fishermen approached Billy Joe in an overture of peace, but they were rebuffed. Ever since the confrontation on the bay, Billy Joe started keeping a rifle in the pickup. The Vietnamese were buying guns of their own.

Bằng had received threats from men he suspected were part of the Ku Klux Klan, and someone had burned a cross along the bay. Just a year earlier, a photojournalist published a bombshell series of photos of Houston Police Department and Galveston County Sheriff officers wearing Klan hoods over their uniforms, the identifying numbers on their badges and squad cars concealed with masking tape. He didn't know whom he could trust, so he went to Walmart and bought a pistol.

Most evenings after they got in from the bay, Bằng, Sáu, and their friends would sit out by the docks and drink a couple of beers. One night after their altercation on the water, Billy Joe drove up in his red Ford pickup with three or four others in the back and shouted, "You need to get outta town! Time to get out of here!"

"Fuck you! I ain't moving nowhere!" Bằng snapped, responding for his friends.

Billy Joe eyeballed them before easing off into the pitch-black roads of Seadrift.

DIANE WILSON FOLLOWED REPORTS OF THE STILL-GUSHING IXTOC I oil spill with mounting dread over what would happen if it reached Seadrift. There was, in the emerging nomenclature of spills, a forty-mile-long "tongue" of oil jutting out from the main slick, periodically lapping at the coast as winds blew the slick toward American waters. When it reached the southern shores of Texas at South Padre Island, Mexican officials predicted that they would have the well capped by mid-September, but this was, at best, a hopeful guess. Tourists stepped around tar balls peppering the beaches; the island's Dockside Deli responded to the newly arrived crude with a new addition to its menu—Oil Slick Soup: broccoli bobbing in chicken broth between pools of soy sauce. Those who swam in the water emerged with a "brown goo" clinging to their feet. The most popular way to remove it was by dousing their skin in lighter fluid.

But instead of focusing on the massive slick headed toward their bays, the White fishermen were obsessed with the Vietnamese.

One morning, while working with Donna Sue at Froggie's, Wilson got a call from a Vietnamese woman, asking if her husband might be allowed to shrimp in the nearby bays and sell to her. "Sure, why not?" she said, thinking nothing of it, but Donna Sue was furious.

"The Vietnamese are gonna ruin the bays!" she exclaimed.

"How?!" Wilson asked.

"They're going to shrimp at night!" Donna Sue retorted, which ran-kled Wilson: every White shrimper she knew did that. She realized there weren't any Vietnamese shrimpers yet for the simple reason that fish houses refused to buy their catch.

By then, she'd finally saved enough for a down payment on a shrimp boat, securing a balloon loan from the bank for $10,000. It was a terri-fying amount of money to owe, but she knew the bays better than just about anyone, and saw the boat as a pathway to a better life. She chris-tened it the *SeaBee* and became the first female shrimper of Seadrift. She never wanted a deckhand, because it would've meant having a man on her boat, and she knew they had an incurable need to take control. They couldn't help telling her where to drag or where the catch was better. Whatever the subject, they talked too much for her, so she shrimped alone, scanning the watery horizon for gulls feeding on shrimp and learning how to gauge a squall. Whenever she wasn't on the boat or tend-ing to the kids, she worked at Froggie's, mending nets, unloading the daily catch, and adding to her collection of mutated specimens.

Wilson sensed something ugly brewing among the White fishermen. Forty times a day, she'd hear them talking about "slopes" and "gooks" over the CB radio, but she wrote it off as a bunch of hardheaded men barking.

But it wasn't just talk. Late one Saturday night, Sáu and his brother Chính were drinking at the Paradise Bar when a shrimper with too many drinks in him pulled a knife, screaming that the Vietnamese were steal-ing food from the mouths of his children. By the time the sheriff showed up, Sáu and Chính had dragged their attacker out to the parking lot for a pummeling. After spending the night in the Port Lavaca jail, Sáu went back to the bar and bought a revolver for $35 from another patron. Chính, who had a wife and one-year-old son back home, bought a .22 rifle.

Sáu told his brothers that trouble was coming.


ON JULY 22, BILLY JOE TURNED THIRTY-FIVE. BETH AND HER SIB-lings gave him a new button-down white shirt, but he wasn't in the mood for much of a celebration.

On August 2, Billy Joe came upon Sáu's car parked outside the hardware store in town. He slashed its tires and waited for Sáu to come out so he could tell him he'd been the one who did it.

As Sáu went off in search of the justice of the peace to file a complaint, Billy Joe trucked some rigging over to the boatyard to weld it to his boat. He fired up his welder's torch, unaware that his helmet had a small scratch. When he eventually removed it, his right eye was in excruciating pain, the result of welder's flash: UV light had leaked through and burned his cornea. It felt as though his eye was filled with sand, and every time he blinked, it would scratch and burn.

Judy brought him to the hospital in Port Lavaca, where he was given dilating drops. That night, he fell into a deep sleep, not waking until early the next afternoon.

On August 3, Police Chief Bill Lindsey added a chat with Billy Joe about slashing Sáu's tires to his to-do list. It was a police force of two, so the job required a constant triaging of each citizen's problems.

By early evening the pain in Billy Joe's eyes had subsided, so he trudged out the door to visit a relative staying at the Seadrifter Inn. As he drove to town, the waters of bay glinted in the sunset out his driver's-side window. Out his passenger's side, great fields of white-capped cotton unfurled inland, interrupted only by the expanding petrochemical plants. The harvest would begin soon.

He eased his truck over a bridge spanning an irrigation canal and turned down Main Street toward the docks. When he pulled up to the Seadrifter Inn, he glanced over and saw Sáu.


SÁU AND HIS BROTHERS CHÍNH AND TÀI WERE THERE WITH SOME friends, Sen and Hiển, excitedly testing the engine on a new boat Sáu had just bought. By then, they could tell Billy Joe's truck from a distance, so they urged Hiển, who was only fifteen, to run for Chief Lindsey.

Hiển scampered off as Billy Joe pulled into the parking lot and down to the water's edge, blocking Sáu's boat on the launch ramp. He glared at the men for an uncomfortably long time before hopping out.

"Who is this guy?" Billy Joe asked, calmly pointing to Sáu.

No one replied.

Billy Joe walked over to Sáu.

"What's your name?"

Sáu didn't answer.

"What's your name?!" Billy Joe asked, getting agitated. He kept asking but each time was met with silence.

Finally, Sen blurted out Sáu's name, but Billy Joe, in a rage, was no longer interested in talking. He struck Sáu, who bolted around to the back of his car, which was parked with its boat trailer close to the ramp.

Sáu reached for the trailer hitch, trying to unfasten it from the car so they could escape, but Billy Joe stomped on his hand, pinning it to the hitch.

"If you don't move out of Seadrift," Billy Joe shouted, "I'm going to cut your throat!"

Sáu stood up and folded his arms, what he saw as a Vietnamese form of demonstrated politeness.

Billy Joe drew a knife and swung at Sáu, cutting him across the chest. He pushed Sáu to the ground, beating him as he shouted, "Leave Seadrift! If you don't, I'll shoot you in the open sea!"

Chính jumped into their car and turned it on. Sáu managed to pry himself free from Billy Joe, leapt inside, and the two sped off, leaving their brother Tài in the boat.

Sen stayed there with Billy Joe, trying to mediate the situation, urging him not to fight, telling him, "Everyone can live in peace in Seadrift."

"This town is my town!" replied Billy Joe, though he'd come only a few years before Sáu. "This land is my land! This house is my house!

"We helped you in the Vietnam War, but you were defeated!" he continued. "Now you're coming here, and scaring my wife and children!"

Sen stayed there, listening to Billy Joe. There was still no sign of Hiền or Chief Lindsey, but he felt that the situation was subsiding, and hoped that Sáu and Chính would clear out of town for the rest of the night.

Bằng was sitting in front of his trailer drinking beers with a friend when Sáu and Chính pulled up, kicking up a cloud of oystershell dust behind them.

Sáu burst from the car and shouted, "Where's my gun?"

# 7

# "No, Man . . . No!"

Sáu raced into his room, grabbed the loaded .38 revolver from his closet, and filled his pocket with a fistful of bullets. He wedged the gun in his waistband as Chính emerged from the bathroom with a .22-caliber rifle.

Bằng saw that Sáu was bleeding from his chest, but the brothers sped off before he could understand what was happening. Instinctively, he grabbed his pistol and took off in search of his friends.

Sen was still talking with Billy Joe when Sáu and Chính roared back into the parking lot by the docks. Less than five minutes had passed. Sen raced over and pleaded with Sáu and Chính to drive home, but within seconds Billy Joe was yanking at Sáu's door. Sen tried to step between them, but ducked out of the way when Billy Joe started throwing punches.

The door was ajar, just enough for Billy Joe to land a blow on Sáu, who scrambled out of the car. The two started brawling, but Billy Joe soon dropped Sáu to the ground.

Sen was in a panicked state, desperately hoping the police would arrive to break up the fight, but in the melee he saw Sáu regain his footing and draw his revolver.

Billy Joe backed up several feet.

"No, man . . . No!" he pleaded.

POLICE CHIEF LINDSEY WAS THREE BLOCKS FROM THE WATER-front, looking for Billy Joe at that very moment, when Bằng screeched up alongside him and shouted, "There's going to be trouble at the docks!"

They were a half block away when they heard gunfire.

Sáu's first bullet tore through Billy Joe's liver, stomach, and heart.

Billy Joe stumbled back toward his truck and held his hands up; when Sáu shot him again through his left biceps, he collapsed to the ground by his tailgate, just a few yards from the cold water of the bay.

Sáu jumped into his car and drove off, leaving his brothers at the scene of the crime.

When Bằng and Chief Lindsey arrived moments later, Lindsey crouched down and felt Billy Joe's throat for a pulse. Bằng sped off in search of Sáu.

As the paramedics raced to the hospital with Billy Joe, Lindsey drove to the Vietnamese trailer park in search of a suspect.

JUDY APLIN WAS AT HOME WITH THE KIDS WHEN THEIR NEIGHBOR ran up to the front door screaming, "Billy Joe's been shot! We gotta go to the hospital, now!"

The hospital was twenty miles away in Port Lavaca, only blocks from where she'd first met Billy Joe. It was only yesterday that she'd taken him to the same hospital to treat his welder's flash.

When she arrived, the emergency room doctor sat her down and started talking, and she went numb. He brought her into the room where her husband was laid out on a table, awaiting autopsy. After identifying his body, she emerged into the hospital's parking lot to find Beth, Cheryl

Ann, and Billy Joe Jr. waiting nervously in the backseat of their neighbor's car. As she told them, the car erupted with screams.

IN THE MOMENTS AFTER THE SHOOTING, SÁU PULLED OFF TO THE side of Bay Avenue and hurled his .38 into the water. Chính's .22 rifle, which hadn't been fired, lay in the backseat.

He drove back to the trailer park, fished the bullets from his pocket, and tossed them in the weeds behind his trailer.

When Bằng pulled up, he found Sáu sitting on the hood of his car in a blood-soaked shirt.

"What happened?" Bằng screamed.

"He's dead," Sáu said in a daze.

"Man, we gotta go!" Bằng snapped.

Sáu didn't move off the hood. "I'm not going anywhere. I'm waiting for the police to come get me."

Bằng was beside himself, and frantically tried to explain the Ku Klux Klan to Sáu, the burning cross he'd seen, and how they'd react if they found out that a Vietnamese guy had killed a White fisherman. Bằng was worried that the Klan might show up before the police ever did, or that they themselves might be Klansmen.

If Sáu wanted to turn himself in, that was his decision, but better to do it in a town far away from Seadrift, where nobody knew the Aplins. Bằng finally talked him into his car and the two disappeared down the oystershell road leading out of town.

Moments later, Chief Lindsey pulled up to the trailer park and found Sáu's car and Chính's rifle. Chính was arrested as a probable accomplice, but Bằng and Sáu were nowhere to be found.

# 8

# Seadrift Awakes to Ashes

Bằng and Sáu drove up back roads, never speeding for fear of attracting the police, who were surely prowling for suspicious drivers in the wake of the first murder in Seadrift's history. They arrived in Houston close to midnight. Bằng pulled up to the bus station, gave his friend $100 in cash and a white button-down shirt, and said goodbye. He was exhausted, but he knew how bad it would look if he was discovered out of town, so he turned around and headed back to Seadrift.

By the time Judy and her children returned home, their house was filled with members of the Aplin family and other armed men, some of whom had worked as deckhands with Billy Joe. In the hours since Billy Joe's killing, the men flooding into their home had convinced themselves that the Vietnamese of Seadrift would be coming to kill the rest of the family, so they barricaded the doors with tables, drew the curtains, and loaded their guns. When Beth walked through the living room, someone barked at her to get down and crawl on all fours.

Beth, Cheryl Ann, and Billy Joe Jr. crept into their parents' bed and wept. In the middle of the night, there was a noise outside on the street. Beth scampered over to the window and peered out to find a cougar loping across the road.

When Bằng finally pulled into town around two a.m., his four-door Ford was in rough shape, its engine block smoking after five hours on backcountry roads. The police were waiting for him with handcuffs, and took him to the county jail, where Chính was already in custody.

CHIEF LINDSEY KNEW THEY'D HAVE TO FIND SÁU, BUT HE FELT AS though the situation was well enough under control. The only wild card was how the White residents of town would react to the killing of Billy Joe Aplin.

ACROSS TOWN, IN A SMALL MESQUITE GROVE BEHIND AMASON'S bar, Richard Haight, a thirty-four-year-old sanitation worker, was drinking and smoking weed with a small group of angry Seadrifters. Timbo Blevins was there with a couple of his brothers, Billy Don and Michael, and their cousin Peanut. Hubert Cady and Pudd Milam. One of the Chatham boys. They all crabbed or shrimped or had family in the business, and they all knew Billy Joe.

As the empties piled up and the weed ran thin, the men's anger curdled into talk of revenge. About getting rid of the "chinks" and "gooks." The moon was nearly full, and in the dark of the mesquites, Richard took a long hit off a joint and exclaimed, "Well shit, if we're gonna do it, let's do it! What're we gonna do? Wait till daylight and do it? It's two o'clock in the morning!"

That set them all in motion. They rustled up several empty liquor bottles, filled them with gas, and wedged diesel-soaked rags into the mouths of their firebombs. One of the men, a Vietnam veteran, suggested that anybody who squealed about what they were about to do would be killed. They all shook on it.

They emerged from the grove and marched over to the home of Ray Mooney, cutting across the lawn to the garage, above which was a small apartment rented by a Vietnamese family.

Richard fumbled with his lighter. He was pretty messed up from the booze and weed, but he managed to light the diesel, watching it burn down toward the mouth of the whiskey bottle. At the last second, he and four others whipped their firebombs against the side of the garage apartment. The glass shattered, drenching the siding with gasoline as it ignited.

"Go fuck yourselves, you sonsofbitches!" Richard and the others hollered. "You shot our friend!"

Screams soon emerged from within the apartment. When the door burst open, Richard saw what looked like twenty people spilling down the staircase, five-year-olds, ten-year-olds, elderly, all of them screaming.

Some of the Vietnamese picked up rocks and oyster shells and started hurling them at Richard and the others, who had already started scampering off.

They still had plenty of firebombs ready to go, though.

They regrouped and moved down to the harbor. They all knew which boats belonged to the Vietnamese—the one Richard firebombed was painted a pretty red. They set fire to three boats before running off in different directions.

Richard didn't want to walk past Ray Mooney's burning house, so he crept along a drainage ditch lousy with rattlesnakes, desperately hoping to get home before anyone spotted him.

He emerged onto Dallas Avenue and was passing the volunteer fire department just as the siren, perched atop a thirty-foot pole out front, began to wail.

Richard was pretty familiar with the siren for two reasons: first, in the early 1960s, his stepdad, then mayor of Seadrift, had arranged for Union Carbide to donate the siren to the town; second, he was one of the town's volunteer firefighters, and the only one authorized to drive the fire truck.

Just then, another firefighter screeched into the lot and shouted,

"Ray Mooney's house is burning down! Are you gonna drive the damn truck or what!"

"I guess I'm gonna have to, ain't I!"

"Where you been?" the firefighter asked.

"Ain't none of your business where I been," snapped Richard, who knew he smelled like diesel and gasoline.

By the time they pulled up to the fire, three or four other volunteer firefighters had joined them. They were all wearing their helmets and firefighting gear; Richard was in shorts and a T-shirt.

As he extinguished his own fire, he glanced nervously around at the onlookers—none of the Vietnamese were there. He didn't think the damage to the garage was that severe, but he knew it'd be classified as arson as soon as they found the broken whiskey bottles in the weeds.

Once home, he collapsed into his bed, unable to shake the image of the kids running down the stairwell. As he drifted off, he remembered that volunteer firefighters got a bonus of $2.50 for every fire they put out.

THE SUN ROSE A FEW HOURS LATER OVER A TOWN IN TURMOIL. SÁU was still at large. Boats and a home had already been firebombed. One of the police department's two squad cars was having trouble starting.

Diane Wilson watched her fellow Seadrifters descend into a spasm of hate but didn't know what to do other than keep her head down. One of her high school classmates, Timbo Blevins, walked into her friend's home sopping wet and announced that he'd just burned one of the Vietnamese boats. She saw young men she'd once babysat brandishing rifles. Billy Joe's father, B.T., told a reporter, "Just as long as there's one gook left in a fishing town on this Gulf Coast, there's going to be trouble." He fought back tears before warning, "There's going to be war."

Most of the Vietnamese in town were frantically packing their things, queueing at the gas station to fill their tanks and buy last-second provisions. Their home phones were ringing with threats. "You killed my brother, and I have to kill you," an anonymous caller told a seventeen-year-old girl working at the crab-picking plant.

"We're just barely keeping our heads above water," sighed Mayor Rayburn Haynie, who worked as a shipwright in town when he wasn't acting in his official capacity. "I don't have the power to protect them," he told a reporter who asked about the fleeing Vietnamese. Chief Lindsey agreed: the town was "a big powder keg with a short fuse," and his tiny force would be "hard-pressed" to protect any Vietnamese who remained.

Haynie issued a curfew for the first time in the town's history. Nobody would be permitted out between the hours of nine p.m. and six a.m.

THE VIETNAMESE FAMILIES WHO DECIDED TO STAY REARRANGED the trailers into a large rectangle, creating a compound that could be guarded more easily. They pulled their crab traps out of the water and stacked them by the hundreds in the compound, then returned to the waterfront to pull their boats out, that they might keep watch over them. To protect the compound, Vietnamese fishermen gathered their weapons and patrolled the trailers in shifts. Chief Lindsey had his constable blockade the road leading to the trailer park, hoping to keep the White and Vietnamese Seadrifters separated.

As some families loaded their belongings and children into trucks and left, reporters poured into the little town.

A photographer from the Associated Press went down to the waterfront and found Là Thanh Nhí and Đặng Thành Vinh kneeling on the planks of the dock, staring at what remained of their capsized boat, a charred husk jabbing up from the seabed. Mộng Huỳnh, whose boat was also torched, had another problem: someone had pulled his motor out of the water and wouldn't give it back unless he paid $1,000.

RICHARD HAIGHT WOKE UP WITH A SPLITTING HANGOVER AND A sense of dread. He didn't want to go to prison. When he saw some of the others in town and told them he was out, they called him chickenshit. Later that night, despite the curfew, someone torched a boat that was being stored in the backyard of a Vietnamese home whose occupants had already fled. Rumors swirled that Verlon Davis's crab-picking plant was about to be bombed.

Some 120 of the 150 Vietnamese who had settled in Seadrift in the previous three years fled town within forty-eight hours of Billy Joe's killing. Some who remained told a local reporter that they would have left, too, if they could have afforded to.

That 10 percent of the town's citizens had fled in terror wasn't exactly the best postcard for Seadrift; Mayor Haynie certainly wasn't helping in his interactions with the press.

"They're so *different*," he began. "They're human beings, but . . ."

The mayor paused.

"I don't want to see them pushed out of town, but . . ." Haynie again paused. "I won't go looking to bring 'em back either."

But the mayor did have one grudging acknowledgment: "They're the hardest-working people here, I'll give 'em that."

Except they were no longer there. And with no Vietnamese employees, the crab-picking plant closed down.

BẰNG SAT IN A JAIL CELL IN PORT LAVACA, UNSURE OF HIS FATE. HE knew enough about the law to understand that he'd broken it by helping Sáu escape from Seadrift. When they brought him into an interrogation room, he admitted that he'd taken Sáu to Houston, but he lied, telling them that Sáu had forced him by gunpoint to drive him out of town. He was released the following day.

In between making funeral arrangements and trying to explain to her children why their father had been killed, Judy Aplin dodged reporters stalking her in town. Her father-in-law, B.T., had no problems sounding off: "My son died standing up for his rights . . . and as long as these two shoes stay on these two feet, I will do the same thing. Regardless of the cost."

Billy Joe's sister Noopie sat on the front steps of her trailer and wept as she told a news crew, "These people . . . they don't think like us! They're just not our kind of people, and they're vicious, cruel people, and they're gonna take and grab what they want at anyone's expense. They've already went as far as murder!" His brother Doc told a reporter that he used to view the Vietnamese as "compassionate and hospitable . . . but now with my brother lying dead, I almost have guilt feelings I felt that way."

ON SUNDAY NIGHT, THE CASKET HOLDING BILLY JOE'S EMBALMED body was delivered to the Aplin home and wheeled into the living room for visitation.

Beth, Cheryl Ann, and Billy Joe Jr. cowered in their parents' bedroom, unwilling to come out. When Beth finally emerged, she saw her dad in the coffin and bolted toward the kitchen, training her eyes on the floor and walls, anything to avoid seeing his body. He was wearing the white shirt they'd given him for his birthday two weeks earlier.

On Tuesday, a hearse delivered Billy Joe's coffin to the cemetery. That same day, a police officer up in Port Arthur, near the Louisiana border, was sitting in his patrol car when a young Vietnamese man came up to him and said, "I killed a man in Seadrift."

The bewildered officer took Sáu Văn Nguyễn into custody.

THE DAY AFTER THE FUNERAL, CHIEF LINDSEY AND A DEPUTY QUIetly approached the Outlaw Motel, making their way to the room of Bobby Vandergriff, a local crabber who'd recently told a TV crew, "Somebody's gonna take care of those Vietnamese . . . kill 'em."

They'd received word that the crab-picking plant was about to be bombed. Verlon Davis had hired around-the-clock security to protect the plant, even though it was shuttered. He doubted any Vietnamese would return in the current climate, and he was himself persona non grata, vilified for his role in bringing Vietnamese to town in the first place. He started carrying a snub-nosed .38 in his coat pocket.

Chief Lindsey burst inside and found Vandergriff with two other crabbers in their twenties, three five-gallon cans of gasoline, and blasting caps. They claimed they weren't after the crab plant, but confessed that they were planning to douse the docks in gasoline and torch it all.

In the days since the killing, Chief Lindsey hadn't taken an hour off. But as he drove home, he sensed the worst of it might finally be behind them.

# 9

# The Klan Comes to Seadrift

IT MIGHT'VE ENDED THERE, BILLY JOE IN HIS GRAVE, SÁU AND Chính behind bars. One small-town fisherman killed by another, a tragic event, but one that cast a short shadow.

For the White fishermen, there was a way things were supposed to play out. Texas justice: quick trial, harsh sentence. The obnoxious news crews would finally clear out and things would go back to the way they'd been before. The Vietnamese who'd fled the firebombings would stay gone, maybe even giving up fishing and trying their hand at something new in a faraway town. The White fishermen would have the bays back to themselves.

But nothing happened that way.

WHEN THE JUSTICE DEPARTMENT APPROACHED THE LOCAL DIO-cese of the Catholic Church—which had played a role in resettling refugees—to help mediate between the Whites and Vietnamese, a priest from San Antonio paid a visit to Sáu and Chính, who were languishing in the county jail, unable to find a lawyer willing to defend them. Early the following morning, the priest sat down in the pew behind one of his most faithful parishioners and told him it was his Christian duty to represent the brothers. Pat Maloney, otherwise known as the "king of torts," was one of the best trial lawyers in the country. He knew the wheels of justice were "damn square most times . . . those poor guys that came to court without a good attorney got sold down the river," so he accepted the case, but refused any money.

Within days, Maloney successfully moved to change the venue of the murder trial, arguing that the brothers stood no chance of a fair trial in any of the fishing towns along the coast. But Sáu's and Chính's relief was soon extinguished by news that they'd be tried in the ultraconservative town of Seguin, 150 miles inland, which Maloney decried as "redneck" and a "plaintiff's purgatory."

Maloney thrashed through the voir dire process of selecting a jury, getting numerous prospective jurors to admit that, while they under-stood the constitutional presumption of innocence, they just didn't like the Vietnamese. "I'm certain I couldn't be fair," said one juror, who wouldn't explain why. "Well, I just don't feel like people should come to this coun-try to begin with," said another. "You don't know these two Vietnamese, do you?" Maloney countered. "No." "Are you telling the Court . . . that you just don't like Vietnamese at all, that you couldn't be fair to these two defendants?" Maloney asked in exasperation. "Well, right," the juror an-swered. Another juror acknowledged a bias against Vietnamese but promised that "by God," he would try to overcome it. "See," Maloney replied, "but God isn't doing the picking. I am."

When an all-White jury was empaneled, they could feel the screws of Texas justice turning.

Police Chief Lindsey told a reporter, "If those boys don't get a rea-sonable sentence, there's probably going to be open warfare . . ."

AS IT WAS, THOUGH, MALONEY'S REPUTATION AS A COURTROOM brawler wasn't exaggerated. On the first day, he threw members of the jury on their heels, provocatively suggesting they were too biased to render a fair verdict and defying them to prove otherwise. He destroyed the prosecution's depiction of Billy Joe as a gentle family man by calling a

Sáu (right) and Chính (center) Văn Nguyễn arrive in court to be tried on murder charges.

former Seadrift constable who described him as "a big ole fighter with a
bad reputation for being rough and tough." According to the constable,
it was common knowledge that Aplin had been threatening the Vietnamese in town. Verlon Davis's wife, Georgia Ann, testified that "Billy
Joe told me he wanted to get rid of all the damn gooks." Maloney even
managed to get the prosecution's eyewitnesses—three teenagers driving
by the docks when they saw Billy Joe pummeling Sáu—to concede that
Sáu "wasn't trying to start any trouble."

When the trial turned to the fateful day Billy Joe smashed the crab
traps, Maloney wondered whether Aplin had even confronted the right
guy: Sáu and Bằng had testified that the traps had actually been dropped
there by another crabber, Thảo. Could a simple mistake have set Billy Joe
on a course that would lead to his death within weeks? It was a crucial
point, one that reporters covering the trial ignored wholesale: only one
local paper mentioned it, near the bottom of an article. Judy took the
stand to argue otherwise, but during a recess, Maloney had Sáu and
Chính switch seats. When they resumed, he asked Judy to point to the
man who had dropped his traps between theirs—and who had killed her
husband—and she pointed to Chính.

The prosecution's case was simple: Sáu couldn't rightfully claim self-defense because he had escaped from the docks after being assaulted by Billy Joe. Why, when he was out of harm's way, did he get his revolver and return to waterfront, if not with cold-blooded, premeditated plans of murder?

In attacking this, Maloney didn't need to rely on any courtroom antics; he simply put Sáu on the stand. Speaking in a quiet voice, Sáu gave the jury an equally plausible explanation for why he returned to the docks: he wanted to protect his brother from the man who'd just cut him open. It wasn't until Billy Joe started beating him again that he drew his weapon.

"Put aside your prejudices of these two foreigners," Maloney urged the jury, "and give them justice."

Maloney summoned Shakespeare in his final remarks, from *Henry VI*: "Even the smallest worm will turn when trodden upon."

"As little as they are," he said, gesturing at his 115-pound client, "a man can only be pushed just so far. This has been a tragic case of a man who would not have it end any other way. Billy Joe Aplin pushed, cut, threatened and beat until he got his."

He took Billy Joe's knife, stabbed it into the railing alongside the jury box, and rested his case.

Three hours later, the jury shuffled back into the courtroom and delivered their verdict: not guilty, lawful self-defense. The room erupted, a discordant peal of joy, shock, grief, and fury. Sáu was trembling as the interpreter translated the verdict. He began to cry. He'd hoped all along to be acquitted, but in the final two days of the trial, he was overcome with dread that he would spend the rest of his life in prison. He thanked each of the jurors as they filed past him.

In that moment of bewilderment and rage, Judy Aplin was glad she didn't have a gun. She hustled her children into a car and disappeared, while B. T. Aplin, the patriarch of the family, spoke to media gathered outside the courthouse, proclaiming that Sáu's acquittal "gave the Vietnamese a license to kill."

"The Vietnamese just declared war." He predicted "a whole lot more problems everywhere," and said he'd just spoken with shrimpers who were starting to carry guns on their boats.

BẰNG DROVE SÁU AND CHÍNH UP TO HOUSTON, WHERE THEY CELE-brated their freedom, drank a few beers, and said goodbye. Despite their exoneration, Sáu and Chính knew they could never return to Seadrift. They left the state of Texas for good around midnight.

When the verdict hit town, Police Chief Lindsey instituted a new curfew and called up reserve deputy sheriffs and retired law enforcement officers. TV and print journalists were already racing back down to Seadrift from all over the country, and he didn't want them to find more homes or boats on fire. He sure as hell didn't want another murder. "We're getting ready for the worst," a city councillor said.

That night, Joe Surovik, a marine extension agent friendly with just about every fisherman on the bay, came home to find a number of trucks parked around his house, filled with members of the Aplin family. They had tanks of gasoline and a double-barreled shotgun and plans for re-venge, but Surovik wanted nothing to do with it. The Aplins then asked Butch Hodges, a Vietnam War veteran and commercial fisherman, if he would lead the charge to "burn 'em out," but Hodges declined.

When dawn broke without any incident, it seemed to many as though the worst was past. After several peaceful days, the curfew was lifted, and the town groped its way toward something resembling nor-malcy. Some of the Vietnamese began to return, now that fears of a violent backlash were subsiding.

BUT THEN, SEEMINGLY OUT OF NOWHERE, A RUMOR STARTED SNAK-ing through town, in whispers over coffee at the diner, between barrels of crabs down at the docks, and over CB radios out on the bays: the Ku Klux Klan was coming to Seadrift.

Nobody understood who had invited them or why they cared so

much about a dead crabber, but the Grand Dragon of the Texas Klan, a highly decorated Vietnam War veteran named Louis Beam, announced that he and a group of Klansmen were coming down for a "fact-finding mission" over Billy Joe's death and "irregularities" in the trial. Someone from Seadrift, he claimed, had driven up to his headquarters near Galveston Bay to ask for his help.

Several nights before the Grand Dragon's expected arrival, the town's one thousand citizens crammed into the elementary school's sweltering auditorium for an emergency city council meeting to figure out how to respond. A Boy Scout leader said his kids were terrified. Junior high schools were pulling out of basketball games in Seadrift for fear of running into the Klan.

Diane Wilson watched in dismay as B. T. Aplin addressed the crowd. "All we're after is truth and justice, and we hadn't got it. Whenever you can't get nothing done about law and anything else, there's people watching it," he said, referring to the Klan. "I don't think they want to hurt anybody. They're good people."

His words didn't offer much reassurance. By a unanimous vote, the council approved a resolution condemning the Klan and urging them to stay out of Seadrift, and the auditorium erupted into cheers.

WHEN BEAM ANNOUNCED THAT HE WOULD IGNORE THE TOWN'S request and come anyhow, the news crews returned.

The day before his arrival, Richard Haight, who was never questioned over his role in the firebombings, looked out his front window to find his Hispanic neighbor, who worked at the Union Carbide plant, loading up his wife and kids to clear out of town. He couldn't help being amused by all the sudden shock over the Klan invading Seadrift—he knew they were already there. When he'd worked as a sanitation truck driver, he occasionally found Klan robes in the trash. Once, when he was checking water meters for the city, a homeowner emerged in full Klan regalia and tried to recruit him.

Louis Beam and his "fact-finding team" showed up one late November morning to find a throng of cameras waiting. He spoke of conspiracies, alleging that a great injustice had occurred. During the trial, the sheriff had sheepishly acknowledged that he'd lost Chính's .22 rifle, an embarrassment, even though it had never been fired and the coroner attested that Billy Joe was killed by Sáu's .38. But to Beam, it suggested a cover-up—that the government was siding with the Vietnamese. He wondered whether there was a third shooter, a theory that Billy Joe's father took up after the trial.

The Aplins had had their day in court, but Beam wanted a do-over, calling for a "new investigation." If he wasn't pleased, he warned, the Klan would come back to Seadrift in the hundreds to "dramatize our concern."

"Would the Klan be here today if Billy Joe Aplin was killed by 'Joe Smith'?" a news reporter asked the Grand Dragon.

Beam looked down for a moment as he considered his response.

"I don't think that if a Seadrift fisherman had been killed by a 'Joe Smith,' I would be here."

"Would you encourage them to fish somewhere else?" another reporter asked, referring to the Vietnamese in Seadrift.

"For their own good, I plan to encourage them to abide by the standard accepted practices and regulations that the fishermen locally have."

"And if they say no?"

"Well, if they say no, then they'll bring the wrath of God on their head, I'm sure," Beam said, his arms crossed.

B. T. APLIN, WHO HAD CONVINCED HIMSELF THAT HIS SON WAS killed as part of a grand conspiracy after discovering secret members of the Viet Cong, took it a step beyond a mere investigation: "There will be no peace on the bay until there are no more Vietnamese," he said. "You cannot find any shrimper out there who doesn't have a gun now."

Seadrift soon receded from the national media, but things never returned to normal—something had been unstoppered in the minds of many White Seadrifters. A month or so after the acquittal, an anonymous appeal over the CB radio channel invited shrimpers and crabbers to a "social gathering" of the KKK in Seadrift, where new Klansmen would be inducted. Fishermen driving by would curse at Georgia Ann Davis for her role in managing the crab-picking plant that had brought the Vietnamese to town. Verlon still carried his snub-nose .38 with him wherever he went; there was talk of burning a cross in their front yard. "I got news for them," Georgia Ann told a reporter. "If they step foot in my yard to burn a cross, everyone will end up in jail or a hospital!" The Vietnamese trailer park was now illuminated by powerful floodlights throughout the night and ringed by No Trespassing signs.

Diane Wilson knew who the real enemy was. By then, she was certain that the petrochemical plants were behind the die-offs in the bays and mutations she'd locked away in her freezer. She felt "dumb as a hammer" for taking so long to see them for the danger they were, but now that she was alert, she saw threats rolling in from every direction. To the north, on the day of Sáu and Chính's acquittal, the *Burmah Agate*, a tanker filled with sixteen million gallons of Nigerian crude oil, collided with a freighter and exploded. As millions of gallons seeped into Galveston Bay, the flames seemed impervious to firefighters' efforts. To the south, the Ixtoc I well continued to gush, months after the blowout. And on land, the Formosa Plastics Group of Taiwan announced plans that December for a $100 million plant to manufacture PVC—polyvinyl chloride—on property purchased from Alcoa overlooking Lavaca Bay, where Billy Joe first came to suspect the plants as being behind his mutated crab. But all Wilson's fellow fishermen could talk about was "the Vietnamese problem" and the fact that they were on the verge of breaking into shrimping.

WHILE BẰNG, SÁU, AND CHÍNH WOULD NEVER COME BACK, ENOUGH Vietnamese families returned for the crab-picking plant to reopen.

Judy had kept her distance from the Klan, refusing to talk to journalists trying to find out why the KKK had taken such an interest in her husband's death.

Beth never told anyone what she knew.

If she had, she might've talked about the time her dad took them to their first Klan rally, over a year before he was killed. She remembered the fish fry, the angry speeches, the tense drive back.

She might have told them about the ceremony where her dad and mom swore an oath to the Klan.

They might've spotted the smoke curling from the Aplins' grill up into the sky over their tiny home as Judy loaded their belongings into the truck, readying to move yet again.

Inside the grill, Billy Joe's Ku Klux Klan robe went from white to black to nothing.

AS 1980 APPROACHED, LOUIS BEAM WAS INVIGORATED BY WHAT he'd stirred up in Seadrift. In the ten years since he came back from Vietnam, he'd never stopped fighting. After checking out the John Birch Society, the Minutemen, the White Citizens' Councils that emerged in opposition to integration, the American Nazi Party, and the National States Rights Party, he concluded that the KKK "reflected the very best ideals of white civilization" and signed up. He brawled with antiwar pro- testers. He was arrested on charges of bombing the Pacifica radio station in Houston for its antiwar stance. When he watched the fall of Saigon on television, he got a BORN TO LOSE tattoo on his arm, believing his government betrayed those who had fought. Convinced that commu- nists were on the brink of invading a weakened America, he formed a private militia called the Texas Emergency Reserve, training Klansmen in the bayous and grasslands in biological warfare and ambush tactics.

But he was looking for something bigger. He kept losing his day jobs whenever the press printed his name, and he dreamed of moving into full-time Klan work. For it to happen, though, he'd need a dramatic in- crease in the number of dues-paying members. And for that, he'd need more publicity. And as much as the media loved to film White men in robes and hoods, burning a cross in the middle of a dirt field just didn't grab their attention as much as it used to.

But the controversy Beam churned up in Seadrift had drawn national nightly news coverage, leading to a new Klan chapter in town there. The initiation ceremony was held on a small dock, on the outskirts of town, owned by B. T. Aplin, who declared to a reporter: "In my heart, I've been a Klansman all my life."

The Vietnamese of Seadrift had mostly fled without putting up much of a fight—if Beam moved quickly and dramatically enough, they might be driven from the coast entirely, before they broke into the more lucrative industry of shrimping. And he didn't plan to stop there.

Seadrift was the template. From his Klan headquarters just up the road from Galveston Bay, the Grand Dragon salivated for an opportunity to amplify the anger of White fishermen into an even bigger spectacle.

# Act II

# The
# Colonel
## and the
# Felon

Fury comes easily to the white worker. He is ready for battle. But he does not quite know against whom to declare war.

—GUS TYLER, LABOR ACTIVIST (1911–2011)

10

# The American
# Fishermen's Association

A S DAWN BROKE OVER 1980, GALVESTON BAY WAS WHEEZING
beneath what seemed to be a permanent plume of black smoke
snaking from the *Burmah Agate*, still burning off oil a full two months
after colliding with the *Mimosa*. The gigantic tanker—longer than two
football fields—was filled with sixteen million gallons of Nigerian crude
oil, ten million of which had already seeped to the bottom of the bay or
caught fire and darkened the skies above it. Fishermen reported a heavy
"rainbow sheen" drifting from the ruptured side of the vessel, oil that
would eventually drift two hundred miles all the way down to the
Matagorda peninsula, by Seadrift.

This wasn't a remote outpost: one in five Texans lived around Galveston Bay, three million people looking out onto six hundred square
miles of water poured into a shallow basin, freshwater from the Trinity
and San Jacinto Rivers mixing with the salt water squeezing in through
a mile-wide channel known as the Bolivar Roads. Over a thousand sewage and industrial wastewater treatment plants discharged effluent into
the bay; along its seabed ran 247 miles of pipeline, crisscrossing 251 miles
of channels dredged for deep-draft tanker ships. Half the chemicals

produced in the country came from plants lining Galveston Bay; a full 30 percent of the petroleum industry was based there.

Only a couple of decades earlier, scientists out of the University of Texas at Austin mapped a five-thousand-acre meadow of seagrass around the bay, a nursery for juvenile shrimp and crab for thousands of years. By the dawn of the 1980s, 95 percent of it was gone.

In early January, a private firefighting firm carried out its fourth attempt to extinguish the *Burmah Agate* by dousing it in chemical foam. When the fire burned through the chemicals, a despondent Coast Guard spokesman searched for a positive way to spin it: "I think you would have to say it's been reduced to a smoldering type fire."

That same week, a National Oceanic and Atmospheric Administration official warned that shifting gulf currents would soon start pushing more oil from the Mexican Ixtoc I onto Texan beaches. Seven months after the explosion that triggered the deep-water spill, the well remained uncapped, leaking fifty thousand barrels of oil a day with no signs of ending. "If the oil happens to be out there when the shrimp hatch," a shrimper told a reporter, "the crop will be wiped out."

ON THE WESTERN EDGE OF THE BAY WAS A PAIR OF FISHING TOWNS, Kemah and Seabrook, separated only by a narrow canal clotted with shrimp trawlers, go-fast boats, and the occasional yacht. At John's Western Point, a run-down tavern by the docks, a sandy-haired barrel-bellied Vietnam veteran named Eugene Fisher drained a pint of cheap beer in a foul mood.

Fisher was a foundering shrimper, about to lose his boat after having fallen several payments behind. The thirty-five-year-old with a bushy mustache planted himself sullenly on a stool as his buddies Jody and David Collins knocked balls around the pool table and listened to him gripe. The Collins brothers, both in their early thirties, originally hailed from Florida but had been shrimping Texas bays since they were teenagers. It was their oldest brother, John, whose salvage boat had hoisted Billy

Joe Aplin's trawler up from the seabed the day the Apollo 11 mission landed on the moon.

Fisher, who'd spent a portion of his childhood at the Boy's Harbor orphanage overlooking the Houston Ship Channel, only made it to the tenth grade before dropping out. A handful of years later, he joined the Marines and deployed to Vietnam, where he was shot twice in the side, twice in the leg, and once in the stomach. After coming home, his life hit the skids with an arrest in Arkansas for larceny, a felony conviction for stealing a car (which sent him to the federal penitentiary in Sandstone, Minnesota, for a couple of years), another conviction for embezzlement, and another arrest for burglary and assault on a police officer, which landed him a two-year sentence at the Nebraska State Penitentiary. When he got out, he returned to the Gulf Coast, taking odd jobs as a welder, carpenter, cement finisher, and swimming pool installer. He was now trying his hand at shrimping, but his timing was rotten.

Shrimping was as bad as anyone could remember. The National Marine Fisheries Service pointed to several reasons: heavy flooding during the period when the shrimp were in the estuaries; the Ixtoc I oil spill; rising fuel costs; and the implementation of a US–Mexico treaty ending American shrimping in Mexican waters, which forced many border-area shrimpers to move north, crowding the bays. And now the *Burmah Agate* disaster.

Jody had been shrimping full time since dropping out of school after the eighth grade. He'd seen a long succession of would-be shrimpers crash and burn after it became clear just how grueling the work was and how thin the margins were. He enjoyed the boom years but budgeted for bad times: for Jody, shrimping was a slow method of starvation.

But Gene viewed Galveston Bay like an ATM. When he needed money, he'd go out for a few hours and make a withdrawal, converting the shrimp he sold into booze, which led to regular barroom brawls. "He's a real redneck," one Seabrook waitress said. "He doesn't like anyone or anything."

Jody tried in vain to teach him that if he wanted to make a living at shrimping, he'd need to be out there every good hour of the day, not just when his pockets were light. But Gene never took his counsel, and was now on the brink of losing his boat.

Gene didn't blame his misfortune on toxic dumping, oil spills, or his own amateur shrimping skills. To him, the real problem was the forty Vietnamese refugees who had recently bought shrimp trawlers to work Galveston Bay.

MANY WHITE SHRIMPERS KNOCKED ON THEIR HEELS AFTER THE terrible season of 1979 sold their boats to the Vietnamese at huge markups—sometimes five times their worth—but then grew angry as the average cost of a trawler skyrocketed as a result. Months before opening day of the 1980 shrimping season on May 15, White fishermen who wanted to buy a trawler could no longer afford one. They resented the Vietnamese for paying so much, and before long, the same rumors of a secret government program funding the refugees that were accepted as gospel down in Seadrift began to ricochet around Galveston Bay.

Gene downed his beer. He made no secret of his hatred of the Vietnamese. "Nobody realizes the hell I go through when I go to the bay in the early morning and in all the boats they're speaking Vietnamese or listening to Vietnamese on their radios," he told a reporter. Jody was a teetotaler—an anomaly among shrimpers—the result of being raised by alcoholics. David drank a little, but preferred pills; he was particularly fond of quaaludes, which he trafficked up and down the coast in small amounts.

"This is not their country. They're guests in this country!" Gene ranted. "Through sheer numbers, they're going to shove us out. This is my town and I don't see where they have the right to take it over in the name of competition."

Gene's hatred of the Vietnamese wasn't just a product of his time in the war: he'd recently started dating Judy Aplin, the widow of the man whom White fishermen along the coast had come to see as a martyr in their fight against the Vietnamese. Jody and David Collins had known Billy

Joe—Jody gave him bait for his crab traps whenever he passed through Seabrook; David had a crush on one of the Aplin sisters.

So long as they were crabbing, the Vietnamese never presented much of a problem to them, but now that they were graduating into shrimping, Gene and the Collins brothers were furious about the competition. "We cannot compete with these people . . . they live off whatever they take from the water. Hell, the water's a supermarket for them!" Gene said in disgust. "They eat what we throw away. They don't throw nothing back. Even the littlest crab, they make some kind of sauce from it."

David always loved the rat-trap bar, its drunks so devoted to their craft that not even a hurricane or crab-filled floodwaters rising up around their heels seemed capable of dislodging them. But that night, they weren't there to brine their brains; they were there to figure out what to do about all these Vietnamese coming to Galveston Bay.

ONLY A FEW WEEKS EARLIER, THEY'D ALL PARTICIPATED IN A TOWN hall organized by mediators from the Department of Justice, which was hoping to avoid another Seadrift by bringing Vietnamese and White shrimpers together. As a gesture of goodwill, Father John Toàn Minh Hoàng, a Vietnamese priest assigned to St. Peter's Catholic Church in Kemah, gathered $500 and a bouquet of flowers from Vietnamese families around Galveston Bay to present to Judy Aplin.

"We know this money can't replace her husband," Father John told the gathering, "but we just wanted to help her at Christmas."

Mediators looked on nervously as Rudy Aplin, Billy Joe's brother, who had just founded his own White supremacist organization dedicated to preventing the resettlement of more Vietnamese refugees in the United States, approached the microphone.

"I cannot accept the gift," Aplin said to a shocked audience. "No amount of money can bring Billy Joe back." The town hall quickly descended into a shouting match. "This is a fight for survival!" David Collins cried, as mediators threw their hands up.

Jody had kept quiet that night, but he harbored deep suspicions that the government was up to something, trying to replace White shrimpers with Vietnamese, and he decided there was no point humoring the feds.

"THE SOLUTION IS NO MORE REFUGEES!" GENE DECLARED, AS SMOKE from the *Burmah Agate* drifted over John's Western Point saloon. "You've got to quit somewhere . . . at the rate the government is bringing in refugees, it's going to look like Hong Kong Harbor pretty soon." He racked the balls and laid out a proposal before the Collins brothers: Why not create a group of White shrimpers to combat the Vietnamese? Just how, they didn't yet know, but they grabbed a scrap of paper and put their names to it, Gene as president, David and Jody as officers.

They called it the American Fishermen's Association.

David smashed the cue ball into the rack, sending the balls gamboling over the chipped felt. He wasn't the shrimper Jody was, but he had dreams of building a new trawler for himself so he could get out of this nickel-and-dime business running quaaludes.

Before he could afford to, he'd need to unload his decrepit trawler on the first sucker he could find. He'd heard of a Vietnamese man who had just purchased a fish house and was looking to buy a boat.

The man went by the name of Nam.

# II

# The Colonel

P HƯƠNG LOOKED UP FROM HIS BREAKFAST WITH STARTLED eyes. His father, the Colonel, had just entered the kitchen with his head shaved, a ritual before a great battle. On the table before them was a cache of M16 rifles and revolvers.

In Saigon, in April 1975, the ten-year-old didn't understand what was happening with the war against the North, only that his father had been fighting for more than two decades. He was the Colonel's firstborn son, from a marriage that dissolved as quickly as it had formed: Phương's mom came from a wealthy family that disapproved of a military man for a son-in-law, even though a baby was on the way.

He'd endured stretches of years at a time without seeing his father; it wasn't until he was four that the families relented and allowed periodic visits. But the Colonel was always off fighting in some different part of the country, so Phương stored memories of his rare visits in the silo of his young mind. The gleaming ceremonial swords he played with when nobody was watching. The way people looked up to the charismatic Colonel. The arresting beauty of his dad's new wife—his fourth—who was a bona fide movie star. Sometimes he'd see her on the cover of magazines on the streets of Saigon and it made him feel close to his father.

But this visit was different. Phương's mother and aunt had told the Colonel that they wanted to flee from encroaching North Vietnamese forces, a plan that he rejected with a fury that frightened the young boy. Phương's uncles, then studying in America and Germany, were also pressuring his dad to help their parents escape, but the Colonel was adamant: the family would stay. He was in command of thousands of young men asked to surrender their lives in the defense of the country—how would it look if his own son was spirited away?

Phương stared at his untouched breakfast of eggs and bánh tiêu while his father gingerly loaded the weapons into a rucksack, tousled his hair, and headed out the door to the front, which was now only sixty miles from Saigon, near the port city of Vũng Tàu.

COLONEL NAM VĂN NGUYỄN HAD BEEN AROUND PHƯƠNG'S AGE when Hồ Chí Minh returned from exile in 1941 and founded the Việt Minh movement to fight for liberation from colonial oppression. For nearly a century, France had deployed a force of just twelve thousand soldiers to force a country of twenty-three million into submission while it extracted rice, coffee, opium, rubber, and valuable minerals from the fertile countryside. A *colonie d'exploitation*, in the official vernacular.

In the early days, Nam supported the Việt Minh. He had just started high school at the prestigious Lycée Pétrus Ky in Saigon when one of his classmates, who had passed out leaflets in support of Hồ's movement, was pulled from class by French forces. Through the open windows of the lycée, Nam heard the cracks of gunfire outside the school gates. He and his classmates rushed out of the school like bees from a broken hive in search of their classmate, but he was nowhere to be found. Days later, the French claimed that the boy had died under interrogation.

A youth movement grew. In 1950, some six thousand students in Saigon marched to protest the arrest of classmates who expressed support for independence. Police cracked down on the protest, arresting 150 and firing into the crowd. After another classmate was shot in the stomach, Nam and his fellow students boycotted class and marched to reclaim the body; the eventual funeral brought three hundred thousand to the streets. As the demonstrations widened, American war planes from an aircraft carrier anchored off the coast buzzed the students, while US destroyers ferried matériel for French forces.

In early 1954, the Việt Minh entered into the decisive battle against French forces holed up in the mountain valley outpost of Điện Biên Phủ. Even with nearly ten thousand troops, American-made tanks, artillery, and bulldozers, and an underground headquarters and hospital, the French failed to anticipate the determination of their colonial subjects to be rid of them. Fourteen thousand men and women lugged thousands of tons of mortars, rifles, and cannons into the hills surrounding the base; twenty thousand bicycles were used to transport months' worth of food. As the battle progressed, President Eisenhower, the first to describe Vietnam as a domino on a map liable to fall under the sway of communism in the event of a French loss, covertly deployed bombers and air mechanics. Two weeks later, the first two American pilots were killed attempting to airdrop supplies to the besieged French troops. The next day, the French surrendered. Two months later, at the signing of the Geneva Accords in Paris, Vietnam was partitioned in two, and millions fled from the north to the south in a matter of months.

Nam, then twenty, had just graduated as a second lieutenant from the Thủ Đức Military Academy. He'd lived under French colonial oppression long enough to support efforts to drive them from Vietnam, but as he grew into fighting age, the battleground shifted: it was more important to defend the South against the communist ideology espoused by Hồ Chí Minh and the North than to expel White foreign forces.

And so he began fighting alongside Americans to keep the domino from falling. After spending a year training in special forces operations at Fort Benning in Georgia, he entered the fight against the North. In the forests of Khe Sanh and Lao Bảo, he pierced his feet on punji sticks and took his first bullet, in his left arm.

While he was promoted up the ranks, the Americans dropped napalm and sprayed the chemical defoliant Agent Orange, destroying villages in increasingly vicious attempts to pacify a people who didn't want them there. When Nam was twenty-seven, he was fighting in the high-lands in Kon Tum when an artillery shell exploded nearby. He looked down at the pulp of his hip and pelvis and was certain he was about to die. He ordered a flanking maneuver and lay on the dirt, waiting for the peal of CAR-15 fire from his men. When at last he heard it, he smiled and passed out. Weeks later, he awoke in a field hospital in Pleiku, shocked to be alive.

Throughout the years of fighting alongside US servicemen, Nam—now a full colonel and a deputy battalion commander of more than two thousand men—paid regular visits to field hospitals to thank wounded American GIs for their heroism. Some had been injured in ground combat; others dropped from the skies in strafed helicopters. He fastened US–South Vietnamese friendship pins to their uniforms and thanked them for their heroism. But by 1973, the Americans had given up on the fight and left the South to fend for itself.

NAM KNEW THE END WAS NEAR, BUT HE PLANNED TO DIE IN THE fight or else in a North Vietnamese prison. He'd divorced the movie star and was in love with another woman, named An, but his ultimate loyalty remained to South Vietnam. That April morning in 1975, as he drew close to Vũng Tàu, heavily armed and head shaved, he found most of his men had already fled the fight. Within the previous few months, his division had lost nearly two-thirds of its ten thousand men as the North Vietnamese Army advanced on the capital.

He sped back to Saigon to defend his family and the capital, but by the time he arrived, Phương was gone.

THERE WERE SO MANY REFUGEES BELOWDECKS ON THE MASSIVE ship—some injured, others passed out from dehydration—that Phương couldn't see the floor. He clambered over bodies until he reached the stairs leading to the blinding brightness of the upper deck.

The day his dad left for the front, Phương's aunt dropped by and asked if he would come with her. She was like a second mother to him, so he joined her without hesitating, thinking they were just going on an errand. He was wearing his most prized possession, a new pair of jeans that his mom had just bought for him, but he didn't pack anything because he didn't realize he was about to become a refugee.

In the chaos of their escape, he and his aunt drifted from the shoreline in an armada of the damned as hundreds of skiffs, shrimp boats, and barges fled the North Vietnamese. Food and water ran so low that fights broke out over husks of bread; others paid small fortunes for a sip of water from gougers passing by in motorboats.

They first fled to the southern island of Phú Quốc, the site of a prisoner-of-war camp that his father had once overseen, which had since been converted into a haphazard refugee camp holding hundreds of thousands. They had planned to reconnect with Phương's mom, who had booked seats on a last-minute flight from Saigon, but she'd been stranded when the airport runway was cratered by Viet Cong shelling. Phương and his aunt boarded another ship and pushed out into international waters.

A week into the voyage, Phương stood on the deck in searing heat as the ship churned east across the South China Sea. To where, nobody really knew, but there was no returning to South Vietnam, which no longer existed. There were more than eight thousand refugees on the ship. There were makeshift toilets hammered out of plywood and bolted to the edge of the upper deck; when it rained, dehydrated passengers licked water off the deck, which was fouled with waste. Nearly every day, Phương witnessed death. He saw people fall over the taffrail into the sea. He saw a small boat filled with people draw too close to the ship and disappear into its propellers. He saw people leap from helicopters moments before they crashed into the ocean.

After two weeks at sea, the ship finally reached the US protectorate of Guam, which had become a staging area for the largest resettlement of refugees to the United States in history. He had no idea what had happened to his dad and mom, but he assumed the worst.

———

IN THE FINAL, CHAOTIC HOURS OF APRIL 30, 1975, AN BEGGED NAM
for a chance to escape. Nam, who had just turned forty, was determined
to fight to the death, but he drove her and his mother down to one of the
last ships readying to leave. Something was wrong, though: his father,
who was coming separately, hadn't arrived at the boat.

Nam tried to go back to the checkpoint to find him, but the South
Vietnamese navy seamen securing the area wouldn't let him leave, despite the fact that he was a uniformed officer and armed. He charged his
rifle, telling them he'd start shooting if they didn't let him go, but a naval
officer approached him and told him it was pointless: South Vietnam
had formally surrendered. Nam stood there, dazed, while his family
shouted at him to board the boat. Finally, someone wrested his car keys
from him, flung them into the water, and pulled him aboard.

As the boat inched out of Saigon, US helicopters darted overhead,
ferrying small numbers of people from the embassy. Nam was so dis-
traught, he gave little thought to where they might be headed. The family farm was surely gone, and he wondered what the North Vietnamese
would do to his father, whom he would never see again. He didn't know
what had happened to his son.

WEEKS LATER, PHƯƠNG WAS STANDING IN A LONG LINE TO GET
breakfast at the refugee camp in Guam when an announcement from the
PA system seized his attention.

"This is Colonel Nam Văn Nguyễn. I am looking for my son,
Phương."

He bolted off to find his aunt, who was already running to the ad-
ministrative office in search of Nam. It was the first time he remembered
seeing his father weep. They had nothing—not even a country—but they
were together again, at the very least.

——

WHEN THEY ARRIVED IN THE UNITED STATES THEY HEADED TO San Antonio, where Nam's younger brother was studying to become a pediatrician. Nam didn't want to go on welfare, so he applied for every job he could find in the classifieds section. The Colonel got a job as a car wash attendant at a nearby Exxon station for $3.10 an hour, drying cars, working as a mechanic, and pumping gas. Since he could speak English, French, Vietnamese, and some Chinese and Lao, he had many repeat customers; within a year, he was promoted to assistant manager.

The whole family moved into a single trailer with three bedrooms: Nam and An slept in one room, Phương's grandmother, cousins, uncles— twelve people in all—in the other two. Phương slept on a mat on the floor.

Everyone worked at the car wash, coming home at the end of the day soaked and exhausted. Phương's first job was drying their shoes with a hair dryer to make sure they didn't stink. Apart from the jeans he'd worn the day of the evacuation, he had nothing left from his boyhood in Vietnam. And when he enrolled at Jefferson Elementary, the White Americans had such difficulty pronouncing his name that he gave that up, too. Phương became Michael, but that didn't stop the White kids from calling him a "chink" and bullying him.

Almost daily, Michael would walk home terrified of encountering a group of about ten White boys who regularly beat him up. They called him Chinese, Japanese, Bruce Lee, tauntingly asking if he knew kung fu before descending upon him; Michael realized they didn't even know what Vietnam was.

He never told his dad about the beatings. When he came home bleeding and bruised, he'd lie and say he'd fallen while playing with his cousin. He knew his dad would be furious if he discovered the truth, but Michael figured it was pointless. Even if he learned to fight back, it was usually one versus ten, so he'd only be inviting a more vicious drubbing.

MICHAEL'S MOM WAS STUCK IN SAIGON WITH HIS STEPFATHER
until the day they escaped by boat to the Malaysian island of Bidong,
home to forty thousand refugees crammed into a space the size of a football field, considered at the time to be the most densely populated place
on earth. When she finally made contact, Nam helped Michael fill out
the paperwork to sponsor her resettlement. When they arrived, in 1978,
they moved into the trailer with everyone else. His stepfather worked
as a mechanic at the station. It might've been an awkward situation,
but Nam's wife, An, who was now pregnant, got along well with Michael's mom.

Eventually his dad saved enough to buy an Exxon station of his own
and a massive Cadillac, and Michael settled into a stable but grueling
routine: up at five to open the gas station at six, off to school until three,
then back to work pumping gas alongside his mom until eleven.

Despite the bullying, Michael was thriving in school; he was the star
of the math team and winning competitions throughout Texas. He was
spending more time with his dad than ever before in his life. The family
regularly piled into Nam's Caddy to pick the cilantro growing along the
highway—a delicacy in Vietnamese cuisine but ignored by San Anto-
nians. Michael and Nam went to the San Antonio River Walk to catch
crawfish. On long weekends, Nam took him deer hunting at a ranch near
Big Bend National Park along the Mexican border, teaching him how to
fire a .30-06 Remington rifle. In the baking heat, he picked off rabbits
while his dad stalked deer.

It was a happy time, which is why his dad's sudden announcement
that he was moving to a town on Galveston Bay called Seabrook came as
such a shock. Michael was fifteen and desperate to soak up as much of
his dad as possible, but Nam had heard there was good money to be made
in the shrimping business. Even though he knew nothing about shrimping, he'd already bought a fish house with a small bungalow overlooking
the bay.

All he needed was a shrimp boat.

# 12

# The Seabrook Agreement

D AVID COLLINS WATCHED AS THE VIETNAMESE MAN INSPECTED his boat. The man wasn't particularly tall, but he had a serious demeanor and walked with ramrod posture. And he didn't seem to know the first thing about shrimp boats.

"What'd you say your name was again?" he asked.

"Nam."

"Nam from Vietnam!" David chuckled. "You see any fighting over there?"

Nam glanced over at the beanpole of a shrimper with a faint smile. He knew the boat was in rough shape, but it seemed seaworthy, at least, which was more than he could say about some of the half-sunk heaps he'd seen.

David's eyes bulged for a moment when Nam agreed to his price: $26,000.

After the payment was made, David complained to a journalist that there were too many Vietnamese getting into shrimping, then used his windfall to start building a new trawler with the best boat mechanic in town, a man by the name of James Stanfield.

The Vietnamese in town already knew Stanfield, having paid him a

Colonel Nam Văn Nguyễn on his shrimp boat,
Seabrook, Texas.

small fortune to patch leaks and resuscitate their engines. Most of the
boats they'd bought had rotten hulls, sinking at sea or capsizing at the
piers amid the high winds. The Vietnamese called themselves "thầy
trọc"—"bald-heads"—on account of the heavy blows to their heads each
repair, towing, and salvage bill represented.

Not long after pressing his boat into service as one of about forty
Vietnamese shrimpers in the bay, Nam discovered that the engine was
beyond repair; Stanfield charged him another $9,000 for a replacement.

At first, he took it all as the cost of business. Nam had heard rum-
blings throughout the Vietnamese community of an incident the previous year involving the killing of a White fisherman down the coast in
Seadrift, but he didn't know anything about the Ku Klux Klan or its
leader, much less Gene Fisher and his newly formed American Fishermen's Association, or the mushrooming anger among White shrimpers

in Galveston Bay against Vietnamese newcomers. Nam and An kept to themselves, fixing up their fish house and bungalow on the Eleventh Avenue waterfront, with dreams of a simple life of sorting shrimp and selling it to restaurants in the Houston area.

But soon after he moved to Seabrook, other Vietnamese townspeople started coming to his fish house to ask for help—his reputation as a high-ranking colonel was so well known among the diaspora that it was impossible for him to live in anonymity.

"Some people don't like us," said Đức Phạm, a shrimper working out of Kemah. "They don't want us fishing here. They chase us." Another reported that Whites had tried to board his boat, telling him that "they don't want Vietnamese fishing in their water."

In a nearly perfect echo of Seadrift, White fishermen complained about Vietnamese habits on the water, that they weren't honoring the unwritten code of the bay. They were cutting too close to other boats, on occasion tangling and damaging nets. They were navigating hazardously in the Houston Ship Channel. They were chatting too much over the CB channels. Gene and other White fishermen routinely described the Vietnamese as secret communists who had infiltrated the refugee program.

As in Seadrift, fish house owners were pressured to stop buying from the Vietnamese fishermen, and in the bars and diners around Seabrook and Kemah, White shrimpers embraced the conspiracy that had seized most fishing towns along the Gulf Coast: that the federal government was secretly subsidizing the refugees. The Vietnamese tried in vain to explain that they didn't even qualify for Small Business Administration loans, and that their only advantage was that they borrowed money from each other through the hui, their private loan clubs.

Not everyone was so unwelcoming, though. After Jim Craig, proprietor of Old World Seafood, made it known that he would do business with the Vietnamese, his docks became known as "Saigon Harbor." Craig, a transplant from Illinois who had spent the previous five years converting the space from a junkyard, felt the stigma from others in town almost overnight, but tried to ignore it: "If a man's working for me, and somebody gives him a hassle, I don't give a damn if he's green or yellow or black! It doesn't make a damn bit of difference—I'm going to stand up for him."

By working together, the Vietnamese found efficiencies. At the end of a day, White shrimpers tended to dump their entire catch out at the fish house and take an average of all sizes of shrimp—jumbo, large, medium, and small—each of which fetched a different price per pound. But before the Vietnamese returned to the docks, they'd tie two boats behind a third, and use the time they were being towed to sort their catch into the right sizes for a more exact accounting.

"The Vietnamese still have the togetherness amongst themselves that we lost twenty-five or thirty years ago," Craig said. "When we lived on a farm in Illinois, if a man next door broke his arm, everybody went and worked for him. If you break your arm now, they're trying to buy you out tomorrow! But the Vietnamese are still helping each other. If their boat sinks, they run out and help each other, and don't ask nothing for it! They all quit working and go together."

White shrimpers saw the same trait in a different light. "I just think it's unfair competition," said Frank Jurecski, a forty-four-year-old shrimper. "They work as a family unit. They have a wife, kids, aunts and uncles working together. Our customs aren't like that."

"The Americans are jealous because the Vietnamese will hustle," Craig told a journalist. His wife, Sandra, agreed: "When it is raining, the American fisherman sits in a beer joint; the Vietnamese are out fishing."

Kids at school started calling the Craigs' teenage daughter a "chink lover."

MICHAEL FENDED OFF THE BULLIES AS BEST HE COULD, WHILE lamenting the fact that his father now lived four hours away. The few years he'd lived with him in San Antonio seemed almost like a lost luxury: he was now reduced to visiting on the occasional weekend, just as it had been back in Saigon during the war. As before, his dad was preoccupied by the growing threat of violence, despite the fact that An was just a few months from delivering their baby. As before, he saw his dad build a small cache of revolvers and rifles, one of which they'd used while deer hunting in Big Bend.

White fishermen insisted that their issues with the Vietnamese were strictly about economics—that race had nothing to do with it—but they often showed their hand in interviews with journalists covering the growing tensions out on the bay. "All it's going to take is for those gooks to run across a shrimper who's had a little too much beer one day and there's going to be big trouble," a shrimper told the *Galveston Daily News*. "The government thinks more of them gooks than the native Americans!" said Kemah shrimper Floyd Eades.

"I'm talking, running off at the mouth, because I don't want to see any violence," Gene Fisher groused. "I don't want to see my friends sent off to the penitentiary, or like Billy Joe Aplin—dead." But, Fisher murmured, accidents out on the crowded waters were "unavoidable."

As more frightened Vietnamese filed into Nam's home every day asking for help, he knew he couldn't ignore the problem. The opening day of shrimp season, May 15, was fast approaching, and he was worried about armed confrontations. After learning about Gene Fisher and the American Fishermen's Association, he decided to form a group of his own: the Vietnamese Fishermen's Association. He didn't have any strategy other than pursuing peace, but he wasn't about to let them harm anyone in his community.

DESPERATE TO AVOID ANOTHER SEADRIFT, THE JUSTICE DEPARTment and members of a task force on Vietnamese refugees convened by Governor Bill Clements organized town halls along the coast. If part of the problem between Billy Joe and Sáu had been a failure of communication, they could at least help by facilitating a conversation between both sides.

Even though the December 1979 town hall had ended in disaster when Rudy Aplin rejected the Vietnamese community's condolence gift to Judy Aplin, the tension in Galveston Bay was reaching such a point that Seabrook's young police chief, Bill Kerber, who had been on the job for only a few months, convened a new meeting at the local school auditorium in late March 1980 to discuss "the Vietnamese problem."

There were, of course, other problems. Five days before the town hall, the Ixtoc I oil spill was finally capped. In the ten months since the deep-water well ruptured, shortly before the killing of Billy Joe Aplin, an estimated 140 million gallons of oil had spilled into the Gulf of Mexico—enough to fill more than 210 Olympic-size swimming pools. The fires consuming the *Burmah Agate* tanker in Galveston Bay were finally extinguished, but not before ten million gallons of crude seeped into the seabed or went up in smoke. Vast and toxic spills and pollutants notwithstanding, all along the coast, ribbon-cutting ceremonies feted the opening of more petrochemical plants, which received tax abatements, freshwater impounded from nearby rivers, and permits to discharge toxic chemicals into the bays.

But as the Seabrook town hall kicked off, the White fishermen had only one thing to complain about: Vietnamese shrimpers. They wanted a ban on issuing new permits. They claimed there was "improper or incomplete screening of refugees," many of whom could not communicate in English. They accused Vietnamese of ignoring boating courtesies and the Do Not Enter signs in parts of the bay. They spoke of secret communists in their midst, and demanded to know just how these refugees were capable of paying so much money for their boats.

The governor's task force offered a few concrete remedies in response: They wanted to help establish an English training center in Seabrook, where Vietnamese fishermen could also learn the local customs of shrimping. There was a plan to open a fish paste factory in town, which would create jobs for both White and Vietnamese residents. State lawmakers hoped to introduce a bill that would freeze the issuance of new permits, but the biennial legislature wasn't due to reconvene until January 1981, a full ten months away.

But the White shrimpers weren't mollified. That night, Fisher's voice rose to the top: "All the ingredients are here for possible violence," he threatened. After the meeting, the governor received an urgent memo from Allen Clark, his assistant, describing the situation in Seabrook as "grave and explosive." Clark had privately spoken with Fisher and determined that the Whites could live "at least in the short-run, with an 'agreed upon' number of boats in the bay."

"The current situation, if it is not to explode," Clark wrote, "requires immediate action in a self-policing limiting of boats in the bay areas . . . any catalytic agent can ignite the tinderbox."

One week before the start of the 1980 shrimping season, a cross was burned in the dead of night beneath the drawbridge connecting Seabrook and Kemah, just yards from Jim Craig's "Saigon Harbor."

A few days later, as a tropical storm pounded the coast, Efrain Martinez of the Justice Department's Community Relations Service booked a room at the Holiday Inn in Seabrook. When his two guests arrived, he locked the door and told them they weren't walking out of there until they'd brokered an agreement. Sitting across from each other, for the first time, were Gene Fisher and Nam Văn Nguyễn.

Nam had brought bodyguards, but the Justice Department mediator made them wait in the lobby. Every fifteen minutes, an associate of Gene's called up to the hotel room to make sure that he was still alive.

For two hours, the two men tried to hammer out their differences. Martinez was hopeful: after months of talking about each other through the media, they now had a chance to see each other as individuals. The two finally settled upon a series of promises that Nam felt the Vietnamese would sign if it restored peace to the coast: they would not build any new boats, they wouldn't cut across the bow of other boats, and would try their best to abide by the unwritten laws of the bay, which Nam would endeavor to explain to the members of the Vietnamese Fishermen's Association.

They emerged from the hotel room that night with a handshake and what would become known as "the Seabrook Agreement." The number of boats working Galveston Bay would be limited to those currently tied up at the docks in Seabrook and Kemah: seventy for the Whites, fifty-five for the Vietnamese.

Over the next eight months, Nam did everything he could to uphold his end, discouraging any more Vietnamese families moving to the area from getting into shrimping, but he knew he wasn't omnipotent. After Southern California, Texas was home to the largest concentration of Vietnamese refugees—by 1980, nearly forty thousand had moved to the Lone Star State, with more coming each week. He had only limited tools at his disposal to dissuade newcomers.

On the morning of May 15, the start of shrimping season, Nam issued an emphatic statement to the press: "I discourage other Vietnamese—don't go into this business! I ask American fishermen not to sell any boats to us." He reassured White shrimpers that the Vietnamese were learning the rules and regulations governing shrimping in the bay. "Given time, I think the programs will work . . . it's not a problem that's going to be solved by leaving it alone, but it won't be solved by guns and knives, either."

The season opened without any violence. When the landings of shrimp outpaced 1979's miserable numbers, shrimpers started growing a bit more optimistic about the future.

BUT AT THE END OF THE YEAR, A FEW VIETNAMESE FISHERMEN moved to the area from Louisiana. Oblivious to the tensions in the bay, they began building a new shrimp boat in Jim Craig's boatyard. As they sawed away, someone tipped off Gene, who pulled up and eyeballed the new boat taking shape.

By New Year's Eve, Gene was making plans for war.

# 13

# A Fragile Peace, Torched

ON JANUARY 2, 1981, NAM WAS EATING BREAKFAST WITH A Vietnamese friend at the Dutch Kettle, the local diner a couple of blocks from the water's edge. He was in high spirits: An had just given birth to a baby girl, Judy, who was back at their bungalow on the waterfront. He was expecting a visit from his son, Michael, who hoped to spend his summer break working at the fish house and taking night classes at the community college.

Their conversation was interrupted when Gene Fisher barreled over to his table.

"Nam! Why are you letting your people build a new boat?!"

"Nobody told me anything!" Nam said. He was obviously frustrated; it wasn't as though every Vietnamese person in Galveston Bay had to get his permission whenever they wanted to fasten a rivet.

"Why are you letting them build a boat?" Gene badgered.

"I didn't tell them to build any boat!" Nam snapped. "I cannot stop them!"

"I don't like them building more boats just like that," Gene told him. "They're gonna get burnt...."

Nam was furious. His Vietnamese friend didn't speak any English, and he couldn't tell if others in the Dutch Kettle had overheard Gene's comment, but he didn't respond well to threats. Gene and other White shrimpers increasingly spoke of violence, and while Nam and his fellow Vietnamese knew how to fight, they just wanted to be left alone. Besides, David Collins, who'd sold him his boat, was also violating the agreement by building a new boat that he co-owned with James Stanfield, but Nam wasn't yelling at Gene about it.

From there, Gene drove over to Jim Craig's fish house, where most of the Vietnamese tied their boats up, and gave him a warning.

"Better watch your boats . . ." he said with a grin. "They're easy to burn."

Craig, a former football player, ursine and short-tempered, wasn't threatened.

"If I catch anyone burning boats here, I'm gonna shoot them!"


SHORTLY THEREAFTER, A VIETNAMESE MEMBER OF NAM'S COALI-tion was docking his boat when a White shrimper told him to leave or else it'd be burned. The Vietnamese shrimper was alarmed, but he couldn't find anywhere else to dock, so he left his boat and called Nam to report the threat. When he returned to the boat the next day, he was relieved to find that they hadn't torched it, but found it stripped of every-thing valuable: his nets, reels, and CB radio equipment.


ON JANUARY 8, SENSING THE PRECARIOUSNESS OF THE SITUATION, Police Chief Kerber summoned Gene and Nam to the station and man-aged to extract a renewed commitment to the Seabrook Agreement.

That day, Nam confirmed to reporters that five of the six Vietnamese boats under construction would replace old boats, which would be re-moved from the bay. The sixth was registered in Louisiana and would fish there, but Nam had persuaded the owner to halt construction on it. Nam said that the Vietnamese would honor their side of the agreement, even if the White shrimpers didn't.

"We hope the American shrimpers do the same thing, but we realize they have the right to build new boats and we don't have the right to stop them. They were here first."

Gene Fisher told a reporter he doubted the Vietnamese would pull their old boats from the water. "Better to burn them, just to make sure," he said.

On January 10, newspapers around the state reported optimistically on Kerber's efforts to bring both parties together with headlines like "Viet, Texas Shrimpers Find Accord."

Later that night, the first boat burned.

EARLY THE NEXT MORNING, LOAN HENDERSON, A VIETNAMESE woman married to a White American in Seabrook, raced down to the docks behind Emery Waite's Fish Market, where her forty-foot trawler, the *Trudy B*, was tied up. She owned the boat with some of her Vietnamese relatives, and had been operating it for only a few months.

Someone had severed the boat's fuel line, allowing roughly one hundred gallons of diesel from the tank to seep into the hull. The fire should have burned the boat down to the waterline, but whoever lit the match subsequently closed the hatch and bolted, inadvertently depriving the fire of oxygen. The boat, which was uninsured, suffered approximately a thousand dollars' worth of damage.

As they poked around and took photographs of the damage, the police noticed that all the *Trudy B*'s tie ropes had been cut, freeing it from the dock. The arsonist either wanted to spare nearby boats from being burned or to guarantee that the blazing *Trudy B* would drift into the bay beyond the reach of any firefighters.

Later that night, several hundred White fishermen and shrimpers attended a fish fry at the Stardust Lounge in Clear Lake Shores, just to the west of Kemah and Seabrook, not far from NASA's Johnson Space Center.

Around eleven p.m., a Kemah police officer on a routine patrol was radioed to be on the lookout for a yellow Opel with a smashed-out back window. The Opel had been at the Stardust and apparently had several members of the Ku Klux Klan in it.

Moments later, the officer was flagged down by a motorist who'd just seen a boat on fire while crossing the Kemah-Seabrook bridge. The officer called for the Kemah Fire Department before he even reached the shrimp boat, which was burning on its port side. The flames stretched the entire length of the white trawler, which was registered to a Vietnamese shrimper.

The fire engine roared up and extinguished the blaze quickly enough for the fire marshal to discover the remnants of a plastic fuel bottle. Whoever started the fire had popped the boat's fuel cap off, exposing its contents to the flames, but the fire had been extinguished before reaching the tank.

"With the current Vietnamese fishing problems," the officer wrote in his report, "this appears to be a racial incident, and the actor or actors might be connected with a racial movement, possibly . . . the KKK."

"There's no doubt in anyone's mind it's arson," Kemah's police chief told a reporter.

The night of the twelfth, wondering if they were in for a third straight night of burnings, both Kemah and Seabrook stationed police officers undercover down by the docks on either side of the sixty-foot-wide Clear Creek Channel.

Strange things happened. After midnight, a white-and-blue 1971 Oldsmobile registered to a White Texan eased by one of the officers with its lights off, driving slowly past where the boats had been burned. A yellow 1976 Fiat with extinguished lights crept by and disappeared into the darkness.

At around four thirty in the morning, a 1977 white-and-blue Ford pickup with Louisiana plates drove down to the dock where the second boat had been torched, unaware that they'd just driven past an undercover officer.

The officer watched in tense silence as four White men hopped down from the truck, whose license plate number he couldn't make out in the darkness.

The men reached into the cab of the truck and pulled out four white robes and hoods, which they donned. For twenty minutes, the Klansmen stood near the docks.

Then, as quietly as they'd come, they removed their robes, climbed back into the truck, and disappeared into the streets of Kemah.

Police Chief Kerber had tried his best to keep a lid on the situation, but now felt it about to boil over. He didn't have trained arson investigators, and feared that more fires were coming.

He called in the feds.

# 14

# Escalations

**B**ARRY FREECE, ARSON INVESTIGATOR WITH THE BUREAU OF Alcohol, Tobacco and Firearms, approached the *Trudy B*, where Chief Kerber was waiting expectantly. Freece had a barely noticeable limp, the result of a couple of shattered bones after a hard parachute landing from his days as a Navy SEAL.

He'd done three tours in Vietnam, working alongside Vietnamese special forces, carrying out ambushes, sabotaging infrastructure, and serving in the Phoenix Program, a ruthless campaign of capture and assassination coordinated by the CIA to persuade Viet Cong to defect. After getting out, Freece trained SEALs in New Orleans while going to night school at University of Holy Cross, hoping to join the ATF. While in school, he wrote a paper on the KKK, and as part of his research, he went into the local headquarters. When the Klansmen realized his training, they sat him down with David Duke, who tried unsuccessfully to recruit him.

In the argot of arson investigations, Freece was a "digger," a point-of-origin guy whose job was to find out how and where a fire started, and to chart its spread. He boarded the *Trudy B*, pried some char samples loose for analysis at the ATF's laboratory, and then set off in search of the arsonist.

Nam was certain that the boats had been burned by White shrimpers.

"We have no way of proving it," he told a reporter. "My people are angry and upset, but we are satisfied with the promise by the Justice Department that they will investigate."

The same day the ATF investigation was announced, though, the Texas governor's task force announced it would look into allegations that Vietnamese fishermen were improperly receiving food stamps. Even though he was privately skeptical, Nam applauded the decision and told reporters that he wanted to get everything "out in the open."

As part of his investigation, Freece showed up at a meeting of White shrimpers at which Gene Fisher spoke. He flashed his badge after the event and spoke to Fisher, who convinced him he had nothing to do with the burning of the *Trudy B.*

When Freece finally wrote his findings, he included Fisher's public warnings about burning Vietnamese boats and appended the local police reports about the dead-of-night Klan gathering at the site of one of the torched boats.

But his report quickly took a turn. "It is interesting," he wrote, "that both of the Vietnamese boats that burned were old boats, while just across the channel are two brand new Vietnamese boats which could have just as easily been set on fire." By Freece's reasoning, if White shrimpers or the Klan had set fire to the boats to harm the Vietnamese, why hadn't they targeted the newer, more valuable trawlers? But his own report stated that the second boat torched was only four years old, built in 1977.

Strangely, the arson investigator dwelled on possible food stamp fraud in his report, and named a Vietnamese fisherman rumored to have more than $200,000 in cash "in an unnamed local bank," who was allegedly on food stamps. He cast doubt on Nam's integrity, relaying rumors of black-market activity before acknowledging that the "information is unconfirmed."

And then, his shocking conclusion: "I feel that the suspects in this case are probably among the Vietnamese fishermen." He listed the names and addresses of each of the Vietnamese fishermen currently building new boats in the area, recommending that they be regarded as possible arson suspects.

———

TWO BOATS HAD BEEN TORCHED AND A CROSS BURNED WHILE
Gene Fisher publicly mused about burning them, but in the assessment
of the ATF, the Vietnamese were the arsonists. Fisher might've been
forgiven for assuming that law enforcement was on his side, or at least
willing to look the other way.

But the Vietnamese, whom he'd started describing as "fire ants," were
stubbornly still *there*. Gene, who knew how quickly the Vietnamese had
decamped from Seadrift after their boats were torched, decided it was
time to turn up the pressure.

He drove over to James Stanfield's place, where the mechanic and
David Collins were hammering away on their new trawler. Across the
bow of the boat they'd painted the name *Miss AKIA*. Plenty of the
White shrimpers knew what it meant. Hell, Police Chief Kerber knew
what it meant. David Collins thought it was one of the funniest names
for a boat imaginable: Miss "A Klansman I Am."

As it happened, Stanfield was the local recruiter for the Ku Klux
Klan, a fact unknown to all the Vietnamese who'd showered him with
money to fix their trawlers over the past couple of years.

Gene didn't care that they were also violating the Seabrook
Agreement—that was only meant to keep a boot on the Vietnamese. As
far as he saw it, the bay was for the Whites only.

"Stanfield!" Gene hollered as he lumbered over to the *Miss AKIA*.
"I need you to bring me to your friend in Pasadena!"


ON JANUARY 24, EXACTLY TWO WEEKS AFTER THE *TRUDY B* WAS
burned, Fisher and Stanfield hopped in a truck and headed out of
Seabrook in the direction of Pasadena, twenty miles northwest of town.
Gene had a new idea, one that might help him get rid of the Vietnamese
of Galveston Bay for good.

They drove up Red Bluff Road, cutting through flatland that was once
carpeted with strawberries but was now strangled with asphalt, oil refin-

ery smokestacks, and massive chemical tanks. The air was so foul most days that Pasadena took on the nickname Stinkadena; some residents coped with it by dumping Air Wick scented oil into their swamp coolers.

Fisher and Stanfield drove past the adult drive-in theater, which had recently been forced by city hall to build a large wall concealing its screen, due to the number of car accidents caused by distracted drivers on Red Bluff. Just down the road was Gilley's, the football-field-size honky-tonk nightclub, whose mechanical bulls were immortalized in the film *Urban Cowboy*, released the previous summer.

In the 1970 census, the year Gilley's powered on its bulls, Pasadena had a population of 89,277, only 45 of whom were Black. This was not a coincidence. For decades, the town had a reputation as a "sundown town," meaning Black people knew to clear out before darkness fell.

The local country radio station had the call sign KIKK, which handed out bumper stickers that were all over town: "PROUD TO BE A KiKKer," with the *K*s in the shape of cowboy boots. Some residents snipped the *i* out.

Fisher and Stanfield eased the truck into the small parking lot of 1619 Red Bluff Road.

Out front, a couple of men in forest-green camouflage fatigues stood guard. A large American flag hung next to a Confederate flag.

The windows of the squat redbrick building were hidden behind plywood adorned with Confederate flags and signs.

The signs read WHITE POWER and KLAN COUNTRY.

Another sign hung over the entrance:

KU KLUX KLAN
INFORMATION CENTER
OPEN TO PUBLIC
SAT. 10 A.M. TO 5 P.M.

Stanfield waited in the truck while Fisher went inside to look for the Grand Dragon of the Knights of the Ku Klux Klan, the man who'd taken their side after Billy Joe Aplin was killed in Seadrift.

Louis Beam was waiting for him.

# 15

# Louis Ray Beam Jr.

LOUIS RAY BEAM JR. SHOULD HAVE BEEN DEAD, IN PRISON, OR on the run, but as the thirty-four-year-old Grand Dragon sat in the headquarters of the Texas Knights of the Ku Klux Klan, fielding questions from a student filmmaker from Rice University, he didn't seem the least bit troubled.

How many times had he cheated death in Vietnam as a helicopter door gunner, three times more likely to perish than soldiers on the ground? One army helicopter was lost for every eight sorties—killing forty-five hundred pilots and crewmen over the course of the entire war—but Beam relished the danger and violence, longing to beat the 102 confirmed kills of Mike Long, whom he described as "the envy of every door gunner in the entire battalion." He survived all the "meat runs," extracting dead soldiers from jungle clearings in the midst of firefights. Survived the day a Viet Cong fighter unloaded an AK-47 into his Huey, rounds impacting a half inch from his head before the chopper crashed to earth. Survived a thousand hours of combat flight time, with twelve confirmed and thirty-nine probable kills, for which he received the Distinguished Flying Cross and the Air Medal with "V" device for heroism.

Did he realize how close he'd come to dying just two years earlier, the rainy February night Chinese vice premier Deng Xiaoping came to Houston? As Deng and his wife rode the glass elevator down to the lobby of the Hyatt Regency in downtown Houston, surrounded by Chinese security forces and members of the US Secret Service, the atmosphere was tense: nearly six hundred Taiwanese protesters were cordoned from the hotel by five hundred riot police officers of the Houston Police Department.

Deng was on his way to a rodeo, part of a carefully orchestrated cross-country tour heralding the opening of full diplomatic and economic relations with the People's Republic of China, a process that had started under President Nixon seven years earlier. But as Deng and his retinue made their way through the lobby toward the motorcade waiting outside, Beam squeezed through the cordon and sprinted toward the vice premier, screaming, "Communist! Communist! Kill him! Kill him!"

He was only feet away from Deng when Secret Service agent Paul Kelly spun around and planted himself in front of Beam, who was reaching into his coat pocket. Kelly, who served in Vietnam as a marine, had a Model 19 Smith & Wesson .357 Magnum revolver and a 9-millimeter Israeli Uzi submachine gun under his own jacket, but figured if Beam was reaching for a gun, he'd already beaten him to the draw, so Kelly balled up his fist and slugged him in the face, sending him to the ground like a sack of potatoes. Beam was set upon by Houston police, who found a can of red spray paint in his coat pocket and a fistful of KKK flyers. As Kelly and the Chinese delegation sped off in the motorcade, the Secret Service agent replayed the moment in his mind: if he'd spotted Beam a half second earlier, he'd have shot him, and by his training, it would've been a justified kill.

Other than a few hours in a holding cell and a charge of disorderly conduct, Beam never spent any time behind bars for attempting to assault a visiting head of state.

NO TIME SERVED AFTER BEING INDICTED ALONGSIDE SEVERAL other Klansmen for allegedly bombing the Pacifica radio station and the local Communist Party headquarters, amid some twenty other explosions targeting antiwar leftists in Houston. Freed on bond, never tried on the charges.

The man was a walking testament to the power of the First Amendment and the reach of the Klan into Texas law enforcement. When he took a photojournalist on a "night ride" with uniformed Houston and Galveston police officers, Klan hoods over their heads, Beam couldn't resist bragging that a member of Houston mayor Louie Welch's "almost immediate family" had been in the Klan for years, "and at the time this man came in, it was generally assumed and agreed upon . . . that there would be no police harassment or interference with any of our activities as a result of Mayor Welch's close kinfolk being a member of the Klan."

It wasn't just law enforcement who seemed to give Beam the benefit of the doubt; the media embraced the fact that he'd attended college as proof that the Klan was evolving into something more sophisticated, maybe even reputable. Only months after Beam's attack on Deng, a reporter described him as a "new generation Klansman . . . college educated, soft-spoken and with an eye on political office as a means of changing the system." One credulous profile that ran in papers throughout the nation admired "the evenness of his voice," which projected "an appealing sincerity that can catch a listener off guard," and then quoted Beam describing his cellmates during his brief incarceration following the Deng incident as a "bunch of niggers."

AT THE DAWN OF THE 1980s, THE KU KLUX KLAN AND OTHER WHITE supremacist groups were in resurgence. The KKK had nearly doubled its membership in four short years since 1975, with ten thousand active members, another seventy-five thousand active sympathizers throughout the country, and hundreds of thousands who read the White supremacist movement's literature. This was, in large part, due to the rising popularity of David Duke, a Louisiana political aspirant who charmed TV audiences and eschewed the public use of the N-word. A Gallup poll showed that the Klan's favorability ratings had climbed from 6 per-cent in 1965—the peak of the civil rights movement—to 11 percent in 1979.

The Klan and neo-Nazi groups claimed that their struggle was now against communism, but their targets were still minorities, and just about anything that rallied them in their previous heydays was now re-christened as communist plots. The forced integration of schools, at-tempted through busing in the 1970s, was a communist plot. Unions were pawns of the Soviets. Interracial marriage—which had received federal protection only in 1967—and immigration were threats to "racial order" meant to weaken the United States in advance of a communist takeover.

Many of the Klan's newest members were Vietnam War veterans, but Louis Beam wasn't radicalized by his service: as far back as junior high, he'd tried to persuade the all-White school's history club to join the KKK. In 1965, the year his mother went on trial for shooting his father with a German .22 pistol during a late-night fight, Beam, still in high school, went to his first Klan rally, in Houston.

It wasn't until he returned from Vietnam that he formally joined the Klan. His well-publicized antics soon caught the attention of national leaders in the White supremacist movement: David Duke appointed him as Grand Dragon of the Texas Klan, introducing him at a Septem-ber 1979 convention in New Orleans as "the epitome of what a dedicated Klan leader in any state should be."

"As I look over the crowd here today, I see some very fine people," Beam told the audience of Klansmen, unaware that law enforcement had someone in the audience secretly recording his remarks. He boasted about the training camps he'd established on Texas land purchased through a special government program for veterans. "We're getting ready to reclaim Texas for the white man!" he shouted to cheers. "You can call us a self-defense force, a security team. But soon the day is coming when Texas will once again belong to us!" His audience roared its approval. "We're gonna take it back!"

He quoted Reverend Robert Miles, a White supremacist in Michigan who had been convicted of a plot to bomb school buses in an attempt to stop court-ordered busing to integrate schools: "I'm gonna have my sack full of heads when I go to the pearly gates!"

"We're eventually going to be required to resort to that ancient right of all white men, so get ready," he said, speaking of a race war he hoped to foment: "It's going to take some fresh blood. Some of it will be our blood, but by God a lot of it is going to be the blood of the enemy," he shouted, to rapturous applause. "This is our country, and we're going to have it again!"

When the cheering subsided, all that could be heard for a moment was the whimpering of a baby. Beam capped off his speech by unfurling, for the first time, the flag of his militia: the Texas Emergency Reserve.

NOT LONG AFTER THE KLAN CONVENTION, BEAM TOOK NEWS crews out to film his militia training at the Lyndon B. Johnson National Grassland near Fort Worth, where twenty-five Klansmen—some of them claiming to be active-duty army officers—stuffed twigs and shrubs into their uniforms and greased each other's faces before practicing reconnaissance, ambushes, hand signals, and moving through a kill zone.

After a brief lunch, Beam led a class on chemical and biological warfare with a white biohazard respirator mask in hand. The Klan leader was consumed by a fear that the United States, after the humiliation of losing in Vietnam, had become soft, and that it was only a matter of time before the Soviet Union invaded. He believed that the Russians would cripple America's conventional defenses with a series of nuclear attacks followed by a land invasion. This wouldn't be stopped by a missile defense shield or negotiations to reduce the nuclear stockpile, but rather by Louis Beam's Klansmen, some of them in their fifties, their uniforms bulging scarecrow-like with shrubbery.

Beam roared at his militiamen to "decimate them! You want to utterly destroy! The closer you can get, you see the blood dripping off their bodies, the more enemies'll be dead, and the stronger this country will be for it! In Vietnam they took ears . . . we're gonna take heads!"

When they weren't training on federal grasslands, the Texas Emergency Reserve used a fifty-acre camp situated on bayou and swampland near the coast. One of the instructors there, John Allen Mosier, had done time for possession of hand grenades, explosives, and military firearms stolen from the Texas National Guard, and would later go to prison for killing his father-in-law for an $800 bounty. Another instructor, Joe Bogart, told the *Houston Chronicle*, "There are only two groups I'll battle with—communists and homosexuals. That's the basic reason I joined the Klan."

One undercover journalist visiting Beam's camp heard the Grand Dragon lay out a dark vision of the future. "We'll set up our own state here [in Texas] and announce that all non-whites have 24 hours to leave. Lots of them won't believe it or won't believe us when we say we'll get rid of them, so we'll have to exterminate a lot of them the first time around."

The camp had operated in secrecy, until they began training Boy Scouts in survival and guerrilla tactics, teaching them how to decapitate enemies with a machete and fire semiautomatic weapons. They taught the boys how to garrote someone with a length of rope. One furious mother reported that instructors discussed a plan to use her sons in a mission to the United States–Mexico border to look for any "illegal aliens entering the country." Other parents reported that their kids had heard the instructors using racial slurs.

At the end of 1980, the firestorm of publicity around the Boy Scouts' training led to a major change in Louis Beam's life: after being fired from his day job at a construction firm, he had decided to go into Klan work full time. He had a wife and a newborn, so he knew he'd need to act quickly to attract new members into the Klan—he was just looking for the right opportunity.

———

A FEW WEEKS LATER, GENE FISHER WALKED INTO HIS KLAN HEAD-quarters.

Fisher was surprised to see the Rice University student film crew, but he'd come to Pasadena with just that goal in mind: getting the Grand Dragon and the cameras that buzzed around him to listen to his complaints about the Vietnamese.

He took stock of the bookstore, where roughly hammered pine bookshelves carried copies of *The Protocols of the Elders of Zion*, technical manuals on land mines, photos of men in combat poses, bumper stickers against busing, posters, and "Running Nigger" targets. Klan robes and hoods were on sale for $27. "KLAN WOMEN: for a Better Community" posters hung on the walls. The latest issue of *The Crusader*, the Klan's newspaper, flags, and SECRET MEMBER OF THE KU KLUX KLAN T-shirts were popular items.

As the student filmmaker's camera rolled, Fisher approached Beam.

"Well, what are the intentions of the fishermen?" he asked Fisher. "Y'all come to us and you're saying that you want help. What exactly do y'all want the governor of this state and the federal government to do?"

"I've asked the federal government to try to stop the flow of legal and illegal refugees to the state of Texas," Fisher said, "into an industry that's already overcrowded by a lot of people."

The Texas legislature was in session at that moment, debating various bills meant to mitigate tensions along the coast, but Fisher was uninterested in the political process. In the previous couple of weeks, two Vietnamese boats and a cross had been burned; Fisher wanted an escalation of the sort the Klan specialized in.

Beam smiled. In the almost fifteen months since his jaunt down to Seadrift on a Klan "fact-finding mission," he'd stopped talking about the trial that exonerated Sáu Văn Nguyễn. The mere threat of the Klan marching in Seadrift had been enough to garner national media attention, which led to new members, which led to more dues coming into his coffers. And here was another White fisherman—a Vietnam veteran, no less—asking him to come to the rescue in Galveston Bay.

After the camera stopped filming, Beam and Fisher began discussing just how the Klan might get rid of their Vietnamese competition once and for all.

The first thing on their list: finding a sympathizer with large enough piece of property to host a major Klan rally against the Vietnamese of Galveston Bay.

# 16

# The Collins Ranch

MARILYN COLLINS KNEW SHE HAD TOO MANY HORSES, BUT SHE couldn't say no. Anytime someone had a maimed, malnourished, or otherwise unusable horse, they brought it to the Collins ranch, an old dairy on twenty-some acres a dozen miles up the road from Galveston Bay. She'd fatten them back up and love on them and ask nothing of them in exchange, not even a quick ride, racking up huge bills in feed and hay and veterinary care along the way. She was never as comfortable as when she was alone in the stalls with her old horses, which is where she was that February morning when she looked out the barn door and saw her husband, Jody, ambling across the pasture with Jim Stanfield, the boat mechanic and local recruiter for the Ku Klux Klan.

When she saw Ralph Yarborough, the local salvage yard owner, towing an old boat across the grass into the dead center of the pasture, she stormed out of the barn and fixed the angriest pair of eyes she could muster on Jody, who repaid her look with a smile.

As she stomped next door to her mother's to pick up her four-month-old daughter, Erin, she replayed the conversation from a few days earlier over breakfast at the Dutch Kettle, when Gene Fisher dropped by their table to tell them about the Klan rally they were organizing in support of White fishermen. There were so many people who might turn out that they were looking for a property big enough to hold it.

Marilyn's eyes widened when Jody volunteered their ranch.

"Do *not* have it on our property!" she snapped at him after Gene left. "We've got a little kid that's gonna grow up here!"

Jody nodded, but Marilyn had been married to him long enough— they'd just marked fifteen years—to understand the weightlessness of her words against her muleheaded husband. She knew that most shrimpers, especially those working the bays in smaller boats that didn't require a crew, were go-it-aloners. This was not an industry based on collaboration, and neither was their marriage.

THE COLLINS FAMILY HAD MOSTLY GOOD YEARS IN THE LATE SIX-ties and early seventies. They weren't wealthy by any measure, but there wasn't a thing in the world Marilyn wanted that Jody wouldn't get her. He looked the other way whenever she showed up with another wasting horse in her trailer, and paid for the hay and veterinary bills without much grumbling. She put up with the shrimping life—his wretched alarm going off at four a.m., the unsteady income, and the occasional infidelity—because she loved this man, because he never said no to her, and because she didn't see how else she could afford to keep her horses without him.

Marilyn kept her distance from Jody's world. She didn't go out on the boat with him, didn't like his younger brother David, and hated Gene Fisher, who kept pestering her to let him grow marijuana on their property. She didn't hang around at the bars or with other shrimpers' wives. She just wanted to be alone on the ranch.

But now Jody's world was walking around her pastures, talking about where generators and lights and the PA system might go. When she returned with Erin, she found Jody in the kitchen with Louis Beam and Jim Stanfield, signing an agreement to lease their ranch to the Klan for a rally on Valentine's Day, 1981. Jody asked for a fee of one dollar.

———

FLYERS FOR THE EVENT WERE SOON POPPING UP AROUND GALVES-
ton Bay. "Haven't you had enough? Aren't you disgusted enough with
seeing the government giving away your tax money to illegals and foreigners while you struggle just to keep your nose above water?" they
asked. "Come out and help us show American fishermen we care. Come
out and see the USS *Viet Cong* go up in flames."

There were estimates of a crowd of fifteen thousand. Jody was summoned to city hall for an emergency city council meeting, where he gestured to a portrait of George Washington and said, "It all boils down to
this guy on the wall . . . freedom of assembly. We are not infringing on
anyone's rights."

The mayor assured worried residents that he would summon the
National Guard if local police couldn't keep a handle on the situation.

AS BEAM HOPED, THE MEDIA POURED INTO TOWN.

"I *went* to my government and worked with them for over a year and
a half, *begged* them to help the situation, do something about it, and they
wouldn't do it," Fisher told a CBS news reporter. His tone was scolding,
his arms stubbornly crossed. "So, I'm a white American. I went to the
KKK. Those boats have to be taken out of the water. Destroyed."

Fisher claimed the government was ignoring him, but by February
1981, Governor Clements and his task force were actively discouraging
the resettlement of new Vietnamese refugees to the Gulf Coast area
while Justice Department mediators were feverishly trying to broker
peace agreements between Vietnamese and White shrimpers up and
down the coast. White and Vietnamese shrimpers in the fishing towns
of Rockport and Palacios had already signed agreements pledging to
work in peace. In response to allegations that the Vietnamese boats were
violating safety codes, the Texas Parks and Wildlife Department conducted a rigorous inspection, but found a greater percentage of White-
owned boats in violation. The Catholic Church was teaching Vietnamese

shrimpers both the official regulations and the unwritten rules that White shrimpers were adamant about upholding. A study was commissioned that definitively proved that Vietnamese were not receiving secret Small Business Administration loans to buy their boats. The Texas Education Agency was sponsoring a pilot program to train Vietnamese to process seafood in Galveston Bay, hoping to encourage some to give up their boats and work on land. The legislature was considering a "Limited Entry" bill that both White and Vietnamese fishermen had been calling for: a moratorium on the issuance of any new shrimping permits.

But these initiatives could work only if everyone involved gave them time. Trust couldn't be won with a few signatures on a nonbinding gentlemen's agreement; it needed to be nurtured and protected. The Limited Entry bill needed to work its way through committees and into law. White fishermen needed to hear, as many times as it took to sink in, that the federal government was not showering refugees with secret loans to buy boats, and that the Vietnamese had the same rights to fish as anyone. Everyone needed a good season out on the water, without hurricanes, oil spills, tanker collisions, or toxic chemical dumps.

But Fisher, the Collins brothers, Stanfield, and others were only interested in Louis Beam and his torch-wielding Klan.

On February 13, Governor Clements announced that he had requested help from President Reagan, the US Coast Guard, the head of the Texas Parks and Wildlife Department, and the bishops of the Roman Catholic Church.

At a press conference later in the day, he was asked if he was worried about the rally.

"No, I'm not worried," the governor replied. "I'm concerned, but I'm not worried. There is a difference."

"If you were a Vietnamese fisherman down at Seabrook, would you be . . . ?"

"Fortunately, I am not," the governor quipped.

"If you were—" the journalist persisted.

"I happen to be governor. That's a little bit better job."

———

THAT EVENING, WITH THE BOAT LYING IN THE PASTURE BEHIND her barn and her beloved horses, Marilyn Collins tended to their four-month-old while Jody slept.

She took Erin over to the window, bobbing her to sleep, while she worried about what tomorrow might bring. She'd been hoping that the rally was just the usual shit-talking of shrimpers, and that they would never actually follow through with it. If the point of inviting the Klan in was to provoke a response from the government, as far as she could see, the government was responding . . . but her husband and his idiot friends had set a process in motion that they couldn't stop, even if they wanted to. Now they were bracing for the potential of fifteen thousand people, the National Guard, and counterprotests by anti-Klan activists.

Out in the pasture, men were at work beneath a waxing moon. One had a bucket of tar-black pitch and a broad brush, with which he painted U S S  V I E T  C O N G across the bow of the boat. Another grunted as he drove a shovel into the soft earth, digging a hole deep enough to support what rested on the ground alongside them—a thirty-foot steel cross wrapped in burlap, ready to burn.

# 17

# A Valentine's Day Klan Rally

T HE ROAD LEADING ONTO THE COLLINS RANCH WAS BUMPY AND lined with armed Klansmen. Some had hunting rifles, others carried AK-47s, AR-15s, and lever-action Enfields. Hundreds upon hundreds of fishermen, locals, Klansmen, and journalists made their way toward the pasture, at the center of which was the USS *VIET CONG*. The air was thick with the smell of fried trout, six hundred pounds of it, along with forty-eight gallons of oysters. Jody had volunteered Marilyn to make twenty pounds of potato salad, which glistened in the sun.

Klansmen dressed in black, known as Nighthawks, were posted at various locations in the woods surrounding the field. The Bandidos motorcycle gang snaked in for a visit. A young boy with a toy rifle slung over his shoulder challenged anybody passing by to a draw-down, while other kids in miniature Klan robes scampered about. In addition to police from Santa Fe and other nearby towns, the Galveston County sheriff sent deputies along with undercover officers. The Texas Rangers arrived as the crowd swelled to some seven hundred.

———

WHILE THEY WAITED FOR THE ARRIVAL OF THE GRAND DRAGON, who had spent the night next door stretched out on the couch in the living room of Marilyn's mother, the media hungrily interviewed shrimpers, Klansmen and their wives and children, and especially Gene Fisher.

"There's a lot of people that's mad because I brought in the Klan," Fisher said. "I just want attention. This is the best way to get it. The KKK is not going to do any more than they're asked to do." He blamed Colonel Nam and the handful of new boats under construction by Vietnamese as the reason he ran to the Klan for help. "He says he has no control over his people . . . and they're going to continue building new boats. They're not going to control themselves whatsoever, so we're going to have to help them control themselves."

"But I've got a dream," said Fisher, basking in the attention: "I'd like to see 7,000 Vietnamese fishing boats tied to an aircraft carrier and towed back to Vietnam. If these people stood up and fought like the people in this country did, they'd still have a country."

"You can leave my racism in there," he added, "cuz I don't like the turkeys."


YEARS LATER, EMBARRASSED TOWN BOOSTERS AND WHITE shrimpers would scoff at Fisher and the others as marginal, but there were plenty of allies openly voicing their support that day. Ralph Boyd, a shrimper working Galveston Bay, said he opposed the Klan but supported White fishermen. His wife, Sarah, echoed his thoughts: "I've always thought the Klan stirred up things and caused things that were not all the best. But Gene has a point. We've been fighting this thing for five years and we haven't gotten anywhere. . . . I don't have a racial conflict with them; mine is economic. They're taking away from my livelihood."

Glorio Villarreal, an employee of the Texas Department of Corrections who fought in World War II, was there to "support all of the fishermen and keep them from losing their jobs, their boats to the chinks."

Ernie Hunt, a Vietnam War veteran dressed in combat fatigues, echoed the sentiment: "They paid us to shoot them, and now we have to support them!"

Nearby, a *Time* photographer took a picture of the mayor of Santa Fe, Jim Wood, as he posed with three Klansmen. The mayor acknowledged that it might be interpreted as siding with the KKK, but said he was "merely sympathetic to U.S. fishermen."

Fisher must have felt emboldened, surrounded by all the armed Klansmen and news crews, because he did little to moderate his remarks. He told the Rice University student filmmaker who'd filmed his first interactions with Louis Beam at the Klan headquarters that the Grand Dragon would "show us the right way to burn [a boat]: it's supposed to burn down to the waterline. You're not supposed to close the hatch on it," an unmistakable reference to the fact that the *Trudy B* hadn't burned completely because the arsonist had closed its hatch, suffocating the flames in its hull. "Now . . . this is just in case the Governor forces us to take our own actions," he added cheekily.


JODY COLLINS WAS HOSTING THE WHOLE AFFAIR, BUT HE KEPT A low profile, avoiding the press and watching it all with a detached amusement. He stared across the pasture at the USS *VIET CONG*, which would go up in smoke soon enough, and thought of his very first boat, a $3,500 junker he bought when he was just sixteen. After a brief stint as a grunt in the army knocking asbestos off generators at an underground missile silo, he fell behind on boat payments. Rather than going bankrupt, he set fire to the boat in the middle of Galveston Bay and swam to a nearby oil platform. With the insurance payment, he was able to crawl out of debt and buy another boat.

Jody took stock of the spectacle. As the sun set, the garbage cans were overflowing with beer cans, greasy paper plates, shrimp tails, and oyster shells. By this point, the crowd had been waiting for hours for the arrival of the Grand Dragon; the excitement was palpable.

Gene Fisher acted as warm-up. He professed not to be a member of the Klan but he could've been Beam's deputy. "I'm white and proud. You can be black and proud, you can be Mexican and proud. I don't know if those Vietnamese have anything to be proud of."

"I'll be here fishing five to ten years from now, even if I have to run over every gook in my way!" he roared, as toddlers in overalls stood by their mothers. "I'm not going to run from this one, and neither are the people with me. They're either going to have to put me in the penitentiary or put me in the grave!"

That got some hollers, but the crowd was clearly hungry for more. At that moment, someone whooped and Louis Beam appeared, surrounded by a covey of ten shotgun-toting Klansmen in fatigues from his Texas Emergency Reserve militia. Beam was short, his face pockmarked and mustachioed, his BORN TO LOSE tattoo hidden beneath a white cable-knit sweater, but as he worked his way toward the podium, the journalists and their cameras and recorders converged upon him like filaments to a magnet.

The Grand Dragon theatrically issued orders to his militia. "Your instructions are to apprehend anybody agitating and bring them to the podium . . . the police will take them away. Now if they don't fire," he continued, "you just hit 'em in the head with your rifle butt, but don't shoot your weapon unless they shoot first . . . understand?"

"Isn't it true that the fishermen asked you all here?" a journalist shouted.

"We don't force ourselves on anybody," murmured Beam as he headed to the podium.

He never read from notes but spoke from his heart, believing God would tell him what to say. "All of you understand, we're not having an anti-Vietnamese rally here tonight!" he said, his eyes twinkling. "You don't think them Vietnamese got them boats themselves here in Seabrook, do you?"

"No!" roared the crowd.

"The federal government brought 'em here!" cried Beam. "You don't think they came from a refugee camp 14,000 miles . . . that they *walked* here, do you?"

"No!" echoed back.

"The federal government *flew* 'em here! First-class all the way!" he shouted. "They are your replacements. They will work for one-twentieth of what you will."

Standing on soil taken away from Native Americans by force and given to White settlers, the Grand Dragon spoke about the perils of Vietnamese and other immigrants. "This country belongs to you and no one else! It was not the Vietnamese who built this country, it was the Anglo-Saxon white Europeans that made this country what it is today. The American fishermen, by birthright, have a right to these waters!"

While a deputy splashed gallons of diesel over the USS *VIET CONG*, Beam donned his Klan robe, which bore the four green stripes of the Grand Dragon on its broad sleeves. Camera flashes revealed a mob of robed-and-hooded Klansmen drawing close in anticipation. Low-hanging clouds and far-off thunder threatened to disperse the crowd, so he moved efficiently. Beam shouted: "This boat . . . is symbolic of the policies of the federal government that are leading to the destruction of this country!"

The Klansmen and White fishermen pumped their fists in celebration as Beam gingerly touched his torch against the slick of diesel.

Grand Dragon Louis Beam sets fire to the USS *VIET CONG* at the Collins ranch, Santa Fe, Texas, February 14, 1981.

"I want the rest of the world to watch this goddamn boat burn!" bellowed Fisher. "We don't like them sons-of-bitches and we don't want them here!"

The men, illuminated by the flames, broke into cheers of "White power! White power!" Beam led them in a chant, reciting the slogan of the Texas Knights of the Ku Klux Klan: "Texas First! White Supremacy! America First! We Will Fight!"

As the paint on the USS *VIET CONG* blistered, Beam told members of the media to take note: "If a burned boat doesn't look like that, the Klan didn't burn it." It was a clever bit of gaslighting: the Klan couldn't have set fire to those boats down in Seabrook and Kemah a month earlier, for if they *had*, the boats would've been burned completely. The same winking deniability pervaded the entire rally: the words USS *VIET CONG* were painted across a boat he claimed was actually a symbol of the US government and therefore shouldn't be construed as a threat against any Vietnamese shrimpers. Gene Fisher railed against "gooks" and the crowd cheered "White Power," but nearly everyone in attendance insisted their grievance was more about economics than race.

AND THEN, BEAM TURNED TO THE BANK OF NEWS CAMERAS AND melodramatically issued what he termed a "Grand Dragon's Dispensation": "We're giving you ninety days. We want to see the Coast Guard and the Texas Department of Parks and Wildlife out there where they should be and start enforcing these laws; or there are some American fishermen who are going to!"

Surrounded by members of his Texas Emergency Reserve, Beam extended an invitation to the White shrimpers of Galveston Bay: "The Ku Klux Klan is more than willing to select out of the ranks of American fishermen some of your more hardy souls and send 'em through our training camps . . . and when you come out of there, they'll be ready for the Vietnamese!" He flashed a jagged smile as the crowd roared.

"No one in their right mind can expect these Americans . . . these

*Texans*, to give up these waters without a fight!" By this point, he was shrieking into the microphone over the roar.

"If you want to hold on to this country, you're going to have to shed some of your blood!

"I promise you, if you don't start looking out for the interests of American citizens first, and forget about these aliens . . . this entire Gulf Coast is going to be a very, very troubled place to live. . . ."

A cannon was fired. The cross, propped up with the aid of Jody's truck, was burned. As the reporters raced to file their stories, dispatching the images of a burning boat surrounded by Klansmen to their papers around the country, Beam's ninety-day countdown clock started ticking—timed to end at midnight before the opening day of shrimp season.

# 18

# The Bald-Heads of Seabrook

THE DAY AFTER THE RALLY, ALL THAT REMAINED OF THE USS *VIET CONG* were a few eyebolts lying in the singed grass behind the Collins barn. As Jody picked up the trash, he felt a strong wind pushing in from the east and figured the ashes of the boat were somewhere between Galveston and El Paso.

Châu Văn Nguyễn, a Vietnamese member of Governor Clements's task force, felt defeated by the Valentine's Day rally. He told a reporter that Gene Fisher had been threatening for two years to get the Klan involved, but he was struggling to accept that it had finally happened. "He always said he would bring them in, and he did." Châu spoke of the "disaster" facing fishermen along the Gulf Coast—inflation, the cost of fuel, and oil spills in the bays: "Those are the major problems . . . not the Vietnamese." Of the twenty thousand commercial shrimpers along the entire US Gulf Coast, only about one thousand were Vietnamese. "These people are a very minor factor, but some have capitalized on it to blame everything on them."

"What Gene Fisher and his colleagues want, I do not know," Châu said with a sigh.

GENE WAS ELATED. HE'D WANTED ATTENTION AND NOW HE HAD IT. Journalists across the country stayed on the incendiary story. Most found him holding court at the Dutch Kettle diner.

"It cost us $2,000 for the rally and we got a million dollars' worth of publicity!" he marveled to a reporter from the *Los Angeles Times*. He sipped his coffee and turned serious. "You got to get these people off the coastlines and into the interior." No longer was it about a mere freeze on new permits or building new boats: now it was about driving the Vietnamese out. "What we are aiming for is a complete halt in the dumping of these refugees in the country," said Fisher as he wolfed down a plate of biscuits and gravy. "I'd rather be dead than lose my piece of the American pie," he groused. "If they're not gone by May 15, I'll be prepared to duke it out with them."

More often than not, the coverage was transparently in favor of the White fishermen's perspective, even after they began marching with the Ku Klux Klan. Hyping a long-form piece on the conflict, *Houston Monthly* posed a question on its cover: "Right or Wrong: Should Americans or Vietnamese Fish Galveston Bay?" While the reporter was conducting interviews with a Vietnamese shrimper, a White shrimper accused him of being on the side of the Vietnamese and threatened to take him "into the oyster shells over there and beat the shit" out of him. The reporter was offended, but not enough to conclude that "BOTH sides are right and NO sides are wrong . . . American fishermen, we are on your side. We want you to earn a living. Vietnamese fishermen, we understand you and wish you luck."

IN THE DAYS AFTER THE RALLY, WHITE SHRIMPERS DID LITTLE TO temper their language. "Our problem is the Vietnamese," said Bo Jones, a shrimper in the area, from his perch at the Kemah Clipper bar on the edge of the Clear Creek Channel. "And the answer to the problem is to get rid of the Vietnamese. They are killing our bay." Jones himself was born in Alabama but saw Galveston Bay as his. He was drinking at the bar that day instead of fishing because of fog, and because he hadn't gotten around to replacing a $10 pulley needed on his boat.

Another shrimper grinned at a reporter while describing the time he sold a boat to a Vietnamese shrimper for $25,000, even though he knew it was decrepit. "As soon as he pulled it out of the water to paint the hull, the bottom fell out because it had so much water in it," the shrimper cackled.

Over at Jim Craig's "Saigon Harbor," a reporter found four Vietnamese applying fiberglass to the hull of a new forty-two-foot boat they were building. A White resident who wasn't even a fisherman wandered past and said, "It's nice they are all grouped together over there so you can get them with one torch."


NAM FELT AT AN IMPASSE. HE HAD PLENTY OF WEAPONS BUT WAS committed to a peaceful solution. He had noticed strange cars parked outside his home, usually with several White men inside. He sensed he was being followed as he drove around town. He didn't feel personally threatened, at least not yet, but after decades of active combat, his threshold for fear was admittedly higher than most.

He began taking preventive measures, secretly renting a couple of properties in case the situation deteriorated and he needed a safe house for his family; his daughter, Judy, was only five months old. Friends in Houston were urging him to flee, but his mother urged him to stand his ground, to be peaceful but clever. "You have to find a way to beat the KKK," she told him. "If you lose, your people here will all be destroyed." She told him that if he died for the cause, it would be just, but that if he took up arms against his detractors—even if fifty Vietnamese died and only five Klansmen—then everyone would blame Colonel Nam.

He was doing what he could for the members of his Vietnamese Fishermen's Association, advising them to ignore the drama, but the Valentine's Day Klan rally had altered the atmosphere in the bay; verbal threats against Vietnamese in town were increasing. It was a difficult balancing act: he didn't want them to flee, but he also didn't want them to fight. There was a heaviness in the air; what it portended, Nam was reluctant to dwell upon. The only thing he could do was keep all parties talking to each other, pleading for patience and caution, which is why he called for a town hall on February 28, two weeks into the Grand Dragon's ninety-day countdown.

A delegation of officials from the governor's office came down from Austin, while the auditorium swelled in anticipation of what Nam had to say. The Colonel's voice was deep and sonorous; he had no need for a microphone as he began his address.

"Ladies and Gentlemen," Nam began, "today I wish to publicly own that a number of Vietnamese fishermen have made certain mistakes in their daily trade and may have infringed on local regulations. By the same token, I am certain that . . . some American fishermen also may have knowingly or unknowingly made mistakes of their own. These mistakes, wherever they have been made, are simple mistakes that are amenable to redress."

Nam had an important announcement to make that day, but he wanted to set the facts straight first, because so much of the media coverage had been slanted in favor of the White fishermen. He agreed, as he had many times before, that there were too many boats harvesting shrimp in the bays. Between that and the terrible couple of seasons of shrimping, impacted by hurricanes and oil spills, he understood why some locals might blame the Vietnamese newcomers, but Nam reminded them of the substantial amount of money his community had pumped into the local economy by way of overpaying for boats, repairs, and fees to tow or scrap those that sank on the open sea. These Vietnamese now called themselves "thầy trọc," the "bald-heads" of Seabrook, after the haircut they'd taken financially over the years.

Nam wasn't above a little score-settling, condemning White shrimpers for refusing to acknowledge that they, too, were increasing the number of boats in the bay—after all, most of those who unloaded their old boats on the Vietnamese used their earnings to build new ones for themselves. He looked out over the audience as he mounted his case. These were not the words of a man running scared. "Many of them did not go out to sea . . . and were never seen on the open sea all year round, but still repeatedly made the ridiculous claim that the new Vietnamese fishermen were depriving them of their livelihood!" The reference to Gene Fisher, who just wanted to drag for shrimp for a couple of hours whenever he needed the money, was inescapable. "They cannot bear to see their new neighbors succeed."

But of all the charges made against the Vietnamese, the only one that stung was the allegation that they were secretly communist, which Louis Beam and others had leveled over the past several months. Nam challenged Beam to recant the "unscrupulous allegation" and glared at the White audience for a moment. "I personally remained behind in Vietnam to fight with my friends until the last American safely left the country, and I finally got out with nothing on me but a field uniform and a lot of outrage!" Nam thundered.

He stared out the audience, then back at his notes. "If, in a moment of impatience," he warned, "some form of violence is allowed to break out against us . . . we would be forced to defend ourselves. Once the trouble has started to snowball, it would be very difficult to arrest it." The crowd murmured and shifted in their seats. It seemed as though Nam was about to respond to the Valentine's Day rally with a counterthreat.

But the Colonel took a deep breath and arrived at his bombshell announcement: in the face of so much harassment and animosity, sixty of the one hundred Vietnamese fishermen in the area were prepared to leave.

If their boats were purchased from them at a fair price, he continued, the Vietnamese shrimpers would pledge in writing never to fish in Galveston Bay again.

# 19

# The Klan Boat Patrol

FOR SALE SIGNS BEGAN APPEARING ON THE CABIN WINDOWS OF Vietnamese trawlers. As soon as they could find a buyer, the Vietnamese would leave, and Gene Fisher and the White shrimpers of the American Fishermen's Association would have the water to themselves once again. After Nam's announcement, a string of reporters wanted to know whether he, too, would leave.

He was torn. He liked living in Seabrook. "The reason I decided to come here is I like to have free trade," he told a reporter from the *Los Angeles Times*. "We feel bad . . . it makes me feel sorry to come to this area."

As the journalist sat in Nam's home, twenty feet from the water's edge, a steady procession of Vietnamese shrimpers came by to sign their names to the list he was compiling of the boats, their condition, and the desired price.

One of them, Sư Đỗ, was twenty-seven years old and lived on his shrimp boat. He was frustrated and didn't understand why he should leave. "I guess what it comes down to is that if I do better than you, then you don't like me," he said, reflecting for a moment. "I like it around the water. I hate to leave."

Lam Trường An, a twenty-eight-year-old former sergeant in the South Vietnamese navy, was blunter. "The American fisherman is lazy." An, whose twelve-hour day started at six thirty, thought the Whites were "mad because they like to work from 9 a.m. to 3:30 p.m."

As more and more shrimpers shuffled in to add their details to the list, Nam stared out the window past his boat onto the dark water of Galveston Bay, alternating between confusion and anger. He thought of Judy and Michael and all that his family had already gone through, as well as his mother's entreaty not to give in to the Ku Klux Klan. What would become of the Vietnamese who chose to stay if he abandoned them? He was normally decisive, but he couldn't yet bring himself to add his name to the list.

GENE FISHER, THE COLLINS BROTHERS, JAMES STANFIELD, LOUIS Beam, and the Klan had pushed Nam and the Vietnamese to the point of leaving, but there was a problem: unless the Vietnamese were to suffer another economic blow in the process of abandoning their livelihood, they needed buyers willing to pay the obscenely inflated price the Whites had first charged them for their boats. In selling them a "fleet of old tubs," chuckled dock owner Jim Craig, "they created their own animal."

With the Vietnamese Fishermen's Association offer to leave on the table, Emery Waite, one of the main fish house owners in Seabrook, was burning up the phone lines, trying to find buyers in Mexico. There was talk of an interested party, but with less than two months before the start of shrimping season, there was concern that a deal couldn't be negotiated by the time Louis Beam's ninety-day timeline expired.

"There is tension," said Waite. "One way or another, something has got to happen, or you're going to see an explosion." He acknowledged that White shrimpers had been feeling the combined pressure of a recession, rising fuel costs, the oil spills, and the ban on shrimping in Mexican waters, but he speculated that the Vietnamese were the only one of their problems that they could "literally get their hands on."

Journalists struggled to figure out where Waite fell in the conflict. "Violence won't accomplish anything," he said, "but talking about it *did* at least attract attention. For a long time, they talked about sending the blacks back to Africa. They forced them to the back of the bus with violence. Now the blacks own the bus. We need to be careful that we keep this an economic and not a racial issue," he said in a warning tone. "The feds tend to take the side of the minorities."

**FISHER HAD THE VIETNAMESE ON THE ROPES, AS FAR AS HE SAW** it. Sixty percent were preparing to leave in the wake of his bombastic threats and the Klan's arrival, so he wasn't about to moderate his approach. Better to keep escalating. Two weeks after the rally, he announced that fifty-two White shrimpers were planning to take up Louis Beam's offer to receive military training with the Ku Klux Klan's Texas Emergency Reserve in the weeks leading up to opening day of shrimp season. The militia's camp was shrouded in secrecy, but it had remained operational despite all the bad press surrounding the training Boy Scouts had received in beheading and strangling a year earlier. Police Chief Kerber, trying to keep a lid on the situation, sighed in exasperation when he heard the news. "Combat-ready fishermen, that's all we need."

Louis Beam inspects members of his militia, the Texas Emergency Reserve, during the first Klan rally at the Collins ranch.

———

BEFORE THE BREAK OF DAWN ON SUNDAY, MARCH 15, JODY WAS out on the *Cherry Betty*. He'd bought the boat from a Cajun in Port Arthur a few years earlier, and it was still beat up. The anchor mount at the bow was so rusted it looked liable to fall off; its navy-gray paint was more a memory than anything else. After a few fruitless hours on the water, he tied the boat up under the bridge spanning the Clear Creek Channel, just as he'd been doing since he was a teenager. By around ten a.m., he was home and asleep in bed.

Around the same time, David Collins was having breakfast at the Dutch Kettle when James Stanfield came by his table, commented on the fine weather, and asked if he'd be interested in going for a boat ride. They talked about the annual parade of boats at the blessing of the fleet, where shrimpers decked their boats out in a warmhearted competition, and how the Ku Klux Klan ought to make a similar exhibition. It would be a display of patriotism, they figured.

The boat they were building, the *Miss AKIA*, was still up on racks in Dickinson Bayou, so David called Jody, waking him up, and asked if he could borrow the *Cherry Betty*.

The next call he placed was to Jo Ann Oliphant-Curran, a reporter from the *Santa Fe Express News*. He trusted her. Four days earlier, he'd called her with a tip to be at a vacant lot just west of Kemah later that night. For several hours during the day, as neighbors, fishermen, and pleasure-boaters drove past, he toiled away in a vacant lot next to the restaurant, digging a large hole. After darkness blanketed the coast, he returned with a twelve-by-four-foot cross wrapped in diesel-soaked burlap. To ensure that it burned, he fashioned two crude igniters with a time delay by strapping a kitchen match to the butt of a cigarette with a rubber band. He lit the cigarettes, took a drag, set them on the burlap at the foot of the cross, and bolted. He'd have about five to seven minutes before they burned down, just enough time to head over to a bar and establish an alibi.

When the police arrived, Oliphant-Curran was already there, snapping pictures that would run on the front page the following morning.

The officers approached the blazing cross with plans to kick it over, but had to sprint back to the safety of their squad cars when the AR-15 shells David had scattered into the burlap—to "give it a little character"—began cooking off. Oliphant-Curran never revealed who'd tipped her off.

"Hey, Jo Ann!" David said into the pay phone. "C'mon down to the canal and look for the *Cherry Betty*. You won't miss us. And bring your camera!"

TRẦN VĂN PHÚ WAS VISITING WITH A FRIEND WHO LIVED CLOSE to the waterfront. Phú started shrimping in late 1977 on a boat he'd bought with borrowed money, but a bad couple of seasons had caused him to fall behind on payments and sell it off. He was in great spirits that morning, though, for he was about to return to shrimping as captain on his friend's trawler when the season opened in May.

The two were sitting in the living room when they looked out the window and saw a shrimp boat filled with armed men in white robes skulking down the channel. From a distance, it looked as though there was a body hanging from a noose off one of its outriggers.

THI D. HOÀNG WAS JUST UP THE CHANNEL ON HIS BOAT AT THAT moment. Ever since the fall of Saigon, the former officer in the South Vietnamese navy had assembled car radios at a factory in Houston, saving every penny he could to buy a trawler. After nearly five years, he shelled out $32,000 for his boat, which he was just about to take out when the *Cherry Betty* passed by, filled with hooded men carrying AR-15 rifles. As the stern of the boat passed, he saw what he first thought was an oddly shaped sack of shrimp hanging from one of the outriggers. As it drew close, he made out the ghostly shape of an effigy of a Vietnamese refugee.

SOME OF THE PARTICIPANTS WORE ARMY FATIGUES, OTHERS SECRET MEMBER—KU KLUX KLAN T-shirts or Klan robes and hoods, but nobody concealed their faces that day; they wanted to be seen. There were loads of AR-15s on board.

Someone climbed the mast and unfurled a Confederate flag. Other Klansmen gathered around a small-bore field cannon, the same one that had capped off the rally at the Collins ranch. A small Confederate flag was mounted next to the barrel; a military ammunition case filled with shells rested by its iron wheels. David didn't know whether they were live or blanks, but he was more amused than concerned.

Stanfield had dragged aboard the effigy, what was once a cigar-store Indian, dressed in a pale blue plaid shirt, a dark vest and slacks, and a pair of worn cowboy boots. They fitted a noose around its neck, threw the rope over one of the outriggers, and hoisted it up into the air under the flag of the Confederacy. Its neck canted to the right as it dangled over the Klansmen.

The wind was whipping in from the west, so as he headed toward Galveston Bay, David tried to keep the *Cherry Betty* a safe distance from the shallows and a sunken boat that was constricting the channel. When they arrived at the bridge, just by the Kemah boardwalk, they had to wait several minutes for it be raised.

John Van Beekum, a photojournalist for the *Houston Chronicle*, was taking the day off. A month earlier, when he'd covered the Klan rally, Van Beekum had dropped in to a seafood place on the boardwalk that served up the best shrimp sandwich he'd ever had in his life. That Sunday, piloted as much by his gut as by anything else, Van Beekum drove back down for a day on the bay front. He had just tucked into his sandwich when he heard some people hollering and laughing on the boardwalk. He glanced over and saw a boat with about twenty armed men and women wearing Klan robes.

He leapt up from the table and sprinted to the parking lot, snatching his camera from the backseat and praying there was enough film. By the time he got back, the crowd along the boardwalk had grown. There were bystanders snapping pictures of their own, men grinning with cans of beer in hand as one of the Klanswomen raised her arm in a Sieg Heil salute.

The Klan boat patrol as it passed the Kemah boardwalk en route to Colonel Nam's home.

Van Beekum started snapping. Nobody in the uniformly White crowd seemed particularly disturbed by the display. Stanfield stood at the bow of the *Cherry Betty* in his robe and hood, with his face unconcealed, proudly crossing his arms. Others mugged for the cameras, shouldering their shotguns and AR-15s.

OVER AT "SAIGON HARBOR," JIM CRAIG WAS IN A PANICKED STATE, imploring the Vietnamese to get out of their boats and clear out of town until the Klan boat disappeared. It had only been a couple of months since Gene Fisher had made the veiled threat about how easily the boats docked there could burn; now he feared the worst.

The small police forces of Kemah and Seabrook were flooded with calls about what was happening. Chief Kerber didn't have a police boat at his disposal, so he dispatched squad cars to follow the *Cherry Betty* along the waterfront. There was no sign of the Coast Guard.

SOME OF THE KLANSMEN DIDN'T HAVE THEIR SEA LEGS AND WERE already getting seasick, but David pressed on. Upon clearing the channel and entering the bay, he steered north, piloting the boat toward the fish houses and piers of Seabrook.

They pulled up along the Eleventh Avenue piers in Seabrook, stopping just behind Colonel Nam's home.

Nam and his wife, An, were out. His son, Michael, had just returned to San Antonio after a visit. Inside, Phương Phạm, An's thirteen-year-old sister, was there, babysitting Judy, who was asleep in the nursery. Phạm was in the kitchen, talking with a friend on the phone, when she peered out the window and saw a boat full of armed Klansmen staring and pointing at her, rifles in hand.

She dropped the phone. She'd started studying American history that year and had recently learned about the KKK, so she knew enough to be afraid. In a panic, she snatched up the sleeping baby and ran out the front door onto Eleventh Avenue.

The Klan boat glided on.

Toward the end of the patrol, David Collins steered the *Cherry Betty* past the mile marker, well into Galveston Bay.

As the Klansmen loaded a shell into the cannon, Jo Ann Oliphant-Curran, the reporter from the *Santa Fe Express News*, snapped picture after picture, until the cannon was fired. The blast left her momentarily deaf, but she soon heard the cheers of everyone on board as David Collins shouted, "Let's hear it for the American fishermen!"


WHATEVER RESERVATIONS NAM HAD ABOUT LEAVING SEABROOK disappeared in the wake of the Klan boat patrol. He was done. He had tried to be a force for peace. In meeting after meeting, he'd absorbed the fury of the White shrimpers who wanted the Vietnamese out, unflappably rebutting their conspiracy theories while conceding the mistakes that the Vietnamese had made over the years.

But it seemed as though everyone was aligned against him. The governor's solution was to find them jobs inland so that they'd leave the bays. When the trawlers were torched in January, the arson investigator concluded the Vietnamese had burned their own boats in an effort to garner public sympathy. Gene Fisher was threatening to "run over every gook" in his way, and Louis Beam was about to train shrimpers with his militia so that they would be "ready for the Vietnamese."

With a sigh, Nam walked over to the list of Vietnamese boats for sale. Under the heading "Declaration to Sell Boat," he added his twenty-eight-foot boat with a diesel engine and two nets for $35,000, factoring in the $9,000 he'd sunk into it after buying it from David Collins.

Truth be told, he'd sell it for anything; to hell with waiting for a fair price. He was leaving Seabrook, as soon as he could.

"I cannot argue, because this is not my country," he told a local television reporter, his voice hollowed out. "I am too tired to argue."

"I lost my country," he added. "I left my family in Vietnam. I worked very hard to save some money to invest in here . . . and now, when I leave, I'll lose more."

THE NEXT DAY, A WEALTHY WHITE MAN SEVERAL STATES AWAY was sipping his morning coffee and reading *The New York Times*, when he saw a picture of a boatful of Klansman menacing Vietnamese refugees. He got on his motorcycle and started racing along the Gulf Coast to Seabrook.

# Act III

## 90 Days

If we can't have this country, nobody gets it! It's ours or no one's! It's ours by right, by conquest, by heritage, by culture, by race, it's ours! We will not yield it!

—LOUIS BEAM, FROM *PORTRAIT OF A KLANSMAN*

## 20

# The Cookbook Salesman
# from Montgomery

MORRIS DEES OPENED THE THROTTLE ON HIS 1976 BMW MOTOR-cycle and blasted south out of Montgomery, Alabama, toward the Gulf Coast. With its cockpit array of analog gauges like a fighter plane, his bike was built for the expressways, but he soon tore off onto a local road, jammed a Willie Nelson tape into the deck, and carved a westward path along the coast.

When he was a boy, picking cotton in the fields alongside Black tenant farmers on land his dad rented outside Montgomery, he never would've dreamed of owning such a valuable bike. The Dees family was poor, but the White men around Morris taught him his "skin color automatically made him better." His great-grandfather was buried down the road in a Confederate grave. His grandpa joined the Ku Klux Klan in the 1920s. His uncle Lucien, who ran a country store where he charged Black customers more than White ones for the same goods, kept his Klan robe hanging up in the back room. Segregation was the natural order of things, Morris thought, and he wasn't much bothered by it.

In Alabama, your last name was about as important as the amount of land you owned, but Morris, whom everyone called Bubba, had neither going for him. What he had, though, was a preternatural ability to make money. He fed table scraps to the piglets he got as a six-year-old and soon had more pigs than the family table could sustain, so he talked his grade school cafeteria into giving him wheelbarrows full of leftovers. He did the same with chickens, cattle, and horses, and the small Dees ranch was soon overrun with livestock.

But he wasn't destined to remain a backcountry hayseed. He was crowned king of his junior high. By high school, he stood six feet, with an angular face and a strong jawline. He played on the high school football team, hunted for raccoon in the palmetto swamps along the Tallapoosa River, and skinny-dipped in Solomon's Pond.

As a teenager in the 1950s, he had a front-row seat to the birth of the civil rights movement. He was a junior in an all-White high school in May 1954, when the Supreme Court decided *Brown v. Board of Education*, officially ending segregation in public schools. A few months later, he was introduced to George Wallace at the Whites-only inaugural ball of Governor "Big Jim" Folsom, a drinking buddy of his dad's. "Bubba," his dad said, "Judge Wallace is going to be governor someday." Morris liked the idea of becoming a politician, so when he learned that both Folsom and Wallace had studied law at the University of Alabama, he made up his mind to follow their path.

He was hustling across campus at the University of Alabama in Tuscaloosa in the fall of 1955 when the first ripple of the *Brown* decision arrived in the form of Autherine Lucy, the first Black person ever admitted to a public university in the history of Alabama. Morris looked down from the steps of the student union building as a mob of some five hundred White men and women attacked the car in which Lucy was being escorted on her first day. When she emerged, she was pelted with produce, a brick narrowly missed her head, and eggs shattered on her dress and in her hair. As the day went on, the mob swelled to over three thousand, chanting, "Hey, hey, ho, ho! Where the hell did that nigger go? Hey, hey, ho, ho! Where did Autherine go?" Lucy was evacuated from campus, facedown in a patrol car. That night, while the mob burned a cross on campus and flipped parked cars, the university's board of trustees gathered in a hotel room downtown and voted to suspend her. It was for her own safety, they told her.

Morris might have been troubled by the episode, but he wasn't remotely interested in confronting social injustice. During his junior year, he ran into a first-year law student named Millard Fuller at a meeting of Alabama Young Democrats at the Student Union. He offered Fuller a ride home that night, and the two quickly realized that their true love wasn't in politics but in business. They sensed a fierce entrepreneurial streak in each other, and began spitballing ideas for new businesses they could start, spurring each other on until one of them realized it was two a.m. With a handshake, the two created Fuller and Dees on the spot, with one motto to govern their decision-making: "to get rich."

They sold Christmas trees, holly wreaths, and pine cones dipped in paint. They launched the Bama Cake Service, soliciting orders from their classmates' parents for birthday cakes, which they delivered to dorm rooms. They folded their first $50,000 into dilapidated houses near campus, which they fixed up and rented to students. The pair bought a small apartment building and soon filled it with students. They purchased a vacant lot and trundled in an eyesore of an army barracks building they'd found, adding several more apartments to their inventory. Within a year of meeting, the pair went from painting pine cones to owning a city block's worth of real estate and an ever-expanding portfolio of mail-order businesses.

MORRIS HADN'T GIVEN UP HIS POLITICAL AMBITIONS, THOUGH. IN the fall of 1957, he invited George Wallace, then a judge, to speak to a campus group he'd formed. When Morris approached him after his remarks with an offer to help with his upcoming race for the governor's mansion, Wallace responded by naming him his statewide student campaign manager. After all, Morris's dad had covered Wallace's $500 filing fee as a show of support.

Instead of starting law school, in the spring of 1958, Morris took the semester off to help Wallace. He also mounted his own campaign for the state's Democratic Executive Committee and was one of the youngest people running for office that year—he hadn't yet turned twenty-one. While traveling the state and pressing the flesh, he also became campaign manager for MacDonald Gallion, who was running for attorney general as a staunch segregationist with a plan to create a private, segregated school system. Millard Fuller also hit the trail on behalf of Gallion, giving more than seventy speeches to all-White groups. In the county courthouse in Fayette, he addressed a gathering of robed Klansmen so large that a PA system had to be rigged so that those outside could hear his pro-segregation address.

Newspaper advertisements listed Morris among eight other candidates who would "back your Democratic Senators and Congressmen in their fight to maintain segregation." He appeared in another paid print advertisement promising to "Protect the Rooster" from Dixiecrats and Republicans: at the top was the symbol of the Alabama Democratic Party—a rooster, crowing beneath a banner emblazoned with the words WHITE SUPREMACY.

Dees wasn't particularly dejected when he lost his race; he returned to school, earned his law degree, and hung his shingle with Fuller, just down the hall from George Wallace's private office. But their eyes were on business, not law.

All the small hustles fell away once Fuller and Dees struck the mother lode, in the form of selling cookbooks to high school chapters of the Future Homemakers of America. On the first day of sales, 1,000 orders came in. On the second, 1,800. On the third, 2,200. They branched out, publishing cookbooks for other organizations, and before long, they were selling 500,000 cookbooks a year. The company eventually had to send a panel truck to the post office to gather the sacks of mail filled with orders and checks. They even managed to sell cookbooks with blank pages for gullible customers to record their own recipes.

They bought the former Atlantic National Life Insurance Company building with cash, and mounted a sign so huge that FULLER AND DEES became part of the Montgomery skyline. Once their sales topped $1 million, they bought nearly three thousand acres of property together, stocking it with cattle and riding horses. They paid cash for a pair of brand-new Lincoln Continentals. They bought speedboats, and then traded those in for larger ones. "This was a goal we had set long ago and we finally made it," a jubilant Fuller recorded in his journal. "Now we want ten million!"

FULLER WAS STARTING TO RECOGNIZE THE "TERRIBLE WRONGS IN the social system" of the South, but he and his partner coveted money, not change. "I had to keep it covered up," Fuller wrote in his diary. "It would be bad for business if rising young lawyers and businessmen spoke out for social justice and equality."

In 1965, Martin Luther King Jr. called for a march from Selma to Montgomery to push for voting rights. Dees sure as hell wasn't going to march, but he did offer to help Fuller shuttle ministers who had come from out of state to Selma. The two had made so much money that they could "afford to be at least a little moral," Fuller wrote. On the way, Dees's license plate was logged by state troopers, who visited his mother later that night with a warning against "messing around" with the civil rights movement.

Four days later, Dees and Fuller left their office to watch the twenty-five thousand marchers stream into Montgomery. They found a spot near the front steps of the state capitol, where Governor Wallace had roared, "Segregation now, segregation tomorrow, and segregation forever!" in defiance of the *Brown* decision. They were waiting for King to speak when Dees's uncle James stomped over.

"I know all about you," his uncle seethed, aware of the fact that the two had driven clergymen to Selma. "You're nothing but a bunch of nigger lovers." James drew his coat back to reveal a .38 concealed in a brace harness. "I oughta take this gun and kill you both here on the spot . . ."

James once shot a family friend five or six times in a feud, taking five or six bullets in return. Both men went to the hospital, both recovered, and the police were never summoned. Dees, concerned for Fuller's safety, shooed his business partner away and tried to ignore his uncle. When

King appeared, he was surrounded by ministers all wearing the same blue suit, hoping to confuse any would-be assassin. Dees didn't know if his uncle had come with plans to shoot King or other marchers, but he knew that the community that once showered him with praise and awards was now turning on him.

Not long thereafter, the Klan burned a cross in front of the Fuller and Dees headquarters, accusing them of secretly printing materials supportive of the civil rights movement.

BY THE TIME HE CLEARED NEW ORLEANS ON HIS MOTORCYCLE, Dees was getting tired. He pulled off the road at Lafayette and checked into a Motel 6 on the edge of the Atchafalaya Basin.

In the dozen years since the Klan had accused him of something he'd never had the courage to do—fighting for civil rights—he now found himself just a day's ride from taking on one of the most important cases of his life. And to think he owed his transformation to a snowstorm.

In early 1968, Dees was stranded by a winter storm at the Cincinnati airport. He found a copy of Clarence Darrow's *The Story of My Life*, and began reading about the renowned trial lawyer's work: fighting the death penalty, representing striking coal miners, and defending a science teacher charged with the "crime" of teaching evolution. Darrow wrote that his "sympathies always went out to the weak, the suffering, and the poor" and that he "had little respect for the opinion of the crowd."

Dees thought of all the times he'd looked the other way when the civil rights movement beckoned. He never marched. He hadn't printed materials in support of the movement. When Black and White activists were being jailed, beaten, and killed, he hadn't put his law degree to work to help them—he'd once even represented the ones doing the beating. He wasn't known by anyone in the movement because he wasn't part of it.

Despite the major civil rights legislation of the 1960s, Dees knew, as he later wrote, that little had changed in the Deep South; the power structures remained firmly in White hands. Blacks were denied access to credit, high-paying jobs, and decent education and housing. As he read through the memoir, waiting for the storm to pass, Dees learned that Darrow had given up a lucrative position with the Chicago and North Western Railway company in order to follow his conscience and represent its workers who had gone on strike for higher wages and safer work conditions. "I was a good lawyer wasting my time trying to make a few more million dollars," Dees wrote. "I had made up my mind. I would sell the company as soon as possible and specialize in civil rights law."

In March 1969, eleven years after the two bumped into each other at the University of Alabama, Fuller and Dees sold their business to the Times Mirror Company for $6 million (equivalent to over $40 million today). Dees announced that he was retiring to the practice of law. He was thirty-two years old.

THREE MONTHS LATER, HE FILED SUIT AGAINST THE YMCA IN Montgomery for discriminating against Black children. There was a sordid past to the case: in the late 1950s, faced with federal orders to integrate public facilities, the city dispatched bulldozers to fill public pools with earth rather than let Black and White children swim together. After discovering a secret arrangement between the city and the local Y to keep the races from "overlapping," Dees won a federal injunction against the YMCA, forcing them to integrate.

He sued his hometown newspaper, the *Montgomery Advertiser*, for its practice of segregating wedding announcements and obituaries—Whites in the "Society" section, Blacks relegated to a "Negro News" page. The practice was soon discontinued.

By early 1971, he and Joseph Levin, with whom he'd handled several cases, were being referred to as "crusading lawyers." They opened a practice together, agreeing to charge only those who could afford it and representing everyone else pro bono. By the end of the year, the law firm of Levin & Dees became the Southern Poverty Law Center, with a bluntly stated mission: "to seek legal remedies for inequality and injustice for poor people."

Working out of a converted dentist's office in downtown Montgomery,

Morris Dees.

the center took on the state government in a case dealing with the sterilization of two adolescent Black sisters without their knowledge. The center represented textile workers stricken with brown lung. They took on death penalty cases that won them few friends. They successfully sued Alabama's Department of Public Safety for its failure to hire a single Black state trooper since its establishment over four decades earlier. Dees sued Governor Wallace for hiring only three Black Alabamians to fill the state's 738 governmental posts. He represented Joan Little, a Black woman who murdered her jailer after he tried to rape her while she was being held on breaking-and-entering charges; she became the first woman in American history acquitted on grounds of using deadly force to resist sexual assault.

Reporters from around the country focused their floodlights on Dees—his Southern charm, his good looks, his wealth—each piece making him shine a bit brighter. One wrote that his voice "flowed with the quiet, steady wash and pull of the tides and waves upon the beach." Another marveled at his "honey drawl." He made each of them feel they were getting the untold story, and gave interviews out at his ranch with his shirt off while photographers snapped away.

In the beginning, Dees didn't draw a salary, but he also didn't personally bankroll the organization; the nonprofit relied upon contributions. Within a couple of years of its founding, it had a small team of lawyers and a $195,000 operating budget, most of which came from direct-mail solicitations of subscribers to liberal magazines. With each mailing, he carefully tracked the response rate to learn which appeals yielded the biggest haul.

But the glory days of sending a panel truck to gather sacks of mail from the post office were seemingly behind him: it was easier to sell someone a book of dessert recipes than it was to get them to write a check to keep someone from being executed.

That all changed in 1979.

ON MAY 26, A LARGE GROUP OF KLANSMEN DESCENDED UPON A peaceful march by the Black residents of Decatur, a small town in the northernmost part of Alabama. The local police provided little security, and gunshots soon broke out in the melee.

Curtis Robinson, a Black maintenance worker for city hall, was driving with his wife and five children when he inadvertently turned his car onto a street thronged with Klansmen. When a robed man ran toward him and began smashing his car with a club, Robinson drew his gun and shot him. The Klansman survived, and Robinson was arrested.

Dees took the case, assuming it'd be a straightforward self-defense acquittal, but Robinson was sentenced by an all-White jury to two years of probation. Dees was livid: "This verdict makes history—it's the first time a black man has ever been convicted of shooting a robed Klansman who advanced on him with a raised club." He was tired of the impunity with which the Klan bullied people, and worried about the apparent rise in the organization's activity around the country since the end of the Vietnam War. He hired a full-time researcher to monitor the KKK, calling the new initiative Klanwatch.

As soon as the center began taking on the Klan, something happened: donations flooded in from across the country. A year later, he saw a photo in *The New York Times* of armed Klansmen on a shrimp boat in Galveston Bay.

HE CLEARED LOUISIANA AND CROSSED INTO TEXAS, SPEEDING through the border town of Port Arthur, where Sáu Văn Nguyễn had holed up for a couple of nights before turning himself in as the one who killed Billy Joe Aplin.

As he approached Galveston Bay, the landscape of estuaries and swamps hardened into concrete and steel, chemical tanks and smokestacks, refineries, rail yards, and a baffling skein of highways, overpasses, and bridges.

When he rode down Seabrook's Eleventh Avenue, the homes on pilings gave way to fish houses and seafood restaurants. He motored past the Pier 8 restaurant, where a White man in a red Camaro had recently warned a Vietnamese man that he would soon firebomb Vietnamese homes. Directly ahead was the Clear Creek Channel, where Jody Collins kept the *Cherry Betty* tied up, and where David Collins had launched the Klan boat patrol.

Dees slowed to a stop in front of Nam's fish house, which was filled with bay and gulf fish, and dozens of pounds of shrimp iced down in bright red coolers. Nam had recently leased it to another Vietnamese fisherman and was finalizing his plans to leave the coast.

Dees walked past the fish house toward a small white frame house on pillars. As he approached the front steps, he found three armed Vietnamese men blocking the doorway, glowering at him. When Nam appeared at the front door, the men stepped aside to let his guest in.

## 21

# Allies and Enemies Gather

A S DEES TOOK A SEAT IN NAM'S DEN, HE QUICKLY SIZED UP THE man. He was handsome, with an officer's bearing and deep voice—the makings of a great plaintiff—but he also looked weary. In the days since Nam had made up his mind to clear out of Galveston Bay, the campaign of harassment had only escalated. Four nights after the Klan boat patrol, Vũ Văn Yến peered out his front window to find a cross burning in his yard. Two nights later, Tú Văn Nguyễn saw a cross burning out by the tracks behind his home. Jim Craig, the owner of what locals called "Saigon Harbor," also saw the fiery cross from his trailer. Kỳ Trinh, owner of a fish house in town, was fixing up his storefront when three White men drove up and threatened him. Nam's thirteen-year-old sister-in-law was terrified to return to his home ever since she bolted out the front door with his baby as Klansmen drifted out back.

Nam studied Dees, wondering what this out-of-state lawyer could propose that Nam hadn't already tried in the past two years. More out of politeness than anything else, he agreed to hear the Alabamian out.

Dees knew they had a potentially great case against Louis Beam and the Knights of the Ku Klux Klan—something the Southern Poverty

Colonel Nam with his family.

Law Center was uniquely qualified to press—but he first needed Nam and the Vietnamese Fishermen's Association to sign on. He began by asking Nam about his life, his kids, his childhood, the wounds he'd suffered in his fight against the North Vietnamese, and how he'd battled until the bitter end.

"And now this Louis Beam says *we* are communists?" Nam thundered.

"Beam is a dangerous man," Dees replied, thinking he'd found his opening. "I'd like to talk to you about stopping him." But when Nam's baby daughter, Judy, started cooing from the next room, he could see the Colonel tighten up.

"We don't want to cause trouble, Mr. Dees," Nam said, shaking his head. "We appreciate being in America."

"You're not the ones causing trouble!" Dees exclaimed.

Nam stood up and motioned to the back door, guiding Dees out to the pier that jutted into the brackish water of the bay, cormorants sunning on rotted posts. He gestured at the trawler he'd bought from David Collins: there was a thick coat of white paint over the cabin, and the outriggers were a fading aquamarine, but the hull of the boat was a rusted mess. Dees didn't know a shrimp trawler from an oil tanker, but he couldn't believe the vessel was seaworthy. Several Vietnamese boats were moored nearby with For Sale signs in the cabin windows.

"Many people think it's best if we let the Klan have its way," Nam said.

"I don't think you do," murmured Dees, seizing the moment to lay out his legal strategy. The Southern Poverty Law Center would petition the federal court in Houston for a preliminary injunction to prevent Louis Beam, Gene Fisher, the Collins brothers, James Stanfield, and the Ku Klux Klan from harassing the Vietnamese or interfering with their right to shrimp. To do so, they would throw everything at them, invoking civil rights statutes and the equal protection clause of the Fourteenth Amendment. Dees, speaking excitedly, even thought they could invoke the 1890 Sherman Antitrust Act by showing that the Klan had interfered with the Vietnamese shrimpers' ability to freely engage in commerce. On top of that, he wanted to dismantle Beam's Texas Emergency Reserve by proving it was operating as an illegal paramilitary organization.

This would be a civil, not a criminal case, he stressed; they weren't there to uncover or punish those who set fire to the boats. But if they succeeded, any Klansmen who threatened Vietnamese fishermen would end up dealing with federal marshals.

Nam was moved. After nearly two years of senseless provocation and harassment, it had taken one hour for this Alabamian to present a compelling way of fighting back, nonviolently. But Nam was worried about the possible consequences of suing the KKK, and he asked if Dees thought the Klan would carry out its threats of "blood" at the start of shrimping season.

"I won't lie to you," Dees said. "That's a possibility. But I think the best way to make sure there isn't any violence is by going to court."

Nam had his reservations, but he agreed to put it to a vote with the members of the Vietnamese Fishermen's Association. If they approved, the Southern Poverty Law Center could file suit in their name against the Klan.

As Dees strode back toward his motorcycle, he was confident that

Nam was up to the fight, but he worried about whether the other members of the association would give him the opportunity. The start of shrimping season—and the Grand Dragon's deadline—was only a few weeks away. If they agreed to sue, he'd have to work at a break-neck pace.

THAT EVENING, NAM WAITED QUIETLY AS THIRTY-FOUR MEMBERS of his coalition filed into St. Peter's Catholic Church in Kemah, which was overseen by Father John Toàn Minh Hoàng, the priest who had collected donations from Vietnamese around the bay as a Christmas gift for Judy Aplin, which the family spurned.

Many of the Vietnamese were frightened that local law enforcement might also be secret members of the Ku Klux Klan, so they were loath to report the rash of threats made against them, but they did confide in their priest. Father John kept a rough catalog of events and was growing increasingly concerned: on several occasions, he'd been called to a Viet-namese parishioner's home to find a dead cat strung up in a noose, dan-gling from a nearby tree branch. He'd also begun sheltering frightened Vietnamese in his church, telling them, "I promise you will live in peace. They'll have to kill me first."

Nam called the meeting to order, laid out Dees's strategy, and posed a simple question: Should they sue for the right to continue shrimping? Or should they yield to the forces growing against them, sell their boats to the first bidder, and try their hand in another business? After all, Emery Waite, the local fish house owner, was making progress with a potential buyer in Central America; selling their trawlers and leaving might be easier than taking on the Ku Klux Klan in court.

There was anything but consensus. The Southern Poverty Law Center was asking these newly arrived refugees to place their trust in the constitution of a country that hadn't yet granted them citizenship, at a moment when the White residents of Galveston Bay were openly talking about violence and driving them out. Nam's own faith in the American rule of law had taken a blow ever since he'd seen photos of

Houston and Galveston police in Klan hoods, to say nothing of the accusation by the feds that his fellow Vietnamese fishermen had burned their own boats.

But when it came down to the vote, the coalition decided to stand their ground and sue the Klan.

HOURS LATER, EXACTLY TWO WEEKS AFTER THE KLAN BOAT PA-trol and six weeks after Louis Beam torched the USS *VIET CONG* at the Collins ranch, a man crept down to the waterfront, carrying a jug of diesel. It was two thirty in the morning.

Freddie was a brick mason, whom everyone called "Bean" on account of his love of Mandrax, a prescription sedative also known as quaaludes and more popularly as "beans." His buddy David Collins had given him the nickname back when the two were involved in some trafficking.

He slipped past the fish houses toward the docks and headed for the *Trudy B*, the forty-foot shrimp trawler owned by Loan Henderson that had been partially burned in January. The boat was valued at $25,000 and was on Nam's list of vessels for sale; Loan was tired of the threats and wanted to get out of the business.

Whoever set fire to the *Trudy B* back in January had inadvertently smothered it when they closed the hatch. A month later, when Louis Beam torched the USS *VIET CONG*, he'd told reporters that *Klan*-burned boats burned all the way down to the waterline, and that "if a burned boat doesn't look like that, the Klan didn't burn it."

Freddie tiptoed onto the dock, the planks creaking as he approached the *Trudy B* in the darkness of a crescent moon. Two other boats were tied up abreast of it, but Freddie wasn't interested in them. He splashed diesel around the upper deck and along the left-hand side of the boat's cabin.

He set the diesel afire and scampered off, leaving the hatch open. A northerly wind fed the flames as they devoured the cabin, burning clear through the gunwales and hull down to the water's edge, leaving only the charred vertical ribs of the boat exposed.

## 22

# Unquiet before the Storm

The *Trudy B*, destroyed by arson.

THE CARCASS OF THE *TRUDY B* WAS DRAGGED FROM THE PIER and beached. One of the boats tied up alongside it, owned by a shrimper named Thị Nanh Nguyễn, was scorched along the flank. Barry Freece, the ATF arson investigator who previously concluded that the Vietnamese had probably torched the boat in January in an attempt to win public sympathy, was called back down to Seabrook.

Nam was furious. The Vietnamese in town were "very sad and scared," he told a journalist, but they would not do anything in retaliation. "If we wanted violence, we wouldn't have offered to sell our boats and leave!"

Nam was certain the Klan was behind it. "They got some good training at the rally," he told a reporter. "There's no doubt in my mind who set the fires. It sure wasn't Vietnamese."

"Those are unfounded allegations," Louis Beam scoffed to a journalist who relayed Nam's comments. "He better be advised of not adding fuel to the fire . . . this is merely a propaganda ploy on the part of Mr. Nguyễn."

James Stanfield, local Klan recruiter, professed shock. "I was surprised as anyone when I heard about the fires . . . since the rally, everything has been going along smoothly down there. The Vietnamese will sell their boats, and I see a smooth transition."

Even though the boat had burned in January, Loan Henderson had not bought an insurance policy on it; she couldn't have expected it to be torched twice in less than three months. "Why would they burn an American boat?!" she indignantly asked a reporter. Since she was married to a White American, she thought her boat should be regarded as American, and therefore exempt from the arsonist's match.

At first, Seabrook Police Chief Bill Kerber resisted jumping to any conclusions. "It looks like some people are already blaming the Klan for the activity, according to news reports, but we haven't even determined that it is arson yet." Hours later, though, he, too, was certain the fire had been set deliberately.

When Freece met with Nam as part of his investigation, he asked if Nam would submit to a lie detector test about whether the Vietnamese had burned their own boats. Nam, incensed, said that he would sit for one when Gene Fisher did. Fisher refused.

NAM HOPPED INTO HIS TRUCK AND DROVE INTO HOUSTON TO PICK up Michael, who had traveled up from San Antonio to compete in a math tournament. When they got back to Seabrook, Michael was startled to learn that his dad, An, and their baby daughter were no longer living in the waterfront bungalow, but had moved to a secret safe house.

Michael had planned to spend the weekend pitching in at the fish house, shuffling the ice and sorting the daily catch, but Nam showed him a window in their home that had recently been shot out and told him about the boats that had just been burned. It was too dangerous to be seen in any public setting.

Nam drove Michael over to a neighborhood he'd never visited, two miles north of the fish house. As they eased down an oak-lined street, Nam studied each of the parked cars.

"Dad, what's going on?" Michael asked nervously.

"The KKK has been following me," Nam said calmly.

"The KKK?"

"When you're here, always watch everywhere you go," his dad said, glancing in his rearview mirror. "Look left, look right, back and front, see how people are acting."

Nam gave the street one last scan and parked the truck in front of a house Michael had never seen. He fished out a pair of keys for his son, but warned him never to enter through the front door, in case the Klan had someone parked on the street. The electricity to the house had been cut—Nam didn't want anyone thinking it was occupied—and there were heavy curtains blocking the front windows.

Michael gathered his backpack in bewilderment. He'd recently read about the Ku Klux Klan in high school, but he thought they existed only in history books. Before getting out of the truck, he asked his dad where he, An, and Judy were living.

"I can't tell you, Michael," Nam said.

"But why?!"

"Because if they capture you, I don't want you to know where I am."

Michael sat in silence.

"There are candles inside," Nam said.

Michael hurried inside as his dad sped off. As he closed the door, he noticed a baseball bat leaning behind it. The sun was starting to set, so he drew the curtains tight, lit the candles, and got started on his homework for the weekend.

THE DAY AFTER THE *TRUDY B* WAS TORCHED, LOUIS BEAM ANNOUNCED that the Klan would hold another rally at the Collins ranch on May 9, six days before the shrimp season's opening day and the end of his ninety-day deadline. The next day, a White man in a red-and-white Ford pickup truck drove up to My's Seafood, aimed a pistol at its Vietnamese owner, Đoi Thi Đỗ, and threatened to kill her.

Dees, racing against the clock, knew that newspaper clippings weren't enough to form the factual basis for the suit. If the center was to succeed, they would need more than just a picture of Klansmen on a boat; they'd need to know the names of those in that picture. They'd need to document the power structure of the local Klan, and map out in precise detail just how the campaign of harassment against the Vietnamese had been carried out. They would need to find people who had trained with Beam's Texas Emergency Reserve. They would need the Vietnamese fishermen to testify, even if it meant risking reprisals. They'd need to find witnesses— White, Vietnamese, Klan, or bystander.

In the wake of the center's first case against the KKK, Dees had assembled Klanwatch, a small group of researchers specializing in digging up intelligence on the organization. As soon as the Vietnamese Fishermen's Association agreed to file the suit, he summoned his Klanwatch team to Seabrook to start investigating.

RANDALL WILLIAMS WAS BORN IN THE MIDDLE OF NOWHERE IN Chambers County, Alabama. He was raised Southern Baptist, a Wallace supporter, and racist, in a part of the country that despised the federal government for enforcing the integration of schools. On the day President John F. Kennedy was shot, Randall and his classmates in the seventh grade were brought into the auditorium, where a small television was tuned to the news of the president's critical condition. When Walter Cronkite delivered the news that Kennedy had died, the teachers and students applauded and cheered. When Randall was sixteen, he was desperate to date a girl at his church, so he did the altar call and said he felt moved by the spirit. They baptized him and gave him a Bible. By the time he finished it, he found it impossible to reconcile what the book said with what his preachers claimed it said. He read himself out of the church and, eventually, out of his racist mindset.

He took a job as a reporter for the *Alabama Journal* in Montgomery after college, and quickly sensed that every story—where new schools, jails, or landfills were built—seemed to revolve around race. He grew frustrated with the constraints of a daily newspaper. The problems he was seeing were structural and systemic, far more complicated than could be conveyed in eight hundred words, so he left journalism to work for the Southern Poverty Law Center as the head of the newly created Klanwatch.

He worked closely with another young employee by the name of Mike Vahala, a recent Yale graduate from Indiana, going undercover to Klan rallies throughout the Deep South, wearing ratty clothes and blending into crowds. After one of their first rallies, the pair hopped into their car and joined a caravan of Klansmen en route to a cross burning, driving for a half hour out into the country, where they turned onto a private road that cut across a pasture into the woods. It was pitch-black, and the only other people there were hard-core Klan, with rifles and pistols everywhere.

It wasn't until they were in the shadowy seclusion of the woods that they realized they hadn't prepared any cover story. They were terrified that they might be identified as outsiders—maybe even federal agents. Their concerns soon dissipated, though, when they realized the Klansmen had built themselves a steel cross that was so tall that their small membership didn't have enough muscle to raise it. Williams and Vahala suppressed grins as they watched them grunt and sweat, mud and diesel soiling their ceremonial robes, while the cross lay dormant. When it was finally hoisted with the help of a rusted-out pickup truck, the cross bent. The Klan leader began to speak, his words muffled by his robe, but he soon forgot his lines and had to consult a KKK manual to refresh his memory.

**BUT WHAT WAS HAPPENING IN GALVESTON WAS DIFFERENT FROM** angry men dancing around a burning cross in a field of dirt. Someone had firebombed Vietnamese boats. Refugees were being threatened at gunpoint. Louis Beam was threatening "blood, blood, blood" and offering to train armed White shrimpers.

Williams and Vahala booked rooms under false names at a nearby Holiday Inn and got to work. They quickly learned that the Dutch Kettle was the local hot spot for shrimpers, and began parking themselves in a booth each morning, poking at sausage links and grits while they eavesdropped on conversations. More often than not, they found Gene Fisher, the Collins brothers, and Stanfield. They sipped lukewarm coffee and scribbled furiously in small notebooks they kept in their lap.

Williams's southern accent was an asset, but he didn't know a thing about how to talk to shrimpers. When he first ventured down to the docks and tried talking to a White shrimper about the troubles with the Vietnamese, he was brushed off as an outsider at once. If he had still been with the *Alabama Journal*, he would've been ethically obligated to introduce himself as a reporter, but he was operating under a different set of parameters with the center; he didn't even need to identify himself as an employee. He wasn't a lawyer, governed by the rules of professional conduct. He wasn't looking for evidence that would be admissible in court; it would be used only to justify subpoenas that would drag people in for depositions under oath.

So as far as Williams saw it, he had a wide berth. The next time he went down to the docks, he told shrimpers that he was a reporter writing a story about their clash with the Vietnamese. But Williams didn't tell them he was writing for *The New York Times*; he told them he was writing for *Playboy*.

Everyone started talking.

———

BUT THE CLOCK WAS TICKING. WITH THE *TRUDY B* STILL SMOLDER-
ing and danger mounting, Dees wanted to file the suit as quickly as possible. Williams and Vahala were turning up all kinds of leads in their
investigation, but he knew he would need a Houston-based co-counsel,
an attorney who could bring local knowledge and relationships to the
effort, to say nothing of lending office space and filing motions. In his
mind, there was only one man for the job.

## 23

# The Vietnamese Fight Back

IN MAY 1968, A MONTH AFTER DAVID BERG OPENED HIS LAW OFfice, his beloved older brother, Alan, was murdered. The two used to skip school and drive down the Gulf Freeway to Galveston, passing the day on the beach and making big plans for the future. Alan covered most of David's tuition with gambling winnings; his suspected murderer, Charles Harrelson, was allegedly hired to collect on an unpaid debt owed to the Galveston Mafia.

While he waited for Harrelson's trial, David desperately tried to distract himself, sitting in the cool dark of movie theaters in the middle of the day, unable to focus on anything other than Alan. Without a client base, he dropped into the courthouse to watch renowned trial lawyers try their cases. When Harrelson secured the feared attorney Percy Foreman, David had a premonition that justice would be denied, and he descended into a depression so severe that he stopped talking about his brother. His relationship with his father frayed. His sleeping hours were tormented by nightmares. His marriage suffered.

He threw himself into his practice, writing wills and handling divorces until he got his first criminal case: a young man arrested with heroin in his pocket. When his client's father, a brain surgeon, paid his fee of $2,500, Berg didn't know "whether to shit or go blind." After he got his client off, Berg took on more and more drug cases, eventually becoming the lawyer a generation of young Houstonians knew to call when they got busted. Business came in from around the state; the ACLU threw him cases that nobody else would take.

Berg marched against the Vietnam War, but he always felt embarrassed that he'd been able to avoid the draft by way of a medical deferment. When he realized that the Klan-ridden Houston Police Department was stopping protesters for no reason "other than [their] long hair," often planting throw-down drugs if none were found in their vans, he put his law degree to work.

He took on the case of Danny Schacht, who staged a skit against the Vietnam War in front of an armed forces induction center in Houston, dressed as an army officer whose insignia were turned upside down. Later that night, FBI agents arrested Schacht on charges of "unauthorized wearing of a distinctive part of the military uniform." Berg took the case all the way to the Supreme Court, successfully getting Schacht's conviction unanimously reversed. He filched a pair of quill pens from the counsel's table before emerging from the courtroom in a daze; he was twenty-seven years old.

He returned to Houston lionized by his success, but deadened by the news that Harrelson was found not guilty. After the acquittal, though, something happened to Berg: he was willing to fight anybody. He didn't care about personal risks that might come with taking on a case. His practice thrived, and he became chief legal counsel for the ACLU. "When there are strong forces marshalled against someone," he told a reporter, "my natural instinct is to step in between that person and the forces and say, 'over my dead body.'"

MORRIS DEES WAS A HERO TO BERG, IN NO SMALL PART BECAUSE of his willingness to take on death penalty work and other unpopular cases like that of Joan Little, the woman who murdered her jailer during an attempted rape. So when Dees pulled up to his law office to ask for help representing the Vietnamese fishermen against the Ku Klux Klan, Berg didn't hesitate in signing on as co-counsel. In the division of labor, he and his partner, Philip Zelikow, would draft motions and help flag useful legal precedents.

With his team in place, Dees wrote a letter to Nam to brace him for what lay ahead. The coming weeks would require an exhausting and contentious series of depositions, in which everyone involved in the conflict would be grilled by lawyers on either side. He couldn't rule out the possibility of a violent reaction. The men trying to drive the Vietnamese out of the bay had already resorted to extreme measures; naming them in a federal lawsuit wasn't likely to tame them. Dees wanted to make sure his clients didn't lose their nerve in the face of whatever dangers closed in upon them.

"I want to thank you and your people for allowing us to represent you in your struggle against the Ku Klux Klan," he wrote. "I personally have handled many tough and unpopular cases . . . but never have I been so proud to represent a group of more worthy people.

"This battle we are in together will be won as much in the minds and hearts of the people of Texas and our nation as in the Court," he warned. "If we can generate a passionate feeling in the public for your cause, the bright light of public opinion will cause those who should protect you to be more aggressive and those who would harm you to be more fearful.

"I know that pressures are heavy on you and your family. You know the way of patience and struggle. I can almost assure you that the day will come soon when you will feel the heavy burden lifted."

Dees also scrawled out another letter on his legal pad for his assistant to put on Southern Poverty Law Center letterhead and disseminate to donors, writing as if from behind enemy lines. "The SPLC Klanwatch project filed suit . . . against the KKK. Three Vietnamese boats were recently burned by unknown arsonists. The Vietnamese fear for their lives. The Klan is training in paramilitary camps with semi-automatic weapons. Urgently need $25,000 to fund suit and employ guards to protect fishermen. Please rush all you can afford today."

ON APRIL 16, 1981, THE VIETNAMESE FISHERMEN'S ASSOCIATION filed its suit, calling for an emergency injunction from the federal government to protect their rights to fish. The suit named Gene Fisher, Jody Collins, David Collins, James Stanfield, Louis Beam, and the Knights of the Ku Klux Klan as defendants. Beam's "Grand Dragon's Dispensation," tied to the opening day of shrimping season, was less than four weeks away.

Nam stepped out of the federal courthouse on Rusk Street in Houston to a bank of news cameras. Dressed in a crisp black suit with a black tie, he read from a prepared statement.

"I have stated in the past that I and other members . . . would voluntarily leave the Galveston Bay area if this was necessary to prevent our property from being destroyed, to protect the lives of our families, and to be able to carry on a livelihood free from harassment." Until their boats sold, though, he said the Vietnamese would "seek the protection of the laws of this nation that were written to protect the free operation of a person's business, and that protect a person's life and property from illegal acts.

"We Vietnamese came to this country seeking a land of freedom where we could raise our families in peace," he said, a stern look on his face. "Those of us who have settled in the Galveston Bay area have worked hard to be good citizens and to spend our time in productive work. We have come to love our new home and to hope that, for us and for our children, the American dream will become a reality."

That night, they all braced for the reaction from the people they had named in their suit.

## 24

# The Speedboating Lawyer
# and the Judge

THE NEXT DAY, LOUIS BEAM ASSAILED THE VIETNAMESE AS "only idiots" who filed a "totally unfounded lawsuit," telling a reporter that their problems wouldn't be solved in a courtroom—but by leaving the coast. "I'm not a prophet or a seer," Beam said. "Violence is possible, but it is avoidable at this point."

Beam repeated his claim that he wasn't targeting Vietnamese like Nam and the plaintiffs, but rather the "Viet Cong" he imagined had infiltrated the US refugee program, except the facade frequently slipped. In one interview, Beam hissed that the Vietnamese would get "a lot better fight than they got from the Viet Cong." In another, he boasted that the Klan would "expose these Vietnamese for the parasites they have become upon our society."

Gene Fisher echoed the sentiment, claiming to be happy for the opportunity provided by the lawsuit to expose a government conspiracy to help Vietnamese shrimpers at the expense of Whites.

By this point, Dees was comfortable with TV cameras swarming him whenever he emerged from a courthouse. This was now a national story: Walter Cronkite was running updates on the *CBS Evening News*.

Producers from 20/20 were already making plans to film the next Klan rally at Jody Collins's ranch.

James Stanfield and David Collins held an impromptu news conference, proclaimed that they "welcomed the lawsuit," and then set out in search of a lawyer willing to represent them.

SAM ADAMO WAS A LIBERAL AND OPPOSED TO THE WAR IN VIETnam, but knew he didn't have it in him to dodge the draft. His brother had dropped out of college to join the Marines; he survived the war but was never the same upon his return. When the lottery came, though, Sam's number was high enough that he never went.

After graduating from law school, he spent five years as an assistant district attorney in Houston before opening up a private practice as a criminal defense lawyer. Within a few years, he had a thriving practice, fighting against the death penalty and against overreach by law enforcement officers. In the late 1970s, after successfully representing someone charged with trafficking narcotics along the Gulf Coast, he was approached by a DEA agent in the courthouse hallway.

"You gettin' that boat of his for your fee?" the agent asked.

"What boat?" Adamo's client owed him quite a bit of money but had never mentioned anything about a boat.

"We got pictures of him shooting around the bay in one of those cigarette boats!"

When Adamo brought it up, his client groaned and said, "You want it?"

Adamo never saw the purpose of go-fast boats, which seemed like a pointless way to burn gas at a time when it was costlier than ever, but he was curious . . . and his client owed him. As soon as he took it out on the water, he was in love. Other lawyers golfed; Adamo chased after adrenaline, racing down to the waterfront whenever he had a free afternoon. It was dangerous, exhilarating, and a hell of a way to burn off courtroom stress. A photo of Adamo at the wheel of his boat as it launched off a rolling wave from a passing oil tanker into the air above the waters of Galveston Bay made the cover of *Ahoy: Texas Boating* magazine. He wore a motorcycle helmet to protect his skull from whipping against the dash when the boat slammed back down to the surface at a hundred miles per hour.

He kept his boat docked at a marina by the Clear Creek Channel, a forty-five-minute drive from his law office in Houston. He never knew if his client had actually been involved with drug trafficking, but after suspecting that the boat wasn't performing as well as it should, he brought it to his boat mechanic, who poked around and found a number of secret compartments that had taken on water.

His mechanic's name was James Stanfield.

ADAMO DIDN'T KNOW MUCH ABOUT STANFIELD PERSONALLY— their conversations revolved almost entirely around boats, weather, and ailing engines. That changed in April 1981, when Stanfield showed up in his office grumbling about being sued.

"Whaddaya mean?" Adamo asked.

Stanfield showed him the complaint. Adamo's eyebrow arched when he read that Louis Beam and the "Knights of the Ku Klux Klan" were named as defendants, prompting his mechanic to acknowledge his role as the Galveston-area recruiter for the KKK.

It didn't make sense. Adamo had seen him joke around with Black customers. Stanfield had always been friendly with one of Adamo's Black employees. He'd never heard Stanfield speak in a bigoted way about anyone.

"Every lawyer has a right to a client," he joked with a sigh. He wasn't going to do it pro bono, though. Stanfield told him that one of the Collins brothers was in the midst of another suit involving a car accident that was likely to settle at around $10,000. *Good enough*, thought Adamo.

Adamo knew some would judge him for taking on the case, but the ethical bar for rejecting someone seeking his legal help was high. Besides, he'd grown thick-skinned over the years; every criminal defense attorney walks into a courtroom knowing that at least half the people there hate them. He had a warts-and-all view of humanity, particularly with respect to what he saw as situational ethics—many people who had once scorned him for taking on a particular case later came running with open checkbooks when a family member was in trouble with the law. As he saw it, he represented a lot of good people who made bad judgments. The businessman who celebrated a big deal with too many drinks and got picked up for drunk driving wasn't a bad person to him; neither was the addict who shoplifted jewelry to pay for his habit or the wife who killed her husband because of physical and mental abuse.

He knew James Stanfield. He didn't know the Collins brothers or Gene Fisher, but they seemed harmless enough. As for the Klan, he took a broad view of free speech rights, and found something redundant in the notion of injunctive relief: there was no need for the federal government to warn people that it was illegal to burn boats or assault people.

SHORTLY THEREAFTER, LOUIS BEAM ADDRESSED THE MEDIA WITH a defiant air: "Texas citizens will not yield their birthright, their jobs, and their livelihood without a fight. Period." He touted the May 9 Klan rally at the Collins ranch, which would now double as a fundraiser to cover the legal fees for their defense. This time, though, Richard Butler, the head of the Aryan Nations, would speak, alongside Jerry Paul Smith, a Klansman who had been acquitted after killing several protesters at an anti–White supremacist rally in Greensboro, North Carolina, two years earlier.

While the lawyers girded for battle, they awaited announcement of which of the nine federal judges of the Houston Division of the US District Court for the Southern District of Texas had been randomly selected to hear the case.

JUDGE GABRIELLE KIRK McDONALD WOULD FOREVER WONDER JUST how random it was when it was announced that *Vietnamese Fishermen's Association v. Knights of the Ku Klux Klan* had landed on her docket. McDonald was the first Black judge appointed to the federal bench in

Texas, the third in the entire South, and the third Black female federal judge in US history. After graduating first in her class from the Howard University School of Law, she worked as a staff attorney with the NAACP Legal Defense Fund and in private practice, bringing discrimination cases against both labor unions and major corporations in Texas, such as Monsanto, Union Carbide, and the Lone Star Steel Company.

McDonald wasted no time in scheduling hearings to commence on May 11, which left lawyers on both sides only a few weeks to conduct depositions that would form the factual basis of the suit.

In the spirit of legal bonhomie, Sam Adamo and his law partner, Richard Cobb, offered to host the depositions at their law office in downtown Houston. The first were scheduled for April 30, the sixth anniversary of the fall of Saigon and the beginning of the refugee crisis. Dees and Berg drafted subpoenas for Louis Beam and Gene Fisher, the two Vietnam veterans at the heart of the campaign to drive the Vietnamese from the coast.

## 25

# Guns and Depositions

ON APRIL 30, 1981, THE FIRST DEPOSITION OF *VIETNAMESE FISHER-men's Association v. Knights of the Ku Klux Klan* was held in a conference room at the law office of Adamo and Cobb, a short walk from the Hyatt Regency where Louis Beam had nearly been killed in his attempted assault on Deng Xiaoping two years earlier.

Morris Dees was accustomed to all sorts of things happening in the course of a case. One of his first clients after law school once came into his office with a hangdog look: the judge was threatening to lock him up if he didn't start paying his alimony, and his ex-wife had started seeing someone new. His client kept mumbling that he was going to go outside and kill himself, but after trying to reason with him, Dees exasperatedly pulled a .38 from his desk and handed it to him. "You don't have to go out . . . you can just shoot yourself here." The man pushed back his chair, stood up, closed his eyes, and pulled the trigger. *Click.* He slumped into the chair, drenched in sweat; the two sat in a long silence before his client returned the unloaded pistol with a grateful look.

But the first day of depositions got off to an especially chaotic start.

While they waited for the lawyers to arrive, Nam and three Vietnamese plaintiffs took a seat at the large conference table alongside Williams and Vahala, the center's investigators. A spindly White man soon walked into the room with a camera slung around his neck and, without saying a word, began taking photographs. Williams instinctively pulled a newspaper up to cover his face; as head of the Klanwatch, he needed to be able to dip in and out of Klan gatherings anonymously. If the man was in any way connected to Louis Beam, he risked blowing his cover.

The unknown man took pictures from several feet away, and then drew uncomfortably close to Nam and the other Vietnamese shrimpers, snapping away with his 35-millimeter Miranda. From behind his newspaper, Randall asked the photographer to identify himself, but the man only muttered something about being a soldier.

Williams barked at him to get out of the room, but when the photographer ignored him, he stood up, his newspaper still raised, and went off in search of Dees.

Dees stormed in, livid. Depositions were not public events, and he wanted the man ejected, but not before he had a chance to grill him. Under oath, the man identified himself as Russell Gregory Thatcher, there at Louis Beam's request to document the proceedings "for posterity." He denied any involvement in the Klan other than attending the occasional rally, but added that he was a self-proclaimed minister of the Aryan Covenant Church.

"Are you what we would call a Nazi or neo-Nazi?" Dees asked.

"Yes, I am a Nazi."

When Dees asked him about his camera, Thatcher admitted to taking several pictures of the Vietnamese plaintiffs.

"Would you remove them, please?" Dees asked.

"No, I will not." Thatcher replied coolly.

Dees moved that the court seize the camera, but the only representative of the court present was Mary Truman, a court reporter transcribing the proceedings. She wasn't about to wrest a camera from the Nazi's hands. Thatcher refused until Sam Adamo prevailed upon him to hand it over, and the room was readied for the deposition of the Grand Dragon of the Knights of the Ku Klux Klan.

Louis Beam arrived in his Klan robe, joined by a black-robed chaplain of the Aryan Covenant Church named "Father Joseph," who opened the deposition with a prayer.

"State your name, please," Dees started.

"I respectfully decline to answer on the basis of the protection afforded by the Fifth Amendment."

Dees rolled his eyes. He'd heard the Fifth invoked plenty, but not for answering something as simple as one's name. These depositions, which began with a court official swearing in deponents under oath, were not prosecutions but fact-finding expeditions meant to provide the court with a truthful account of who said what and why. Beam's lawyers could object to any of Dees's questions for the record, but Beam would still be required to answer. Only if Judge McDonald subsequently sustained those objections would his response be kept from being entered into evidence. Beam had every right to invoke the Fifth Amendment to avoid incriminating himself, but courts didn't tolerate "fanciful" or "imaginary fears" of self-incrimination; no judge would construe stating one's name as worthy of the Fifth.

Dees was hoping to avoid the tedium of filing motions to ask the court to force Beam and his codefendants to answer, a time-consuming exercise at a moment when they didn't have the luxury of time.

"I don't want to waste my time on the record," he snapped at Adamo's partner, Richard Cobb, "because you've told me all your witnesses are going to do this for a different reason.

"No further questions," Dees grunted. "We'll see you in court at ten o'clock in the morning," he continued, signaling his intent to ask Judge McDonald to compel Beam's testimony.

"May I make a statement?" Beam asked.

"Yes, you can," Dees replied eagerly.

"No," Cobb jumped in, turning to his client. "I advise you not to make any statement at this time."

"All right," Dees said, gathering his things, baiting Beam. "Let the record show that the witness is refusing to testify . . ."

"Let the record show Morris Dees is an anti-Christ Jew!" sneered Beam, as the court reporter bashed away at her stenotype.

EVER SINCE THE DEPOSITION BEGAN, NAM HAD BEEN STUDYING Louis Beam, looking for some sign of recognition. It was the damnedest thing, but he was certain they'd met before, a dozen years earlier back in Vietnam, when Nam visited Beam in an army field hospital after his helicopter was shot down in 1968. Now the man upon whom he'd pinned a flag of appreciation was trying to drive him and his fellow Vietnamese out of business.

But something else was troubling him: Beam was sitting awkwardly. Nam studied his torso and saw the unmistakable outline of a holstered revolver.

Nam leaned over and whispered into Dees's ear, "Beam's got a gun."

Dees was momentarily flummoxed. "Are you sure?" he whispered, his mind racing. Was Beam dumb enough to try something in his lawyer's conference room, in the middle of a deposition at which a court reporter was present? As much as he hoped the Grand Dragon was all bluster, he couldn't take any chances.

While Beam and his lawyers waited in awkward silence for the next question, Dees and his side of the table worked out a plan in hushed tones. Dees would ask Adamo and Cobb to determine whether their client was armed. If Beam tried anything, then they'd all shove the conference table against him to pin him against the wall, giving them the chance to either disarm him or escape.

Williams and Vahala looked at their boss in bewilderment. Vahala was fresh out of Yale. Williams was a journalist at heart. But Nam and the other Vietnamese just nodded—they were ready.

Dees took a breath, his muscles tensed.

"We'd like counsel at this time to determine whether this witness came into the deposition armed."

After a brief silence, Dees pressed his inquiry.

"Mr. Adamo, would you determine whether your witness is armed?"

Beam shot to his feet and shrieked, "You don't have permission to search my body unless you've got a permit!" before bolting from the room.

Dees turned to the wide-eyed court reporter transcribing the proceedings and said, "Let the record show that this witness has a weapon under his Klan robe. He's in here in full regalia Klan robe, and obviously he has a shoulder holster with a weapon sticking out under it . . . unless his counsel refutes it." With this, Dees pressed Cobb and Adamo into a corner.

"It's not up to counsel to admit or deny what's under somebody's clothing," ventured Cobb. "I'm not clairvoyant, nor do I have X-ray vision, and am certainly not in a position to grant anybody permission to search someone else's body . . . and I see no weapon."

"That's the end of this deposition," Dees fumed.

IT WASN'T THE MOST AUSPICIOUS START TO THE SUIT. LATER THAT night, David Berg drove home to a town house he was renting. He had recently divorced, and it was his night with their two sons, twelve and ten years old, who were inside with the nanny. By the time he pulled into the driveway, it was dark. He noticed that the small gate in front of the house was ajar, and sighed—he was always harping on his boys to keep it shut.

As he worked the key into the lock, he noticed something wedged into the doorframe. He tugged it out and saw an image of a hooded man on a black horse with the words:

YOU HAVE BEEN PAID A SOCIAL VISIT
BY THE KNIGHTS OF THE
KU KLUX KLAN
DON'T MAKE THE NEXT VISIT
A BUSINESS CALL

Berg whirled around and noticed two men in a red-and-white pickup truck parked across the street, eyeballing him. He remembered that a few weeks earlier, someone driving a red-and-white pickup truck had brandished a pistol at Đoi Thi Đỗ, the Vietnamese owner of My's Seafood, and a blinding rage overcame him.

The truck sped off, but before he realized what he was doing, Berg sprinted back to his Mercedes and took off in pursuit of them. Berg supported gun control measures, but he wanted nothing more in that moment than to kill them. He floored the accelerator, chasing after the truck, having no idea what he would do if he caught up with them, but the thought of his sons being exposed to any kind of danger threw him into a berserker fury.

His Mercedes's diesel-powered engine was slow to accelerate, though, and he struggled to keep up with the pickup. After only a few blocks, the men in the pickup shook Berg from their tail.

He drove home, exhausted and frightened. He had never been happier to put his arms around his boys, but he didn't want to hug them so tightly as to scare them. That night, he had them sleep in sleeping bags in a loft space in his bedroom. As they slept, he thought back to one of his first cases, involving a former Rice University student who was arrested while taking part in an antiwar protest in 1967; the Ku Klux Klan shot his home with so much buckshot that Houston Police thought it had been bombed. Berg slipped out onto a balcony overlooking the street and kept guard.

The next morning, Berg tried to keep a steady voice while instructing his boys to pack a suitcase. Until he could find a more secure situation, they would hole up in a hotel.

DEES HAD RECEIVED A THREATENING CALL AT HIS OWN HOTEL room, even though he had asked the receptionists not to give out his name or acknowledge that he was staying there.

They didn't know who was making the threats, but one thing was clear: between concealed guns and Nazi photographers, the law office of

Adamo and Cobb would no longer do for depositions. Dees and Berg filed a motion to hold all subsequent depositions at the federal courthouse under the protection of US marshals.

Judge McDonald granted the motion immediately, forbidding weapons in the deposition room and ordering the neo-Nazi's photographs of the plaintiffs to be held under seal by the court.

## 26

# "You Die . . . You Die . . . You Die"

WITH US MARSHALS MILLING ABOUT THE HALLWAY OUTSIDE their conference room in the federal courthouse, the defendants were much better behaved, or at least unarmed.

Gene Fisher, whose appeal to the Knights of the Ku Klux Klan had set this entire thing in motion, answered questions about his extensive criminal record, but when Dees asked him about the various bills under consideration in the state legislature—among them a freeze on new shrimp permits and an establishment of a two p.m. curfew—Fisher confessed that he hadn't known anything about the legislation until it was announced on the radio.

If his entire purpose in involving the Klan had been to make enough noise to get lawmakers to "pay attention," as he'd said on so many occasions, he was curiously uninterested in directing that attention to practical remedies. Had he bothered to pay attention himself, he would've realized that the bills were drafted weeks before he first drove up to the Klan's bookstore in Pasadena in search of Louis Beam.

As Dees cycled through the defendants, waiting for his rematch with the Grand Dragon, he teased out a familiar litany of complaints. Gene called the Vietnamese "parasites" without the same rights as the White shrimpers of Texas, while denying having animosity toward the Vietnamese in general. Stanfield denied that his beloved Klan would burn boats, despite the fact that they had publicly torched a boat only weeks earlier while describing it as "in-service training." Jody Collins denied being a member of the American Fishermen's Association, even though he'd signed on when Gene first proposed it at John's Western Point tavern. He also denied being a Klansman, even though he'd let them hold the Klan rally at his ranch, he was preparing to host another one there in the coming week, and he'd allowed his trawler to be used for the Klan boat patrol.

As things were wrapping up for the day, Dees mentioned that he had received a threatening phone call in his hotel room the night before.

"Yeah, I heard you did!" Collins said. "I figure you were staying at the Hyatt."

"The Hyatt?" Dees said. "How'd you know? That's where they made the threat!"

"High-priced lawyer like you out of Montgomery, Alabama, ain't gonna stay in the fuckin' Holiday Inn!" Collins said with a grin.


ON MAY 3, LOUIS BEAM ARRIVED AT THE COURTHOUSE DRESSED IN a short-sleeved shirt and tie and carrying a bag. In the hallway outside Judge McDonald's courtroom, he found a scrum of cameras and reporters asking if he had indeed worn a pistol under his Klan robe at the first, aborted deposition. He smirked and said he'd only been carrying a Bible under his robe, but that he had held a cross up between himself and Dees. The man was "possessed by Satan," Beam said. "If those demons get loose, we might need five or six U.S. Marshals."

Upon arriving in the courthouse conference room, he reached into his bag and pulled out his neatly folded white Klan robe, which bore the three green stripes of the Grand Dragon. Alongside his robe was a Bible.

With a federal marshal standing guard in the corner, Dees began the deposition with a discussion of Beam's arrest record. In 1970, wresting a Viet Cong flag in a scuffle with antiwar demonstrators: released without charge. In 1971, indicted by a grand jury for the bombing of the Pacifica radio station: charges dropped. Indicted for blowing up the headquarters of the Socialist Workers Party in Houston: charges dropped. In 1975, arrested on charges of false imprisonment after a White mother and father asked for his help in "getting their daughter back" after she moved in with a Black man: charges dropped. "An act of chivalry and honor," Beam explained, clearly enjoying the conversation. "Let's see . . . I was arrested for assaulting the chief murderer of 55,000 American and Vietnamese soldiers in Vietnam," he continued, referring to his 1979 attempted assault on Deng Xiaoping, then vice premier of China. Released and sent on his way.

When Dees turned to his conflict with the Vietnamese shrimpers, Beam claimed he was only there "to enforce fishing laws," but when pressed, he didn't know what specific laws were being violated.

"The reason I gave the 90 days," Beam offered, was that "people are very upset along the Texas coast. There is a great potential for violence there. I want to avert that, if it's at all possible. So, I served as a moderating influence. That cannot be disputed."

When Dees grilled him about the torched boats, Beam said that it "wouldn't surprise me a bit if a Viet Cong or former North Vietnamese agent doesn't toss a fire bomb in those boats." The arsonist might even have been an agent of Hồ Chí Minh, in the former helicopter gunner's imagination, spitting after saying the name of the Vietnamese leader.

WHEN DEES WAS FINISHED, BEAM ANNOUNCED THAT HE HAD A statement to make to "clearly delineate what is happening here in this dispute.

"From the outset, I think that [it] should be made clear that what is happening here today is proof of the Klan's claim that this country is disintegrating and degenerating. Anytime—"

"Talk slower now . . . the lady has to take it down. She can't write as fast as you talk," Dees interrupted, needling the Grand Dragon. "You have to talk slow . . ."

"Anytime," Beam continued, flustered, "an out-of-state agitator, anti-Christ Jew person is allowed to come into the state like yourself, Demon Dees, to come into the state and ferment discord between Texas people"—presumably meaning "foment"—"it is proof of our claim! No anti-Christ Jew should be allowed to ask a Christian anything for a court of law!"

Dees wasn't Jewish, but he didn't bother correcting him. Every thirty seconds, though, he made a point of interrupting the Grand Dragon to tell him to slow down for the sake of the court reporter transcribing the deposition.

Beam forged ahead, explaining that he was "not the enemy of the Vietnamese. I have set at their table. I've held their children." Only a week earlier, he described them as parasites, but now he wanted the court to know that "the issue is not Louis Beam opposed to the Vietnamese. It's Louis Beam versus Morris Dees, anti-Christ Jew."

Beam turned his attention to the Vietnamese. As far as he was concerned, the problem had already been resolved when Nam announced 60 percent of the Vietnamese shrimpers would get out of the business as soon as they sold their boats. "They have nothing to fear with me," he said, gesturing at Nam and the Vietnamese plaintiffs sitting across the table from him. He just wanted them to "keep their agreement" and move from the coast. "There's not enough fish to go around. I'm asking the Vietnamese to stick by their word as honorable people. If they said they would sell the boats and move, please do so."

"We are not going to burn you out if you don't move," he continued, "but it will show you as having violated your word. And to a Vietnamese, this is a horrible disgrace . . . so, let's give peace a chance."


AFTER THE DEPOSITION, MIKE VAHALA WAS MAKING THE LUNCH run when he encountered Beam standing near their rental car. Upon being spotted, Beam darted off. Vahala nervously crawled down to the pavement to search the chassis of the car for a bomb, got inside, and turned the key in the ignition with dread. When he returned, he left the car with a valet a couple of blocks away.

———

DURING THE DEPOSITION OF DAVID COLLINS, BEAM SAT IN A COR-
ner of the room holding up a book titled *Exorcism*. Dees tried to focus
on his line of questions, but as he glanced over at Beam, the Grand
Dragon seemed to be staring at him in a semiconscious state, pointing a
finger and mouthing the words "You die . . . you die . . . you die . . ."

"This thing is blown all out of proportion," Collins, who piloted the
*Cherry Betty* during the Klan boat patrol, and who had burned two
crosses in the area over the past year, complained. "I didn't say anything
about the Vietnamese. From an environment point of view, this was going to destroy the bay for everybody."

"You've never done any acts symbolically or anything to show any
animosity toward the Vietnamese people?" Dees asked, not knowing
that Collins once made a trip with a friend to a small island off the coast
to gather up rattlesnakes, which he then dropped into the bilges of Vietnamese boats in the dead of night.

"I hollered at some of them running up the creek and beating my
boat against the dock."

Dees knew that David Collins had a mock grave in his front yard,
festooned with a coconut skull on a stake, a Vietnamese flag, and a Confederate flag. "Anything to show general animosity toward these people
like you wanted to bury them or get rid of them?"

"No," Collins said. "I haven't wanted to bury any of them. I have no
desire to bury any of them."


NOBODY HAD SEEN BEAM FOR A COUPLE OF HOURS, BUT AT THE
end of the day, when Dees and Vahala exited the courthouse and began
walking to their car, they realized that the Klansman was following
them, holding a brown paper bag. Dees picked up his pace, but Beam
kept up.

When they made it to the booth of the parking lot, Beam stopped
and watched them. Vahala requested the car from the valet and watched

Beam anxiously while they waited for their car. When it arrived, at last, Vahala scrambled into the driver's seat.

As they approached the exit, they saw Beam advancing toward them. "Floor it!" shouted Dees.

As Vahala screeched out of the lot, Dees saw Beam reach his hand inside the bag, kneel into a firing position, and aim the bag at him. The car careened down the street, and Dees never figured out whether the Klansman had a gun or was just trying to rattle him.

In either case, it worked. Dees called his brother, who ran a company supplying tactical gear and weapons to law enforcement officers along the Gulf Coast, and within a day, he was wearing body armor and carrying a revolver.

AFTER BEAM'S ANTICS DURING THE DEPOSITIONS, DEES FILED A motion that asked for a court-ordered mental examination of the Grand Dragon to determine whether he was insane. He knew it was beyond Judge McDonald's authority but that the press would cover it; he just wanted to embarrass Beam. Asked by a journalist about Dees's charge that he was "mentally deranged," Beam had a simple retort: "He is my enemy and I am his."

ON MAY 4, AFTER ANOTHER DAY OF DEPOSITIONS, DEES WAS GATH-ering his papers and speaking with Nam when the US marshal assigned to the room told him that Judge McDonald's clerk wished to speak to him. Sam Adamo, overhearing the comment, asked if the clerk wanted to speak with Dees about the case or another matter—after all, it would be improper for the court to have an ex parte conversation, with only one side of a lawsuit. The marshal didn't know, so Dees told him to call the clerk down to the deposition room.

When the clerk arrived, he asked both Dees and Adamo how the depositions were proceeding, and whether they expected to ask the judge to weigh in on any Fifth Amendment issues. When the conversation concluded, Adamo, Dees, and the clerk all walked out into the hallway.

About thirty feet down the hallway, Dees realized he'd left his briefcase in the conference room and hurried back to fetch it. Adamo continued to the elevator, but the clerk waited for Dees in the hallway.

"By the way," the clerk said when Dees returned, "the judge has not decided whether to allow Klansmen to wear their robes in the courtroom." He asked Dees how the Vietnamese would react to Klan robes in court.

Adamo was waiting by the elevator when he saw the clerk speaking to Dees. He couldn't hear what the two were discussing, but before he knew it, Dees was waving him over to rejoin the conversation.

Dees, who had not responded to the clerk's question, summarized it for Adamo.

Adamo, incensed, asked the clerk whether Judge McDonald had instructed him to have an ex parte conversation with Dees about the robes.

The clerk insisted that it was his own decision to check with Dees, and apologized if he had done anything improper.

Adamo raced back and began drafting a motion for Judge McDonald to disqualify herself.

DEES COULDN'T BELIEVE IT. MANY, IF NOT MOST, OF THE VIETNAMese were still on the fence about whether they would remain in Galveston Bay. He knew this case could set a precedent for future anti-Klan fights, and he was worried about the very real danger Vietnamese shrimpers faced at the opening of the season. Louis Beam and his private militiamen were the definition of a credible threat. Now there were neo-Nazis crashing depositions, and an upcoming rally headlined by the leader of the Aryan Nations and one of the Greensboro Klansmen who had shot up a crowd of anti-Klan protesters.

A resounding victory in court would knock these groups back on their heels, but a momentary slipup by a clerk had put it all in jeopardy.

# 27

# A Suit on the Brink

JUDGE McDONALD RETURNED FROM AN OUT-OF-STATE JUDICIAL conference to a mess. It was true: she had asked her clerk to sort out the question of whether to allow Klansmen to wear robes during the hearings. She always gave First Amendment considerations a wide berth, but had to weigh them against the fact that Louis Beam had already concealed a weapon under his robe during the deposition. There was talk of installing metal detectors outside the courtroom to keep guns out, but even with the threat of weapons removed, she could hardly allow Klansmen to wear their robes if doing so had the effect of silencing or intimidating the plaintiffs or other witnesses.

But she hadn't asked her clerk to sort it out in an ex parte manner. Ex parte conversations were so totally inappropriate that she wouldn't speak to one lawyer about scheduling a bathroom break if the other wasn't around. As a result of the clerk's sloppy handling of the situation, she now found a motion on her desk calling for her to disqualify herself from the case, claiming the court had demonstrated a bias in favor of the Vietnamese.

But as she read the motion, it was immediately evident that this wasn't a half-baked attempt to throw her off the case. She summoned both parties to her courtroom for a hearing.

SAM ADAMO'S MOTION HAD FOCUSED EXCLUSIVELY ON THE IMPRO-priety of the ex parte exchange with the clerk, but as soon as the hearing began, it was derailed by his client. Louis Beam wasn't there to talk about clerks: he wanted to talk about the color of Judge McDonald's skin.

"I no more have the opportunity and confidence that I could get any fairer trial here in front of you than you would feel were you to go before a Ku Klux Klansman who was a judge," Beam complained to Judge Mc-Donald.

When she asked him to substantiate his claim, he was indignant. "Your race is prejudiced against the Klan!" Adamo cringed. He had sat through enough depositions with Beam to brace for the unex-pected, and figured that the Klansman couldn't resist the opportunity to speak up when national news outlets were in the gallery. He felt like he was on a roller coaster ride, the direction of which he had little control over.

"During my twelve years as a Klansman," Beam continued, "every-where I go I hear [from blacks] 'Death to the Klan.'" The Grand Dragon complained to the judge that this prejudice was "strictly unfounded."

"When did you become aware of my race?" McDonald asked.

"After the suit had been filed."

"You know I am black?"

"Partly black," Beam replied, a reference to the fact that McDonald's mother was half White.

"Let me tell you," Judge McDonald declared, speaking directly to Beam, "I am deeply committed, deeply committed, to equal justice, and you will get it. You are entitled to nothing more and nothing less."

Later that day, as she sat down to draft her decision, she considered Beam's remarks. *Isn't it reasonable for the Klan to feel, given their history, they're not going to get a fair trial before a Black judge?* she thought.

But this wasn't unmapped terrain in the legal world. There were clear tests to be applied when weighing whether a judge ought to be disqualified, and Beam's allegations didn't come close to passing them. Beam had claimed that her past work as a civil rights attorney with the NAACP made her impartiality questionable, but when she asked him to cite any specific statements she had made in the past demonstrating a bias against the Klan, he was unable to.

McDonald quoted from a ruling of Judge Constance Baker Motley, the first Black woman appointed to the federal judiciary. Motley had been Thurgood Marshall's assistant attorney on the *Brown* school desegregation case before President Johnson elevated her to the federal bench for the Southern District of New York. In 1975, Motley drew a case alleging systematic discrimination by a prestigious New York law firm against well-qualified female attorneys applying for jobs. The firm's attorney argued that as a Black woman, Motley had probably suffered from discrimination in the workplace and therefore couldn't be expected to rule with impartiality. Motley recognized the implication of the argument: if women couldn't be expected to rule fairly over a case involving sex discrimination, then neither could men. "If background or sex or race of each judge were, by definition, sufficient grounds for removal, no judge on this court could hear this case," Motley wrote, denying the motion.

And so, McDonald would stay on as judge.

Dees breathed a sigh of relief as he emerged from the courthouse: the suit would proceed. There were only days left before their moment in court, which didn't give him much time to finalize his preparations, but as soon as he returned to his hotel room, he received an urgent call from Nam asking to meet.

Many of the Vietnamese had decided to leave town; it was all getting too dangerous. Nam himself had been tipped off to a meeting where Klansmen debated various ways of assassinating him. One wanted to club him with a baseball bat, but they figured the special forces veteran would be too hard to kill that way. Another wanted to knock on the door and shoot him, but that was ruled too risky to pull off without there being eyewitnesses. The current plan was to tail him until he pulled onto the expressway, where they could ram him off the road, shoot him, and then set his car on fire before driving off.

There was a surveillance car with White men, presumably Klansmen, parked outside his house. Each night, Nam would shinny down the gutter on the back side of his home and slip off in a small boat to another part of town, where he'd hidden his family in a safe house. There was a cruel irony: Over nine thousand miles away, his old home in Vietnam was still under surveillance by the communist government he'd fought for decades. Here, he was accused of being a communist.

His son, Michael, was holed up in another safe house, scribbling away at his homework by candlelight while nervously listening for the footfalls of potential intruders. Whenever he ran out of food, he'd crawl out the back window and creep through the backyard. After scanning the perimeter, he'd climb over the neighbors' fence, cutting through their yard before hiking to a 7-Eleven for chips and a Coke.

Nam had led his community into court with the belief that the constitution would offer them protection, but to reach that potential end point, they were now on a path lined with neo-Nazis and armed Klansmen. Their pictures had been taken. They were being threatened at gunpoint. Many suspected they were being followed around town. Their own lawyers were getting threatened.

AS SOON AS DEES TOOK A SEAT IN NAM'S LIVING ROOM, HE COULD sense something was wrong.

"The elders of our community have asked me to talk to you, Morris," Nam began, a conflicted look on his face. "We want to thank you for representing us, but we have decided to drop our lawsuit."

"Colonel, we've got Beam on the ropes now! We've got a good case here!" Dees pleaded.

"I understand," Nam replied. "But what can a court injunction do? If they want to shoot you in the night, they can."

Dees pressed his case. There were only a few days left before their day in court. The start of shrimping season was just a couple of weeks off. The entire basis for requesting an emergency injunction was the harm Vietnamese might suffer when they resumed shrimping—if they pulled out and left, the case would collapse, handing a resounding victory to the KKK. There would be no action against Beam's Texas Emergency Reserve militia. The Southern Poverty Law Center would miss an opportunity to extract all kinds of invaluable information about the Klan from the proceedings.

Nam explained that the Vietnamese elders had another concern, one that reached beyond the immediate issue of shrimping: if they didn't withdraw from the suit, the animus might spread into the broader community of Vietnamese-owned businesses. Vietnamese florists and restaurant owners worried that White Americans might start boycotting them. Their battle with the Klan had already created problems with their own buyers: Teresita Bartolome, the Filipino owner of Captain Wick's fish house, was so concerned about reprisals that she made it clear to anyone asking that she wouldn't buy any more shrimp from the Vietnamese.

As much as he hoped to knock Beam out in court, Dees couldn't force his clients to remain in the suit. He beseeched Nam for one opportunity to meet with the Vietnamese fishermen and elders in the community to make his case directly.

"I'll see what I can do," Nam replied.

TWO DAYS LATER, DEES WAS LED BY FATHER JOHN, THE VIETNAMese priest, down a corridor to a meeting room in the back of St. Peter's Church. As he gathered his thoughts, Dees reflected on how much he had changed in the twenty years since he'd earned his law degree. Not only had he sat out the civil rights movement as it emerged in Alabama, he'd put his degree to work by helping the other side: in May 1961, one of his first clients was Claude Henley, a White supremacist who had just led the ferocious assault on John Lewis and the anti-segregation Freedom Riders when they arrived at the Montgomery bus depot. Lewis was beaten unconscious; other Freedom Riders were paralyzed for life. When the mob descended on the hospital with a plan to lynch those who'd survived, a nurse gave a victim sedatives because she "didn't want [him] to be aware of anything" if they found him. Dees's old partner Millard Fuller had expressed shock over the mob violence in his private journal, but when Henley came in, he expressed his support for what they'd done. Dees, whose fee of $5,000 would be covered by the Ku Klux Klan and the local White Citizens' Council, enjoyed the publicity—taking the case propelled him to the front page of the *Montgomery Advertiser*—but after a feeble and unsuccessful bid to get his client off, he was confronted by a Freedom Rider outside the courtroom for representing Henley, and condemned for representing the Klansman. The embarrassment didn't compel Dees to change his clients or embrace the civil rights movement: he responded by abandoning the practice of law altogether to focus on selling cookbooks and making millions with Fuller.

But now he was finally in the fight, and on the brink of delivering an important blow against the Klan. He just needed to persuade his clients not to pull him out of the ring.

INSIDE THE CHURCH, FORTY VIETNAMESE ELDERS WERE SEATED quietly in two rows of folding chairs. Dees knew that everything was riding on his next words.

"Sometimes lawyers are called counselors," he began in his honeyed Alabama accent. "I'd like to give you my counsel." But he'd started speaking too quickly for the Vietnamese interpreter, and he had to slow down to regain his composure.

"I don't really know what your vision of America was before you came to live in this country, how you thought you'd be treated here. But I'm ashamed at the way you've been treated. In the United States, all citizens are supposed to be treated equally, regardless of race, creed, or color. It doesn't matter if you're black or Jewish or Vietnamese, whatever, our Constitution provides for equal treatment under the law."

The Vietnamese listened quietly.

"Unfortunately," Dees continued, "just because something is written down on a piece of paper, even if that paper is the Constitution, doesn't mean everyone is going to respect it and abide by it. When I was growing up in Alabama, black folks were second-class citizens. They had to fight for their rights. Dr. Martin Luther King, Jr., and others gave up their lives so their brothers and sisters could have their lawful rights.

"One of the groups that wanted to keep the blacks in their place," Dees said, "was the Ku Klux Klan, the same Ku Klux Klan that wants you to pack up your bags and get out of town. I sure hope you don't think these people, people like Louis Beam and others hiding in their hoods, represent America. Because they don't."

And here he came to the reason why they needed to stand and fight. "I know the Klan. And I know that if your fishermen leave without putting up a fight, Louis Beam and his crew will not stop. . . . Some folks are saying the Vietnamese shouldn't even be allowed to live on the coast. It may be the fishermen that feel the heat now, but you can be sure that if they get the fishermen to give up today, then they'll go after the rest of you tomorrow. 'Why should the Seven-Eleven be run by a foreigner? Why aren't there any Americans employed at the flower shop? This is hurting American business.'

"You have just as much right to be here as Louis Beam or Gene Fisher!" Dees exclaimed. "That is what America is really about. That's what the people who came to this country over two centuries ago as immigrants, just like you, had in mind. That's the vision of America you have to believe in and fight for. You have to—"

HE STOPPED AND TRIED TO READ THE ROOM. ONCE HIS INTERPRETER caught up with his half sentence, the room was silent. Nam and the other elders of the Vietnamese community sat there with impassive expressions.

Dees had no idea what to think. He glanced over at his interpreter, desperate to know whether his words were winning them over.

## 28

# "This Court Is Their Only Hope"

D EES STOOD IN THE BACK ROOM OF ST. PETER'S IN AGONIZING confusion, until a slow, rhythmic clapping broke out among the elders. He didn't know how to interpret it—did they want him to stop speaking? He looked over at Nam, who was also clapping.

Nervously, he looked for an explanation from his interpreter, who smiled and said, "They like what you're saying."

The suit would go on.


FORTY-EIGHT HOURS BEFORE THEY WERE DUE IN COURT, LOUIS Beam, the Collins brothers, Gene Fisher, and James Stanfield had another Klan rally at the Collins ranch. Grass had already started to grow over where the USS *VIET CONG* had been torched only three months earlier.

Kids pranced around in junior Klan robes while their parents poked at fried oysters and boiled fish. As before, armed Klansmen—members of the Texas Emergency Reserve militia—stood guard in the woods surrounding the meadow, which was yielding to mud after a heavy rain the night before. Klansmen waved in a convoy of television crews, but blocked

Sam Rodriguez, a Hispanic American reporter for KHOU-TV, from entering. "The rally is open to white Christians, and he didn't fit the bill," Beam declared.

The crowd was smaller than the previous rally's—only a couple hundred this time—but there was a new group of guests in attendance this time: Richard Butler, the founder of the Aryan Nations, had come down from his compound in Hayden Lake, Idaho, along with Jerry Paul Smith, the Klansman who had killed anti-Klan activists in what became known as the Greensboro massacre, just two years earlier.

Local TV reporter Mike Tracy was conflicted about the fact that there seemed to be more news crews than Klansmen at the rally. "In a way, you feel like you're being sucked in by these guys because they do . . . like to appeal to the media, and probably wouldn't be meeting if we weren't here."

As Klansmen soaked their torches in diesel and wrapped the steel cross in burlap, Beam grabbed the microphone to declare that the Klan would "bring peace to the Texas coast," hurrying his remarks as it became clear that another storm was rolling in.

As they hoisted the cross, a downpour scattered the crowd. Police Chief Kerber, who had been on edge all day, felt a moment of relief as the rain poured, until he heard an explosive peal of what sounded like gunfire. As the Klansmen scattered in search of shelter, Kerber whirled around to find the culprit: a soaked generator that had backfired before dying.

Unable to torch their cross, Beam, the KKK, and members of the Aryan Nations gathered in a large circle beneath the storm clouds and sang the "Battle Song of the American Nazi Party."

> We march and fight, to death or on to victory
> Our might is right, no traitors shall prevail!

Judge McDonald had decided to allow Klansmen to wear their robes—without hoods—but after Louis Beam's antics during the depositions, there was worry about concealed weapons. And so for the first time in the Houston federal courthouse's history, metal detectors were installed in the corridor outside her courtroom.

The twelfth-floor courtroom was already muggy and packed. On one side sat the plaintiffs—Vietnamese shrimpers and their families, in new suits, pressed shirts, ties, and shined shoes. On the other side, the defendants were dressed so shabbily that Dees saw it as a statement of contempt aimed at the very idea of the proceedings: dirty slacks, T-shirts, grease-stained hands. Louis Beam showed up in a suit and tie, forgoing his Klan robe; behind him sat Richard Butler. In his crisp blue suit, Butler might have passed for one of the lawyers except for the fact that he was wearing a swastika armband. Seated nearby were men in black Klan T-shirts, army fatigues, and SS bands.

While they sat in nervous anticipation for the arrival of Judge McDonald, Dees rifled through his legal pad, which he'd meticulously filled with handwritten notes, quotes, newspaper clippings, and references to the deposition transcripts. A tab appeared every few pages, marking the end of one defendant's time in the barrel and the beginning of another. He'd leaned on David Berg and his own team of lawyers for help drafting the various motions that got them to this point, but when it came to working the courtroom, he only trusted his own notes.

Berg leaned back in his chair and glanced at his friend Sam Adamo, wondering how the hell he'd ended up representing Louis Beam and the Klan. He thought back to one of his own cases a decade earlier, when he represented a young Klansman named Jimmy Dale Hutto, who had been detained for months without charges in a psychiatric facility after allegedly plotting to blow up a radio station in California. Berg didn't care if he was Klan or God's gift to the earth: holding someone without charges was what the Soviets did, not the United States.

In the run-up to the hearings, Berg had told Adamo that he always regretted representing a member of the Klan. Adamo didn't know if his opposing counsel was just trying to rattle him, but he seemed earnest. Nor did he know that Hutto's alleged accomplice in an earlier, successful bombing of Houston's Pacifica radio station was none other than Louis Beam. Berg didn't truly regret representing Hutto or object to Adamo taking on the case, but he never passed up an opportunity to throw opposing counsel off-balance.

The charged silence of the room was broken by the sound of a knocker on the other side of the door to the judge's chambers, the traditional announcement that a federal judge is resuming the bench.

Judge McDonald emerged, a regal, confident presence, calmly inviting everyone to be seated. Berg couldn't avoid the profundity of the moment: a Black female judge wearing a black robe, presiding over a case involving White men in white robes. He glanced over at the defendants' side of the courtroom, eyeing the swastikas and SS insignia. He wondered if the men who had left the KKK calling card at his front door were in the courtroom, and what would've happened had he caught up to them during his high-speed chase.

Berg had lost fifty-five members of his mother's family in Auschwitz. He thought of all the anti-Semitic slurs and blows he'd endured on the playground, and all the cops in the Klan-infested Houston Police Department he'd gone up against in his career. He had a personal code: *Fuck with me or my family and I will make you famous.* But as charged as he felt in the moment, he knew he was guided by the rule of law and not by a lust for revenge. Still, as Dees stood to open the hearings, Berg relished the opportunity for a good old Texas ass-kicking.


DEES AND BERG WERE ASKING THE GOVERNMENT TO DO SOMEthing extraordinary: to prevent something bad from happening to one group by potentially limiting the rights of another group. In order to prevail, they'd need to convince Judge McDonald that Vietnamese shrimpers were at risk of irreparable harm at the opening of the shrimp season if she didn't issue an injunction. At the same time, they needed to show that the benefit of protecting their clients' right to shrimp without intimidation outweighed the burden such an injunction would impose on Louis Beam and his Klan, the Collins brothers, Fisher, and Stanfield.

Dees's strategy was two-pronged: to demonstrate that the Vietnam ese were endangered physically, and to show that they had suffered economically. But as this was a civil suit—and one filed with great haste, given the vocal threat of violence at the end of the Grand Dragon's dispensation—this wasn't a trial to determine who was criminally guilty for burning the boats. There would be no inquiry into who'd pointed guns at Vietnamese throughout Seabrook and Kemah, who'd burned the crosses, or who'd fired a round into Colonel Nam's home.

They weren't there to punish the defendants for what they had said or threatened over the past year. At its core was a simple, forward-looking demand by the Vietnamese: leave us alone.

DEES TICKED THROUGH THE EVENTS OF THE PRECEDING MONTHS that had led to this showdown in court: Gene Fisher's confrontation with Colonel Nam at the Dutch Kettle in early January, in which he said the new boats under construction at Jim Craig's "Saigon Harbor" would have to be burned. Fisher's warning to Craig to watch the Vietnamese boats, that they were "easy to burn." The attempted torching, days later, of the *Trudy B*, which was extinguished only when the arsonist closed the hatch and suffocated the flames. Fisher's remark to a reporter that he was prepared to "run over every gook" in his way, if that's what it took to secure his rights to shrimp. Beam's torching of the USS *VIET CONG* at the Valentine's Day Klan rally at the Collins ranch, during which he said, "If a burned boat doesn't look like that, the Klan didn't burn it." The gun pointed at Phước Đặng. The gun pointed at Đoi Thi Đỗ. The crosses burned throughout Seabrook and Kemah near the homes and docks where the Vietnamese kept their boats. The Klan boat patrol, which had so terrified Nam's young sister-in-law that she no longer felt safe to return. The second torching of the *Trudy B*, which burned down to the waterline this time, badly burning another Vietnamese boat moored alongside it.

Dees moved confidently through the courtroom. There was no jury, but he knew the gallery was full of journalists hanging on his every word. By inviting the Ku Klux Klan into Galveston Bay, Gene Fisher, the Collins brothers, and Jim Stanfield had conspired to monopolize the shrimping business for themselves while denying the Vietnamese equal protection and rights guaranteed under both state and federal law. This campaign of harassment had led almost two-thirds of the Vietnamese shrimpers to put their boats up for sale, fearful of the consequences of taking them out when the season opened in just a few days. At the first rally, Beam had warned that things would be "a helluva lot more violent than Vietnam!" and that the KKK might "take matters into its own hands," before telling the crowd, "If you want our country for the whites, you're going to have to get it the way our founding fathers did—with blood, blood, blood!"

Tightening his focus on Beam's private militia, the Texas Emergency Reserve, Dees dragged the Rice University student filmmaker into court to play raw footage of Beam, his face blackened by charcoal as he trained his men in ambush tactics. Beam's exhortations—"When you attack, there is only one thing for the enemy to do . . . die!"—reverberated through the startled courtroom. Thanks to Randall Williams and Mike Vahala's undercover investigation, Dees was able to establish that several armed members of Beam's militia had been on Jody Collins's trawler the day of the Klan Boat patrol, and that Beam had invited White fishermen to come train at his camp. Fisher subsequently told journalists he'd sent members there and would have armed men on boats at the start of the season.

DURING A RECESS, DEES MET WITH PHƯỚC ĐẶNG, A VIETNAMESE shrimper who had been out on the water with his ten-year-old son, Trúc, when a group of White fishermen pointed weapons at them and hurled epithets. Dees could tell that Đặng, who spoke little English, was frightened. Trúc translated for his father, and as they headed into the courtroom, he couldn't resist telling Dees that he wanted to be a lawyer when he grew up.

Dees, with a glimmer in his eye, approached the bench to ask Judge McDonald if Trúc might be permitted to interpret for his father; if there were any mistakes, the court-appointed interpreter could correct the record. When she consented, Trúc relayed his father's damning testimony in flawless English. At one point, when he explained that the White fishermen had also used "dirty hand signals," the earnest boy turned to the bench and demonstrated, startling Judge McDonald, who smiled and let the boy sit in the empty jury box for the remainder of the hearings.

But this wasn't just about personal threats. The Vietnamese had suffered economically when White fishermen pressured fish house owners not to buy from them, to say nothing of the burned boats. Dees accused the Klan of violating the Sherman Antitrust Act of 1890, which was designed to preserve free and unfettered competition in commerce. It was, to the best of his knowledge, the first time anyone had tried bringing antitrust charges against the White supremacist group, but he wanted to throw everything he could at Beam.

But the rushed nature of the entire suit—Dees and his team had arrived only a few weeks earlier—meant that much of his argument about economic injury would rest upon the testimony of one woman in her sixties, named Margaret Anderwald.


ANDERWALD LIVED WITH HER HUSBAND ACROSS THE BAY IN THE Laguna de Oro neighborhood of Galveston, nestled just between Offatts Bayou and the Galveston Causeway, which linked Galveston Island to the mainland. Her husband worked as a cook on an offshore oil rig in the gulf and was frequently gone for weeks at a time.

Their home had a dock on the laguna, and for the past two years they'd permitted a young Vietnamese shrimper named Khang Nguyễn to tie up his boat there. Khang had a wife and small children; the Anderwalds considered them family friends. Over time, Margaret felt a chill from her neighbors but ignored it.

In January 1981, though, she found something unusual in her

mailbox: a Klan calling card threatening to pay her a "business visit." Then the phone calls began. The first caller warned her that Khang's boat would be burned if he didn't move it. Another caller warned her that her own house would be torched. A third asked her if she knew where her children were at that very moment. Yet another told her that she would die that night if Khang's boat was still there.

Anderwald was terrified. Her husband was out in the gulf, and she didn't know how to weigh the death threats. She felt sick as she went down to the dock to tell Khang he had to leave, but couldn't bring herself to say why; she said they needed the space in order to prepare for their daughter's wedding. Khang, bewildered, cleared out in search of a new place to dock.

THE MORNING ANDERWALD WAS DUE IN COURT, RANDALL WILLIAMS drove out to pick her up. By the time they arrived at the courthouse, she was a jumble of nerves.

When Dees emerged during a recess, he found her in the hallway with a ghostly look on her face. She reminded him of his grandmother, "white-haired with glasses, stout . . . an honest soul with a strong religious background," but as soon as he saw her, he knew he was in trouble. Sitting next to her priest, Anderwald announced that she no longer wanted to testify against the Klan. "Mr. Dees, I don't think I can do it. I just can't do it!" She recounted all the threats she'd received. "My heart won't stand it. They're such nice people . . ." she said, referring to Khang and his family, "but I don't think I can stand it."

Dees knelt to the floor and took her hand. "Mrs. Anderwald, you need to get up on the stand, because I'm trying to get the federal court to stop the Klan from doing this. . . . It's your Christian duty."

"I don't think I can, Mr. Dees."

He shot the priest a look, prevailing upon him to encourage her.

"Okay, Mrs. Anderwald. I'm going to go into the courtroom and call your name. If you don't want to testify, that's fine, but you'll have to say so in front of the judge."

When the hearing resumed and the courtroom quieted, Dees exhaled and said, "Plaintiffs now call Mrs. Margaret Anderwald to the stand."

Anderwald rose. Dees walked over to her, and he could feel her trembling as he guided her to the witness box. After swearing her in, he asked some perfunctory questions before asking her about Khang Nguyễn.

Whatever inhibitions she had evaporated at the mention of Khang's name, and her demeanor changed. "We didn't want to make Khang move," she said tearfully, "but we had no choice. . . . His boat had been parked here for two years, and he'd never given us any trouble. But no one wants to have their house burned down or receive threats against their life."

Young Trúc watched from the jury box as her testimony captivated the room.

"We've been ostracized by our neighbors," she said. "We just didn't want any more trouble."

Dees barely had to ask a follow-up. When she stepped down from the stand, Anderwald strode confidently past Beam, the Klan, and their neo-Nazi brethren.

DEES CLOSED HIS ARGUMENT WITH AN INVOCATION OF AMERICA'S past and its promise, chronicling one episode of bloodshed resulting from economic competition after another. He spoke about how the Klan was founded after the Civil War in part to confront the rising power of freed slaves who entered the labor market and began to vote and run for office. He spoke of ordinances passed in 1880s San Francisco designed to drive Chinese immigrants out of the workforce, just two years before the Chinese Exclusion Act banned them from entering the United States entirely.

"But America still lifts its torch," Dees exclaimed, turning to Nam and the other Vietnamese plaintiffs. "They may talk a little different, look a little different," he said, but they had the "pioneer spirit" so glorified in the West.

"This court is their only hope," he continued. "This court represents the power and the promise of law and the Constitution."

As he took his seat next to Berg and Nam, Dees felt both proud and confident. How could anyone examine the madness of the past five months and come to a different conclusion?

And then Sam Adamo rose to defend his clients.

# 29

# Freedom of Speech and Assembly

A S FAR AS ADAMO COULD SEE, THIS WAS NOTHING MORE THAN a big circus for media attention. Dees seemed to love the banks of cameras outside and knew how to charm them, and Adamo's own client, Louis Beam, was just as effective at captivating their attention with a clever quip or terrifying sound bite. They weren't on the same moral scale but they both stood to gain from the publicity.

What mattered to Adamo were the constitutional protections of free speech and free assembly. The First Amendment was not created to protect socially uplifting speech—it existed to protect the free exchange of ideas, however odious those ideas might be.

And as far as emergency injunctions went, he was certain this fell far short of clearing the threshold. Why ask the government to tell people not to do things that were already illegal? Even if an injunction were handed down, the penalty for violating it was a trivial contempt-of-court fine, nothing compared with what they'd face in criminal court.

And what, after all, was the real injury here?

Adamo acknowledged the unpleasant remarks made by his clients over the previous months, but walked through precedents that demonstrated that "abstract injury" wasn't enough to warrant an injunction.

Even though Nam had been tipped off to a Klan plot to kill him by ramming into him on the highway, within the courtroom such talk was just hearsay.

Sure, plenty of nasty things had been said at the Klan rally, but it had happened well within the confines of Jody and Marilyn Collins's ranch—not in a public park. What could be more protected than free speech on private property? Yes, someone had painted USS *VIET CONG* on the boat they burned that night, but Louis Beam had claimed it was a symbol of "the policies of the federal government that are leading to the destruction of this country!" Even more, Beam told journalists at the time that the act of burning the boat was an attempt to refute the allegations that the Klan was behind the botched attempt to torch the *Trudy B*: if it *had* been the KKK, the boat would've burned entirely.


GENE FISHER TOOK THE STAND AND ADMITTED THAT HE HADN'T actually trained at Louis Beam's camp, despite telling a reporter as much weeks earlier.

"Were you lying to the press?" Dees interjected.

"Sure was," snapped Fisher. "I've always considered the press . . . extremely unfair. Well if that's what the press wants—violence . . . not facts—I say, let 'em have it."

Nobody had to like or respect Gene Fisher, but it wasn't a crime to lie to the press.


SURE, ADAMO ACKNOWLEDGED, THE KLAN HAD BURNED A CROSS at the end of the rally, but it was part of a religious service and not intended as a threat against the Vietnamese. Besides, there was nothing illegal about burning a cross.

Adamo wasn't denying reality: *Of course* these things had happened.

Nobody denied that Phước Đặng and Đoi Thi Đỗ had been threatened at gunpoint by White men. But Nam and the Vietnamese plaintiffs couldn't identify the culprits, and they weren't even accusing any of the defendants, each of whom strenuously denied any involvement. *Someone* had burned the boats, but the Vietnamese shrimpers had no hard evidence tying Beam, the Klan, Fisher, Stanfield, or the Collins brothers to the fires. Why should they be punished or have their constitutional rights of free speech and assembly curtailed as a result of the acts of an unknown arsonist?

Adamo acknowledged the claim that the Vietnamese had suffered economically, but he cited a precedent that stated a mere "loss of income" fell short of being considered irreparable harm, the hurdle Dees had to clear in order to get injunctive relief. Even if losing money was enough to warrant something as extraordinary as an injunction, Adamo described the claim as completely speculative—Khang had found another dock to tie up at, after all. And even though one fish house owner had been discouraged from buying Vietnamese-caught shrimp, Jim Craig was still buying anything they brought in.

LOUIS BEAM WANTED TO TAKE THE STAND. BY THIS POINT, ADAMO knew it was futile to try to stop him; he recognized that he was yoked to something much larger than a small-town dispute between two groups of fishermen. Dees had his organization to grow and needed an enemy like Louis Beam to attract media attention, which led to donors. Beam had his own organization to grow and needed an enemy like Morris Dees and the Southern Poverty Law Center to rile up his dues-paying supporters. Adamo knew that Beam would never pass up the opportunity to preach from the stand to a roomful of journalists.

"Until we entered the situation," Beam told the room, "it was a crisis!" In his own telling, the Klan had been a force for peace.

"Did you urge these American fishermen to fight the Vietnamese?" Dees asked.

"No."

Dees leafed through his files, searching for the newspaper clipping with one of Beam's quotes. "You didn't say, 'Before you give up your fishing birthright, you should fight!'?"

"I'm not for giving up anything that our ancestors fought and died for," Beam replied coolly.

The Grand Dragon was clever on his feet. If Dees asked a question with too many clauses, Beam asked him to make it shorter. When asked whether he'd had "much dealings" with Gene Fisher, Beam asked for a definition of "much." He knew not to speculate. Whenever Dees asked for the identities of fellow Klansmen, Beam professed to be the "world's worst" at remembering names. When Dees referenced a comment from the deposition, Beam said, "You better get the deposition out and run it by me and let's see if I said that."

Dees asked Beam if he was opposed to Vietnamese in general, or just those he'd alleged were Viet Cong who had somehow infiltrated the country as refugees.

"I never said no such thing as . . . where did you get that!" Beam retorted. "I never said I was opposed to either one of them! I am for my people. That's who I am, Louis Beam, the Klan. I stand for white people. I'm for my people. That doesn't mean I'm against them."

Dees asked the court to play a portion of video from the Valentine's Day rally at the Collins ranch, to "see if he verifies who he's after here . . ."

"Oh, I know who I'm after," Beam seethed. "You don't need to play anything to say who I'm after—"

"Who is that?" interjected Judge McDonald.

"The federal government and the state government, who has turned their backs on the citizens of this country in favor of non-citizens."

Beam defended his actions as mere nonviolent provocations to force a government response. He was just using "the same techniques that Martin Luther King used—he would go into an area and create tension, and that would force the local community to act."

"I'm not saying that I'm emulating [him]," Beam said of the slain civil rights leader. "I'm just saying that as a student of politics, history, and science, I know it works."

The press gobbled it up.

EVERYONE IN THE COURTROOM ROSE AS JUDGE McDONALD STOOD and disappeared behind the door leading to her chambers to deliberate.

Dees and Berg glanced at each other: Adamo had done an effective job. Now came the excruciating wait for Judge McDonald's decision.

# 30

# The Ruling

DAVID BERG WAS USED TO WAITING FOR VERDICTS, BUT AS HE sat at the plaintiffs' table waiting for Judge McDonald to return from her chambers, he stared out the twelfth-floor window at a dark, foreboding sky with mounting concern. He and Dees had expected a quick decision, but each hour that passed eroded a bit of his confidence.

In the anxious silence of the courtroom, he reflected on what a loss would mean. The Vietnamese would probably leave Galveston Bay or, if they stayed, constantly fear arson or worse. And fleeing might not work. Beam might launch his Klan sea patrol, which threatened to harass Vietnamese shrimpers along the entire Gulf Coast. If the KKK prevailed, they would almost certainly view it as a license to replicate the campaign against any minority in any industry where White men once dominated. Just that morning, newspapers ran reports about leaflets spattered with bloodlike paint that had been posted in a Vietnamese neighborhood in Sacramento with the words: "Vietnamese: you must get out of California State Capital—KKK." The head of the California Klan denied printing the flyers, which had prompted some Vietnamese residents to leave and others to pull their kids from school, but agreed with the message: "We are opposed to the refugees coming here. We don't believe they should be coming here and taking white men's jobs."

But Berg also knew that a victory here would come with considerable unease in its wake. He thought of his sons and the threats that he had received. The red-and-white pickup truck he'd chased. The Klan calling card. Only a few days before, he'd opened an envelope to find a paper that read: "Register Jews—not guns." He accepted a certain level of risk in any case he took on, but he didn't know how the defendants would react in the event of a loss.

It was dark outside when the court reporter and deputy appeared and quietly took their position. Moments later, several loud bangs from a knocker announced the return of the judge. The bailiff, with ramrod posture, shouted, "All rise," as Judge McDonald entered. There was a commotion of sliding chairs and nervous murmurs as all in the courtroom stood to hear her decision.

McDONALD WAS THERE TO DECIDE ON TWO CORE QUESTIONS: whether the defendants should be enjoined from further harassment of the Vietnamese, and whether Louis Beam's Texas Emergency Reserve militia should be permitted to exist in Texas.

As soon as she took the bench, she startled the courtroom with an announcement: the matter of the Texas Emergency Reserve would not be decided that day. She felt she needed more evidence and hearings before she could arrive at a fair ruling, and cited a recent motion by the state's attorney general to join the Southern Poverty Law Center in their efforts to shut down the militia.

Dees was frustrated. He'd hoped to deliver a knockout blow to Beam's militia, but after the courtroom quieted down, he listened anxiously as McDonald turned her attention to the more urgent question of what would happen to the Vietnamese shrimpers when they pushed out into Galveston Bay at the opening of the shrimping season in the morning.

Judge McDonald explained that the Supreme Court had long recognized that there was a narrow category of speech that fell outside the ambit of the First Amendment. These were called "fighting words," which "by their very utterance inflict injury or tend to excite an immediate breach of the peace."

As Dees and Berg had argued, free speech didn't cover "assaultative" or threatening conduct. Since Beam's well-trained militiamen had carried weapons at their rallies and on the Klan boat patrol, they had crossed the line into the common law definition of assault. Dees and Berg had emphatically argued that Louis Beam and the other defendants could say whatever they wanted—however vehemently they liked—so long as they did so without guns. "Guns do not contribute to the free speech of ideas. Threats to life are not rebutted by more speech," they'd written in a memo for the court, adding that they could not recall "any instance where a court has ever been denied, on First Amendment grounds, the power to restrain the conduct of a group of armed men."

Berg's heart was racing as Judge McDonald turned the page and pronounced her decision.

SIDING WITH THE VIETNAMESE, McDONALD GRANTED AN INJUNC-tion against the Ku Klux Klan, Gene Fisher, the Collins brothers, and James Stanfield, forbidding them to put armed men within the personal view of Vietnamese fishermen, their boats, or Vietnamese businesses with the "reasonably foreseeable effect of intimidating" them. They would not be permitted to burn crosses on property "within the geographic area" where Vietnamese shrimpers lived. No robed Klansmen could come within sight of a Vietnamese shrimper. She enjoined them from inciting further acts of boat burning and carrying out armed boat patrols.

Nam exhaled slowly. Like so many of his fellow Vietnamese, he'd come close to fleeing, but he'd never felt as accepted in his new country as he did in that moment. Dees gave him a squeeze on the shoulder as McDonald continued.

She ordered the injunction to be posted in a conspicuous place at the

Klan's headquarters in Pasadena and James Stanfield's boat repair shop. A Vietnamese translation would also be hung throughout Galveston Bay so that they would understand the protections guaranteed them by the court.

Dees and Berg had advanced plenty of arguments and motions over the course of the suit, plenty of which McDonald set aside. She hadn't humored Dees's motion for a mental health evaluation of Beam, or to post US marshals throughout the bay to enforce the injunction. The Sherman Antitrust Act considerations were set aside. She would not be rushed into adjudicating the future of Beam's private militia. But on the core issue of asserting their lawful right to fish without fear of harassment, the Vietnamese prevailed.

"Let me speak to you, Jody Collins," McDonald said, as she turned to the defendants' table. Jody shifted in his seat; Marilyn was out in the hallway, nursing their daughter, wondering why her husband hadn't listened to her pleas to stay away from the Klan.

"I understand the frustrations you have encountered in trying to solve the problems," McDonald said, "but the Vietnamese fishermen are here, and they have the right to be here.

"It was wrong to invite the forces of violence to help," she admonished.

What else was there to say? The matter of Louis Beam's militia would have to wait, but until then, she dismissed the courtroom, which noisily filed out through the metal detectors into the hallway, where a scrum of TV cameras was eagerly waiting.

By the time Dees got there, Beam was already claiming victory before the cameras and promoting a new "celebratory" rally the following night, where another cross would be burned. Despite professing to be pleased, he described Judge McDonald as a "negress masquerading as a federal judge," who had only handed down the injunction "to show sympathy for the Vietnamese. She was just showing sympathy for her people of color."

When the hot lights of the cameras turned on him, Dees likened the Klan's boat patrol to the earliest days of the KKK, when "night riders came to people's homes and children ran out screaming." To him, Mc-Donald's ruling was "a message to the Vietnamese people that the U.S. system of justice and fairness will protect them against thugs."

Adamo's partner, Richard Cobb, scoffed at Dees's remarks, calling them "ludicrous . . . the United States got them out of Vietnam where the Communists would have murdered them—I don't think any further message is needed."

The cameras converged on Colonel Nam as he emerged from the courtroom, a pleased smile on his face. "Today we do not have to fear members of the Ku Klux Klan or other radicals . . . we are able to have freedom and we do not have to fear someone will take this from us."

He glanced down the hallway as Louis Beam and the other defendants sauntered toward the exit. "I think it was better to fight this dispute in court rather than fight on the water."

Later that evening, Dees, Berg, and the rest of the Southern Poverty Law Center team celebrated with Nam and the Vietnamese community. They gave their lawyers ornate wooden clocks carved in the shape of Vietnam to express their gratitude, and invited them down to the docks early the following morning.

A few hours later, Louis Beam's ninety-day countdown expired. Everything now hinged upon whether Judge McDonald's injunction would be heeded or ignored.

# 31

# Fallout

THE MIST WAS STILL HANGING WHEN DEES ARRIVED AT JIM Craig's "Saigon Harbor" in Kemah. After the Klan boat patrol, most of the Vietnamese boats docked there had been put up for sale. With the court now affirming their right to remain, free of harassment, they peeled the For Sale signs from their trawlers and prepared to shove out into the bay. As the sun rose, Dees saw the light glinting off the stars of the police officers Chief Kerber had posted along the waterfront, and he felt proud to be a lawyer.

"We thank God that the Vietnamese people won the lawsuit, but we should accept the victory humbly," said Father John Toàn, who had sheltered Vietnamese inside his rectory during the worst point in the conflict. "It was not a victory against American fishermen, but a victory against the Ku Klux Klan."

Nam handed out copies of the laws governing shrimping—both formal and informal—all translated into Vietnamese, as his fellow shrimpers fired up the engines of their trawlers. "We have to be especially careful because if one person breaks the law, it is seen as all of us breaking the law," he warned.

As a lashing wind whipped in from the northeast, Father John gave

Communion to dozens of shrimpers, prayed for protection of the boats and their crew, and sprinkled holy water on each trawler before it headed out into the chop of six-foot waves, brown diesel smoke puffing up from straining mufflers.

Most of the White shrimpers stayed in that day.

"It's okay for the government to limit car imports but when we try to stop the import of cheap labor we get called bigots and racists," Jody Collins complained to a reporter as he sulked in a booth at the Dutch Kettle. Marilyn picked at her food quietly as her husband accused the Vietnamese of burning their own boats "to get public sympathy."

James Stanfield piped up, denying that race had anything to do with their campaign against the Vietnamese: "We're just asking the government to control immigration . . . it would have been the same if they was niggers, honkies, Indians or anything else." Stanfield and David Collins had finally put their new boat, *Miss AKIA*—"A Klansman I Am"—into the water, occasionally hoisting the flag of the Aryan Nations neo-Nazi group.

Marilyn had been worried that their neighbors and the other new mothers she'd recently befriended would shun them for the Klan rallies they'd hosted on their ranch, but to her surprise, nobody ever brought it up. But she was still fuming with Jody: his actions had only strengthened the Vietnamese shrimpers' position and weakened his own. Slapped with an injunction and a heap of legal fees was not how she anticipated their first year with a baby.

A month after McDonald's decision, one that passed without incident, Dees and Adamo agreed to a deal: in exchange for agreeing to make the injunction permanent, Dees would drop the Collins brothers from the ongoing suit, clearing the battlefield so that all that remained was Louis Beam, the KKK, and their local recruiter, Stanfield. To boot, he would forgo seeking attorneys' fees and court costs, which he estimated at $37,500; the Collinses and their codefendants already owed $35,000 to Adamo's firm. "I doubt if Beam will deal on this," Dees wrote, but "if he can take 'Demon Dees' and 'Rabbi Berg' for three more days, then we will put up with more exorcism."

Beam was nowhere to be found, though, at least not in Texas. Two months after his defeat in court, he was convicted on separate charges brought by the federal government for carrying out war games on federal grasslands, which resulted in a $250 fine and a suspended six-month sentence. He divorced his wife, with whom he had a two-year-old daughter, and complaining of "government persecution," resigned his position as Grand Dragon of the Texas Knights of the Ku Klux Klan. In March 1982, while Judge McDonald was still deliberating the fate of Beam's Texas Emergency Reserve militia, someone claiming to be a deliveryman knocked on his ex-wife's door holding a rubber tree plant. When she answered, he knocked her to the floor, handcuffed her, covered her eyes and mouth, and abducted their daughter. Amid a statewide manhunt Beam bolted with his daughter from Texas, moving into the Aryan Nations compound in Hayden Lake, Idaho, where he began work on a book meant to inspire a new generation of White supremacists.

Adamo accepted Dees's offer, but not before talking Dees into also dropping his boat mechanic, James Stanfield.

There was still the matter of his own fee.

AS ADAMO REMEMBERS IT, DAVID COLLINS HAD A PENDING SETTLE-ment from a car accident that he'd agreed to accept as payment on the case.

As Marilyn Collins remembers it, there was no pending settlement because there was no accident—at least not yet. After being slapped with the injunction, David drove around in search of the nicest car on the road he could find. He pulled in front of a little old lady in a Cadillac and drove in such a way as to get rear-ended. "Adamo knew a doctor," Marilyn said. "Some hospital on the other side of Houston who went along with putting David in the hospital. I think he 'hurt his back,' supposedly. Insurance paid for our lawsuit."

David wasn't a newcomer to insurance scams. Around the same time, after falling behind on payments on his Oldsmobile, he realized he could fetch more by reporting it stolen to his insurance company than by selling it, so he drove it over to Jody's ranch, where his brother flattened it with a tractor and buried it in a sedan-size grave.

Months later, a fire broke out at 1:20 a.m. on Jody's boat, the *Cherry Betty*. At 3:15 that same morning, Kemah firefighters extinguished an attic fire at David's home on West Sixth. Fifteen minutes later, the *Apache Warrior*, a larger trawler owned by their older brother, John— who had salvaged Billy Joe's trawler—caught fire. Shortly after that, David and Seabrook firefighters inspected the *Miss AKIA* and found several gasoline-filled plastic bags in the engine room, alongside candles that had apparently blown out when they toppled over.

Federal arson investigators were once again called in, but no arrests were made. David cashed in on the insurance payment; it would be decades before he admitted to setting the fires himself.

SHORTLY AFTER SHE ISSUED THE INJUNCTION, JUDGE McDONALD received an envelope postmarked Post Falls, Idaho. Inside was a large "Runnin' Nigger" target, a slip of paper bearing the words "RUN NIGGER," a "State of Texas Nigger Hunting License," and a "Boat Ticket to Africa." A letter on "Social Nationalist Aryan People's Party" letterhead addressed to McDonald condemned her ruling in favor of "non white human garbage," and called her a "shame to the nation."

McDonald thought of her children and allowed herself to weep for a moment before summoning the US Marshals. She turned down personal security when it was offered. When the FBI asked if she wanted to prosecute, she told them she wasn't concerned, and to leave the sender of the hate mail alone.

NEARLY A YEAR LATER, ON JUNE 3, 1982, SHE ISSUED HER SECOND injunction, this time breaking apart the Texas Emergency Reserve militia, citing a Civil War–era prohibition on militias. "It is clear to this court that the proliferation of military or paramilitary organizations can only serve to sow the seeds of future domestic violence and tragedy." The order, which prohibited "all forms of combat training," extended to all Klan groups in the state.

"This is not a ho-hum ruling," David Berg told the press. "It just flat shuts down Beam and the Knights of the Ku Klux Klan wherever they are."

"I think the sex appeal to these pathetic people has been the paramilitary aspect," Berg said, never missing a chance to needle Beam and his followers.

DESPITE THE RULING, MORE AND MORE CONFEDERATE FLAGS FLEW from shrimp boats in Galveston Bay, in some cases by owners hoping to signal their Whiteness to the Klan in case of an outbreak of violence. The Klan's crosswheel flag was occasionally spotted flapping over rusted outriggers of trawlers as they broke the waves.

The Klan's membership surged in the year following the injunction, but Beam was gone. It was Gene Fisher, the original shit-stirrer of Seabrook, who lumbered in to fill the void left by the vanished Grand Dragon. After a relatively quiet year since their day in court, Fisher and the Klan marked the opening of shrimping season, on the evening of May 15, 1982, by launching six boats into the black waters of Galveston Bay in search of Vietnamese shrimpers. They code-named their patrols Operation Bad Moon Rising, and claimed to have equipped their boats with infrared cameras to photograph any violators. Fisher touted a $500 reward for anyone aiding in the arrest and conviction of Vietnamese fishing illegally after hours, but the Texas Parks and Wildlife wardens reported no violations.

They launched their boats to "Don't Take Your Guns to Town," Johnny Cash's ballad about a hotheaded young cowboy named Billy Joe who got himself killed after picking a barroom fight with a faster draw.

THEIR OWN BILLY JOE—APLIN—THE ORIGINAL MARTYR OF THEIR cause, was too powerful an image to leave unexploited. Five days after Operation Bad Moon Rising, Fisher and Stanfield filed for a permit for the "Memorial March for Billy Joe Aplin and the American Fisherman—the

Dying Breed." The route they proposed ran down Eleventh Avenue past Colonel Nam's home, My's Seafood—where Đoi Thi Đỗ had been threatened at gunpoint—and the docks where the *Trudy B* had been burned.

Police Chief Kerber studied the route: it had seemingly been designed to pass through the parts of town with the heaviest Vietnamese population. He denied their petition, but when they submitted one with a new route, he approved it.

Flyers appeared around town:

### AMERICANS UNITE

March in memory of Billy Joe Aplin and a dying white fishermens industry. After years and years of whites fishing along the TEXAS coast the government has brought in Vietnamese replacements for them. White people are being replaced by nonwhites all over the United States. One needs but open ones eyes to see the problems that we face as a Race.

When journalists asked Stanfield why they were honoring Aplin, he replied, "The death of Billy Joe was a continuation of the war in Asia. He was a Vietnam War fatality and deserves to be honored as such."

"The Vietnam War has never ended," Stanfield declared. "What we have done is transfer the war from one shore to another."

THE DAY BEFORE THE MARCH, GENE FISHER BECAME THE NEW Grand Dragon of the Klan, replacing Beam. James Stanfield earned the title of Imperial Wizard.

"The Vietnamese have invaded our country," Fisher told one of the many reporters funneling into the Dutch Kettle for an interview. Squeezed into a black T-shirt emblazoned with a Klansman clutching an AR-15, he took a sip from his coffee. "When I was elected Grand Dragon, I decided to bend the fishing pole to the breaking point in this matter." A black trucker's hat with the blood-drop cross insignia of the Klan sat on the booth next to him.

A waitress wearing KKK earrings came by to refill his mug.

"I don't wish to intimidate the Vietnamese," Fisher bellowed as a Vietnamese family ate in the booth behind him, before claiming that he was only fighting the "un-American" way that the Vietnamese were shrimping. "These refugees are practicing communism . . . they all work together for the group. They are Communist in the purest way. I can't compete against that."

Journalists didn't have to cast far to find White shrimpers eager to disavow Fisher. "No way I support Fisher and the Klan," said John Potter, who had been shrimping Galveston Bay for three decades. He told a reporter that he'd never hire Fisher on his boat. "He knows as much about fishing as a housewife in Houston."

POLICE CHIEF KERBER READIED HIS TINY FORCE. HE NEVER IMAGined having so many dealings with the Ku Klux Klan when he first took the job. Now he was catching all kinds of flak for allowing the march to proceed, but he spoke like a cop, unvarnished and preoccupied. He had done everything possible to keep Judge McDonald's injunction from being violated by rerouting the march away from Vietnamese shrimpers, but he barked, "There are no constitutional rights involved here. *I* didn't allow them to have this demonstration; the Constitution allowed them."

Kerber was nervous about the flag-draped coffin meant to symbolize the body of Billy Joe Aplin. He called up Fisher before the rally and asked whether they were planning on hiding any weapons in the coffin.

"Hell," Fisher joked, "you can ride in it yourself if you're worried!"

ON THE MORNING OF THE RALLY, KERBER STATIONED POLICE AT twenty-five intersections along the route. He had called upon nearly ninety officers from neighboring cities, and managed to get a helicopter to monitor the situation from above. Heavily armed SWAT team members seconded from the Pasadena Police Department were perched on roof-tops along the parade route. In the muggy June heat, curious Seabrook residents lounged in lawn chairs in their front yards.

Kerber didn't know how many would show up, but any hopes for a washout were quickly dispelled as dozens of cars filled with Klansmen, women, and children pulled into town. Klan entrepreneurs set up a table to sell KKK T-shirts, flags, and porcelain Klansman figurines. At five dollars a pop, Klan tie-clasps were the best sellers. Bumper stickers proclaiming "The American Dream Is for Americans FIRST!" were also on offer.

One of Kerber's officers took down every single license plate, pulling the names and any police records of each owner. There was Charles Lee, otherwise known as Big Al, whom Beam once described as his "top lieutenant," in his '77 Plymouth. There was Daniel Aplin, down from Grand Chenier, Louisiana. There was Glen Hutto, one of the Klansmen who'd ridden with Big Al and a dozen others on the *Cherry Betty* during the Klan boat patrol.

"We're not marching in defiance of anyone," Fisher told the crowd. "We're marching because we have the right to march, and we want to honor the memory of a slain American."

One hundred twenty marchers carried Confederate, American, and Gadsden flags, some dressed in robes, others in fatigues with KLAN BOAT PATROL shoulder patches, others in black SECRET MEMBER KKK T-shirts. Klan wives pushed their babies in strollers. A young White woman with feathered bangs marched in a white T-shirt emblazoned with bright red words: JUSTICE FROM A NIGGER JUDGE?

Plenty of Seabrook's residents were fed up with the KKK's activities in their town. Some locals spit as Klansmen marched past. Others looked on in bewilderment. "Some of these people look like they've got sense," a local dry cleaner owner commented. "I wonder what they're doing out there!"

"I think they are the dumbest Americans we've got," said another woman watching the procession.

Fisher, Stanfield, and the Collins brothers were among those carrying the empty coffin symbolizing Billy Joe Aplin under the bright Texas sun. David wore a Smith & Wesson cap. Stanfield wore his bright red Imperial Wizard robe and hood.

The Aplin family rode behind the coffin in a copper-colored Cadillac. Billy Joe's brother and sister had come up from Seadrift; his widow, Judy, did not make an appearance.

B. T. Aplin, Billy Joe's father, said that he had come down from Grand Chenier "to show my appreciation for what the Klan did."

DOWN IN SEADRIFT, DIANE WILSON HAD WATCHED WITH A DE-pressed resignation as her fellow shrimpers succumbed to anti-Vietnamese hostility. She loved them, was one of them, but knew they were damned fools. In the three years since Billy Joe Aplin had been buried, the petro-chemical plants had continued their expansion along the bays and into the communities, touting the impressive taxes they paid despite what seemed like an unending series of mishaps, accidental discharges, and explosions. After an explosion at Union Carbide that spilled eighty thousand gallons of Tetralin in July 1980, the plant cleared the wreckage and was humming in no time; months later, a new plant to produce needle coke, used in the manufacture of electrodes, took shape on a six-hundred-acre tract across from Union Carbide.

While White shrimpers were burning crosses and menacing Vietnamese fishermen, Wilson was clearing out room in her freezer to store new mutations that turned up in the daily catch. People close to her were getting cancer, well before their time. The same month Judge McDonald issued her injunction, *Texas Monthly* ran an exposé about the incidence of leukemia in coastal towns—at times quadruple the state's average—wondering whether there was a connection to the petrochemical plants looming over the bays. They gave the affected coastal area a new nickname: the Cancer Belt.

Getting hard data from the plants on the number and scope of toxic discharges was nearly impossible, but Wilson harbored no illusions: she could tell where someone had worked by the type of cancer they had.

Liver and brain cancer usually meant Dow or Union Carbide; Alcoa had the corner on asbestosis and other lung diseases.

But her fellow shrimpers seemed incapable of correctly diagnosing the threat. Months after the injunction, when oysters in the upper bay began dying out, she scoffed as these fishermen blamed irregular salinity instead of the assault on the bays by toxic releases, pesticide-filled agricultural runoff, and years of catastrophic oil spills.

*It can't be the plants*, they told her with increasing vitriol. She grew more and more isolated, and in her isolation she became more convinced that she was right. She resigned herself to the same conclusion Billy Joe Aplin had come to when he realized that too many of his fellow fishermen worked at the plants to recognize them for the threats they were to the bays. Wilson didn't see herself as anyone worth listening to: she was just a mom, a shrimper with a beat-up trawler and a deadbeat husband.

A few years later, a shrimper and Vietnam veteran afflicted with three types of cancer hobbled into her fish house and waved a newspaper article that put her on a collision course with everyone she knew and loved, as she embarked on a nearly suicidal mission against the plants in order to save her beloved bays.

# Act IV

# Poisoned Water

But the oil had come, and it looked like the fish had gone. It had been an even swap.

—WOODY GUTHRIE, *BOUND FOR GLORY*

## 32

# Bill Bailey's Newspaper

DIANE WILSON WAS TOSSING IN HER BED IN HER HUNDRED-year-old clapboard home perched on a swampy ten-acre spread she'd inherited from her father a couple of miles outside Seadrift. She was caught in something between a dream and a nightmare, hovering in a vast Texas expanse of dirt and tumbleweed, dim sky and boiling asphalt, watching a version of herself standing at a crossroads with a grave look on her face. The Diane in the dream didn't speak or move, but something was clearly wrong: far off on the horizon behind her, a skyline of smokestacks exhaled a thick black fog that curled over the earth.

She snapped awake. It was the dead of night but still hot—June could be a cruel month. Her husband was asleep, which was all he seemed to do when he wasn't watching nature documentaries about snakes or shooting them off the banks of the pond out back. At the foot of their bed lay Domino, the family Dalmatian, belly rising and falling, tongue lolling out.

Her five children were asleep in the other rooms. She crept out of bed and checked on her youngest, David, who was three years old but still hadn't uttered a word. She was pretty sure he was autistic, but it was just a hunch—she'd never once been able to afford health insurance.

Diane Wilson on the *SeaBee*.

Even if she could afford a doctor, it wouldn't change anything; Seadrift wasn't exactly humming with services for children with special needs.

As she slipped back into bed, she thought of her dream of the petrochemical plants, but was too tired to analyze anything. Her thoughts turned to the demands of the next morning: As soon as she wrangled her kids into the ancient Sears van she'd bought at an auction and deposited them at school, she'd take the *SeaBee* out for a drag or two of shrimp before heading over to Froggie's, the fish house she managed for her younger brother. Hose off the trawler deck, shovel the ice, mend the nets, load the boxes of sorted shrimp, pick the kids up, dinner, laundry, baths, bed, repeat. After fifteen years of marriage, she had come to see her husband—who never seemed to have escaped the PTSD of his service in Vietnam, and who didn't lift a finger around the house—as her sixth child. Her life was far from boring, but there was a routine to it that occasionally reared its head in an unsettling way to ask, *Is this it? Nothing else new between now and the grave?*

THREE WEEKS LATER, AT FROGGIE'S, HER DREAM BEGAN TO MAKE some kind of sense.

Wilson was waiting for shrimpers to arrive with the daily catch, her white sea boots propped up on the beat-up office desk, a cup of cold coffee resting on her stomach. It was her fortieth birthday, but she wasn't in much of a celebratory mood. The $325 a month she made did little to ward off repo men hoping to seize her truck or bankers waving papers threatening to repossess her home.

By the summer of 1989, Wilson saw modest signs of progress between White and Vietnamese fishermen—a kind of grudging acceptance— in the decade since the killing of Billy Joe Aplin and the seven years since Judge McDonald's injunction and the Klan's memorial march for Aplin. Despite Gene Fisher's boasts to any journalist who'd listen, the Klan kept its distance from the Vietnamese. The Whites were no longer trying to drive them out, but they weren't buying them a round at the bar, either. The only moments when Wilson saw them come together were in tragedy, usually when a shrimper was lost at sea and all fishermen went out to drag the bays, hoping to scoop up the body in their nets.

But shrimping in the bays seemed to be fading as a way of life, for both White and Vietnamese fishermen. In 1982, for the first time, im- ported shrimp—raised in aquatic farms in Vietnam, Indonesia, and Thailand—surpassed domestic, wild-caught shrimp, making it cheaper for restaurants to order prebreaded frozen shrimp from Southeast Asia than to buy it from the shrimpers who docked at Wilson's fish house. The plants continued to erupt, explode, and leak into the bays. At Mus- tang Island, just down the coast from Seadrift, oil from the catastrophic 1979 Ixtoc I spill had hardened into a seventy-five-foot-long tar reef de- void of life. In 1984, a tanker grounded in Cameron, Louisiana, leaked 2.7 million gallons of oil into the gulf, which drifted one hundred miles west into Galveston Bay, coating its beaches and grasslands, killing off marine life.

And to make matters worse, it was another lousy season, which meant less shrimp coming into the fish house, which meant less money, which meant more visits from menacing men on Wilson's property try- ing to take more from her. Only two shrimpers had gone out that morn- ing: her older brother and Bill Bailey. Bailey was a good shrimper even though he was born far from the coast, in Abilene. After returning from Vietnam, where he'd been a fighter pilot's navigator, he coached high school football for a spell, then decided he preferred the solitude of the water.

He liked Wilson—she was married to a fellow vet, her older brother was the most decorated veteran around, and her whole family seemed to work the water.

By noon, Wilson figured Bailey's nets must have come up empty because he hadn't shown up in his trawler. So when she saw his truck kicking up oystershell dust as it sped toward the fish house, she knew something must be wrong.

The first thing she saw of him was his Hawaiian shirt. He was the only person in Calhoun County who wore them, and she loved him for it. The next thing she saw, as he ambled into Froggie's, was a newspaper folded up under his arm.

"Go on, read it," he said, tossing the paper onto her desk and taking a seat by the window. Just two months earlier, he'd been stretched out on an uncomfortable hospital bed up in Galveston when his doctor came in and dump-trucked the news that he had three types of cancer. Nobody knew which one was winning in its destruction of his body, but he was already wasting away. He sat there quietly with his hands on his knees while Wilson read.

The headline: "EPA: Texas Tops U.S. in Industrial Air Pollution."

She read the Associated Press article three times, ingesting more of the horrible news with each pass. The article discussed the just-published Toxic Release Inventory, a federally mandated report from the Environmental Protection Agency that ranked states and counties by the industrial emissions discharged into the environment.

Texas, it turned out, was first in the nation in toxic emissions. And in the county breakdown, Seadrift's Calhoun County, home to fewer than fifteen thousand people, home to her children, was ranked the most toxic place in America.

As Wilson read the article, her anger mounted. Calhoun County accounted for 54 percent of Texas's total of nearly a billion pounds of toxic discharges, some of which came from the Alcoa plant that Billy Joe Aplin had suspected years earlier of fouling the bay and harming the shrimp crop. Aplin had written letters to his fellow fishermen, trying to rally them to fight Alcoa, but got nowhere: the plant was a job creator for the area.

Calhoun County also ranked third for shipping toxins elsewhere, sixth for dumping them in wells, and twenty-first in the nation for dispersing them into the air. Galveston Bay to the north was also choking from 154 million pounds of toxins that had been released into public sewage systems; in all, 660 million pounds of toxic chemicals had been dumped into Texas bays and waterways.

"The Texas sky is used as a giant garbage dump by Texas industries," a Sierra Club official told the reporter, a quote offset by an EPA spokesman in Dallas who said that Texans "should be concerned but not alarmed" by the findings.

Until that point, all Wilson had ever read about "industry" in the newspapers were promotional pieces about the jobs created with each new expansion or about each new gift from the plants to the town: computers for the local police, defibrillators for the town ambulance, schoolbooks for the children. She knew about Alcoa's mercury buried at the bottom of Lavaca Bay, but had hoped the worst of the dumping was decades behind them, despite the occasional mutations she pulled up in her nets. The AP article confirmed that it was still happening—now—and that it was poisoning all of them.

She balled up the paper in a rage and flung it across the fish house.

As she fished around for the keys to her van, Bill watched with a smile on his face, which was burned by the sun.

"Whaddya gonna do, Diane?"

She was halfway out the door when she shouted, "Going over to city hall!"


WILSON WASN'T A PLANNER. SHRIMPERS LIVED IN THE MOMENT, grabbing what they could before conditions changed. You could have a thousand-pound drag in one sweet spot and then come up empty the next twenty days there. She operated instead by her gut—a quick read of where the squall was headed in the next ten minutes—not whether she was socking away for retirement.

She also knew the brain can talk the heart out of things: if you know what's right, better to act on it before you change your mind. She didn't know what to do, but she knew she had to do *something*, and fast, which is why she raced over to city hall, a squat structure just a block north of the hickory grove behind Amason's bar, from which Richard Haight and a gang of Seadrifters had launched their posse to burn the Vietnamese out of town a decade earlier.

As she stomped toward the entrance, the firehouse bell tower—its oscillating alarm donated by Union Carbide—cast a faint shadow across the parking lot like a sundial. As she reached the entrance, the wadded-up newspaper in her fist, she realized she had no idea what she was about to say. She wasn't an activist. She hated talking to people and loved being by herself, sitting in silence on the *SeaBee*, listening to her own thoughts.

She flung the door open to find Fern Dale, who was kin to her in some way she didn't quite remember, but different in just about every other way: she sang in the Baptist church choir, and her husband worked at Union Carbide.

"Fern, I need a town meeting!" Wilson blurted.

"About what?"

"This," she said, slapping the newspaper onto the counter and jabbing her finger at the article.

Fern arched an eyebrow, but pulled out her ledger and wrote down the request, giving Wilson a date for a meeting.

SHE WALKED OUT INTO THE PARKING LOT IN AN OVERWHELMED state, goose bumps and giddy, the way she felt on Christmas Eve, when everything was full of potential. She had just done something so totally out of character that it felt like she'd climbed off the looping merry-go-round of her normal life. As she climbed back into her van, she was startled by how exhilarated she felt to have taken this first, modest step into political action.

As her van jounced along the rutted path leading up to her home in the countryside, she saw her kids out back with her husband, watching as he took aim at water moccasins. He had killed thirty the previous year and was already well past that number despite the fact it was only June.

She didn't tell her husband what she'd just done, because she didn't know how to explain it. By the time everyone was asleep, she collapsed into bed worrying over unanswered questions. Who would come to the meeting? And what was she going to say?

## 33

## Stirring the Pot

DIANE WILSON DIDN'T EVEN KNOW THE NAMES OF THE CHEMI-cals being produced at the plants. She never went to college, but she knew how to learn; she found a notebook and began copying things from the article: 970,000 pounds of trichloroethylene spilled by the US Air Force in Fort Worth; 960,000 pounds of 1,3-butadiene dumped by Texaco Chemical up in Port Neches; 794,000 pounds of benzene dumped by Goodyear at its plant in Bayport, where Gene Fisher lived; 579,000 pounds of methylene chloride dumped by Texas Fibers near Brenham; and another 472,000 pounds unloaded by DuPont in La Porte, where David Collins lived.

She knew nothing of the Clean Water Act or the Clean Air Act. She didn't know her elected officials, or who wielded power in Calhoun County.

What she knew was the world of fishing, so the next morning she began cornering and cajoling every shrimper and crabber she found into coming to her meeting. She called in old favors and promised new ones; the most stubborn holdouts relented only when she offered to mend their shrimp nets for free.

She was in Froggie's when Fern, her relative who worked at city hall, came in and told her she couldn't have the meeting.

"Well, shoot, we can change the day if it's not free then!" Wilson offered.

"No, you can't have the meeting," Fern told her stiffly.

Wilson realized this wasn't a scheduling issue, but a political one.

"All right," she said. "I guess I can move it to the schoolhouse."

"No!" exclaimed Fern. "I need you to take the meeting clear outta town! They don't want it anywhere near here."

She smiled and walked Fern out. As she departed, Wilson lingered at the doorway, trying to stamp out the flickers of self-doubt. But what was her goal, anyhow? To shut the plants down? To have them regulated more strictly? How? What threat was a ragtag group of shrimpers and crabbers to giant corporations with operations throughout the world and armies of lawyers?

She glanced over at the bulletin board, which was cluttered with weathered photos of beat-up trawlers, ancient business cards, and notices. Her eyes settled on a flyer from years earlier touting a meeting with an environmental lawyer out of Houston to discuss ways to fight a new regulation banning the commercial catch of redfish and spotted sea trout. Commercial fin-fishermen would go out of business overnight. Shrimpers pulled those fish up in their nets in nearly every drag; unless they culled them—a time-consuming process—they risked a huge fine if caught by Fish and Wildlife agents. It was a sop to wealthier sportfishermen at the expense of the shrimpers, who had less political power.

Wilson squinted at the flyer, faded by years of sun and salt air, but she made out the name of the lawyer.

WHEN SHE GOT THROUGH TO JIM BLACKBURN, SHE WAS SHOCKED by what he already knew about the Toxic Release Inventory and what was happening in Calhoun County. When she asked if he knew anything about a Taiwanese company mentioned in the article, Formosa, which was operating a small plant on a site next to Alcoa's sprawling plant in Point Comfort overlooking Lavaca Bay, Blackburn told her that they were considering building a new polyvinyl chloride plant in the county to the tune of $3.2 billion. As many as three thousand workers would be needed to build it, and the new plant would add another twenty-five hundred permanent jobs.

To boot, the state of Texas, competing against a bid from Louisiana, was offering some $225 million in tax breaks and incentives if Formosa built its plant in Calhoun County, all to produce PVC pipes, tooth-brushes, and plastic bags. An additional $10 million was promised to broaden the shipping channel at Point Comfort so that Formosa could run deep-draft ships. The dredging would happen in the same spot where Alcoa's mercury had settled after decades of dumping.

The tax abatements were a particularly bitter pill: citizens were giving up revenue for schools, roads, and bridges in order to subsidize the pollution of their air, water, and, ultimately, bodies. County boosters were focused on short-term economic development, but Wilson knew that the long-term cost of this pollution—remediating spills and leaks, combatting illness, and lost income to anyone who depended upon the bays for their livelihood—would be borne by the public.

Blackburn told her that Formosa's proposed expansion seemed like a fine thing to focus on in her meeting. She typed up her first press release, announcing the meeting, and sent it in to the local pa-per. Ignoring Fern's entreaties, she declared that the meeting would be held in the auditorium at the Seadrift elementary school, where the entire town had gathered a decade earlier to voice their opposition to Louis Beam's planned Klan march after the acquittal of Sáu Văn Nguyễn.

Wilson described the meeting's goal as exploring how the toxic emis-sions were affecting the shrimp, crab, fish, and oyster habitats in the bays. If Texas beat out Louisiana, the proposed expansion of Formosa's oper-ation would be the largest in the state's history. She was worried about the health of her fellow Seadrifters. "Hopefully, the meeting will open the way for a grassroots movement that can not only support clean in-dustry but compel the cleaning of industry."

---

SHORTLY AFTER THE ANNOUNCEMENT RAN, A MAN IN A THREE-PIECE suit ambled into the fish house, tiptoeing past shrimp heads and cigarette butts in a shiny pair of black leather dress shoes. Howard Hartzog was the president of the local bank—the man every shrimper approached for a loan—but everyone called him Howdy. Those who couldn't get a loan called him Howdy Doody with a word tucked in between.

Howdy looked down at his shoes while he spoke.

"You send out that press release?"

"Sure did, why?" Wilson replied nervously.

"A banker's prerogative. I just need to go back and tell a few folks that you aren't fixing to have some little vindictive meeting to roast industry alive. Not some renegade environmental group forming in our midst?"

Wilson smiled wide as she struggled for a response.

"So *what* am I to tell them?" Howdy asked.

"Well, tell them they're invited! . . . Heck, I don't care. It's just a meeting."

"Just a meeting," Howdy repeated.

"Well, yeah."

"Well, good. That's good. I'll pass that on, then."


FOUR DAYS AFTER BILL BAILEY WALKED IN WITH THE ARTICLE THAT had set Wilson on this path, the local newspaper ran a follow-up in which industry representatives and public officials declared that the materials dumped by the plants posed "absolutely no health concerns." Doug Lynch, the head of economic development for Calhoun County, was blunt about his priorities to entice Formosa. "You've got to go out and get industry so you can get your share and part of somebody else's." Lynch dismissed Wilson's concerns: "There's always concern with the environment. Sometimes it may be subordinated to other concerns."

Larry Robinson, the president of the Port Lavaca–Calhoun County

Chamber of Commerce, told a journalist that Wilson's meeting ran the risk of blowing up the entire Formosa deal: "If they can't locate here within their 'window of opportunity,' they'll take their project to Louisiana," depriving the county of a lot of new jobs.

The day before the meeting, Wilson called Blackburn in a panic. He said he'd come down and even bring some experts to help answer questions.

"First meetings are always the hardest," Blackburn told her. "You'll get through it."

THE MORNING OF THE BIG DAY, WILSON BAKED A CHOCOLATE sheet cake. It was a little flat, but she knew shrimpers expected cake at a meeting, and everyone already knew baking wasn't her strong suit. David, her youngest son, sat by the front window, running his fingers up and down the screen as she swept through the house, tidying up, hanging clothes to dry on an old trotline she once used to catch catfish near Billy Joe Aplin's favorite crabbing spot on the Guadalupe River.

She was pulling the cake out of the oven when one of her kids hollered from the living room: people were talking about her meeting on the TV. And sure enough, a state senator was adamantly insisting that he would *not* be attending. It struck her as odd—if someone didn't want to come, why did they feel the need to denounce the meeting? Why not just ignore it?

AS SHE DROVE TO THE SCHOOLHOUSE—THE SAME ONE SHE'D AT-tended decades earlier—she was jarred by a memory of her junior high graduation. She'd made salutatorian, but when the principal called her up to give her remarks, she stared out at the crowd, hot under the bright lights, and after a long pause said, "I have forgot the words." She scurried off the stage and never spoke in public again.

Consumed by self-doubt, she resolved to drop the cake off, apologize to Blackburn for wasting his time, and give it all up. But when she pulled up and saw her lawyer hopping out of a Jeep in black cowboy boots with a smile on his face, her nerves quieted; his confidence was infectious.

The day was hot and windless. One by one, beat-up trucks pulled up to the school, their fenders rusted, cargo beds piled with chains and nets and empty shrimp boxes. Turnout was much stronger than expected. They filed into the auditorium, filled their plates with cake, and waited.

She'd asked Blackburn to run the meeting, but she opened with a simple message: "We just want a safe place for our children to live. We don't believe in economic development at any price." Blackburn explained that they had filed a request for a hearing on air permits Formosa had recently applied for as part of its proposed expansion. One of his experts explained that the highest lung cancer rates in Texas were in Calhoun, Brazoria, Jefferson, and Harris counties—the entire coastline between Seadrift and Port Arthur on the Louisiana border, including Seabrook and Kemah and every major shrimping town in between, which was now known as the Cancer Belt.

Wilson was so nervous that she didn't even remember how the meeting ended, other than feeling relief that nobody had disrupted it. When she got her kids loaded in the family van, she felt a wave of pride and peace wash over her.

By the following morning, it was replaced with dread.

# 34

# Chairman Wang Comes to Seadrift

WILSON'S HUSBAND WOULDN'T EVEN SPEAK WITH HER ABOUT her newfound sense of activism. She knew he wasn't happy, but there was nothing new in that. He'd been a wreck for as long as she'd loved him, psychologically disfigured by his time in Vietnam and bolting from the shadow of an alcoholic father and a brother who drank himself to death. He was no stranger to booze and anger, which is why she kept her distance, heading straight to the fish house after getting the kids off to school each morning.

Doug Lynch, the county's economic booster, pulled up in a furor to Froggie's. Wilson was only two weeks into her campaign, if she could even call it that, but she was already getting used to being yelled at by men in nice clothes. She had been expecting Lynch ever since he'd approached her older brother, Leslie, and told him to "simmer that sister of yours down." He'd just grinned at Lynch.

"Do you *know* what it is you're doing?" Lynch snapped at her as he sauntered in. "Have you *any* idea, any notion of exactly what it is? And *who* is this lawyer Blackburn?"

He barely knew Wilson, but he told her that he could resolve her problems for her if she'd just call her lawyer off and withdraw her request for a hearing on the plant's expansion. "I'm just trying to save us a little time and money and nonsense, is all. A hearing is going to do nothing but put a lot of money into a lot of lawyers' pockets."

Lynch reminded her that if Formosa chose Louisiana over Calhoun County for its new polyvinyl chloride plant, they'd lose thousands of jobs, many of which paid over $70,000 a year, far more than any shrimpers or crabbers were making in those days. For a county struggling with nearly 16 percent unemployment, the proposed plant expansion was a lifeline they couldn't ignore. By holding meetings about pollution and talking with environmental lawyers, Wilson was putting those plans in jeopardy. Lynch offered her a job if she'd get rid of Blackburn and drop her crusade.

She didn't know that a year earlier, faced with increasingly violent protests by fishermen and environmental activists back in Taiwan, Formosa's chairman, Y. C. Wang, had flown Lynch, former congressman Joe Wyatt, and seven other Texas officials to Taipei to make a proposal: if his own countrymen wouldn't accept a new plant, maybe these Texans would. She didn't know about all the tax abatements Lynch had offered— five years' worth of county and school property taxes, worth some $132 million. She didn't know about their pledges to help Formosa secure the necessary permits from state and federal authorities allowing the plant to dump its waste into the sky, land, and water.

Lynch was blunt about the stakes: there was no time to worry about the environment. "It's either industry or unemployment. Once we get our economy stabilized, then we can afford to be a little more choosy with who and what we let in."

THE MORE THESE WELL-HEELED MEN GLOWERED AT HER FROM the fish house doorway, the more determined she grew. She called for another meeting with her fellow shrimpers and Seadrifters, hoping to build on the momentum of the first, but as soon as it kicked off she knew she'd already lost them.

The shrimpers, struggling amid another bad season, knew they could get part-time jobs at the plants if things got worse. Given that Alcoa was cutting its workforce from 2,700 to 850, they weren't about to make enemies of what would potentially be the biggest employer in town.

"What you're doin' is killing the gravy horse!" someone shouted.

"I thought an environmental group *helped* a community," someone else cried. "I didn't know its purpose was to tear down everything the community leaders were trying to build up."

On her heels, she told the gathering that she wasn't opposed to the plant's expansion per se: she just wanted to make sure it was done in a way that complied with the regulations . . . and Formosa's track record gave her pause. She rattled through a list of all the recent fines levied by the EPA against Formosa for violating the Clean Water Act, and told the crowd that a member of the state's Air Control Board described the company as having "a serious compliance problem." Was it really so wrong to ask some questions?

Someone accused her of being a paid operative on behalf of the state of Louisiana, hoping to scuttle Texas's deal with Formosa. Men asked her why she wasn't home taking care of her kids. They asked whether her husband or some other man had put her up to all this rabble-rousing. They asked why she didn't just call up Formosa and talk things over with them, as if this was all some kind of simple misunderstanding.

Her fiercest allies were divorced women; married women's husbands were urging them not to get mixed up with Wilson, who was quickly becoming persona non grata. More than once, friends in town told her they couldn't stand with her because they were hoping to get a loan from Howdy Hartzog down at the bank, or because someone in the family worked at one of the plants.

For most of her shrimping life, she'd heard her fellow shrimpers chatter away on their CBs about what they'd seen when working at the plants during the off-season: strange, foul-smelling chemicals dumped in a field behind this plant or in a ditch at that plant. Once she started taking on Formosa in a public way, though, no one would go on the record with her.

But she began getting phone calls from workers at the plants around town, telling her what they'd seen or done. They wouldn't meet her in public, but they shared photos and documents and notes about accidental discharges that were covered up. They told her about colleagues who had been badly injured by accidents and explosions at the plants. Several of them told her about their "insurance policy," the little notebooks they kept to document what they'd been asked to lie about or help conceal, which would be worth a fortune if their bosses ever tried to fire them. But whenever she asked if they'd speak with Blackburn, they clammed up—this "evidence" was meant to help them keep their jobs, not to punish the plants.

WHEN IT WAS TIME TO DECIDE BETWEEN TEXAS AND LOUISIANA, Formosa's chairman, Wang, visited Calhoun County for the red-carpet treatment from Doug Lynch and other leaders. Over a meal of Matagorda Bay gumbo, local crab, and Point Comfort lemon meringue pie, Wang sprung a surprise, telling Lynch that Louisiana had offered him *ten* full years of tax abatements if he decided to build there, compared with Texas's five. Lynch scrambled and talked the county school board into a seven-year abatement, even though the influx of new employees and their children would undoubtedly strain the school's resources. (The school board was already deliberating firing seventeen teachers due to a lack of funding.)

Wang had another demand. Ten years after Seadrift and much of Calhoun County was locked down after the killing of Billy Joe Aplin amid vigilante violence against Seadrift's one hundred Vietnamese refugees, Formosa insisted that the 250 Taiwanese employees needed to help build the plant receive expedited visas. A *Texas Monthly* reporter noted the irony: "Once we regarded foreigners with suspicion; now we court them on bended knee, as long as they bring us a few jobs." The Texans assured Chairman Wang that *these* immigrants would be welcomed with open arms.

———

AND SO IN THE BATTLE FOR WHICH STATE COULD GIVE AWAY THE
most to Chairman Wang, Texas prevailed: Formosa would build the
largest PVC plant in the world at Point Comfort. It would be situated
right next to the Alcoa plant that had dumped so much mercury into
Lavaca Bay that it became the first underwater Superfund site. Jubilant
county boosters predicted that the new plant would be operational
within a couple of years, by 1992.

In exchange, Formosa won a permit from the Texas Water Commission to dump fifteen million gallons of chemical discharge every day,
including sulfuric acid, chlorine, ethylene dichloride, and vinyl chloride,
known to cause cancer, blood clots, and damage to the liver and kidneys.
Formosa assured the public that the chemicals would all be diluted suf-
ficiently enough that the shrimpers' harvest wouldn't be adversely affected. The proverb "Dilution is the solution to pollution" was routinely
deployed by big industry when seeking permission to dump into the nation's waterways. It wasn't until 1969, when the toxic Cuyahoga River in
Cleveland caught fire for the thirteenth time, that the nation finally
passed the Clean Water Act; the Environmental Protection Agency was
established the following year. But nearly twenty years later, dilution was
still being touted as a cure-all.

The day of the big announcement, four hundred residents of the
county were invited for a surprise event at the civic center, which was
festooned with potted plants and flowers. Outside, volunteers inflated a
thousand balloons as camera crews filed in and found Governor Clements, Senator Phil Gramm, Doug Lynch, and other local bigwigs on a
platform around the diminutive multibillionaire Chairman Wang. On a
nearby wall hung a colorful sign that read: TEXAS: AN ECONOMY ON THE
MOVE WELCOMES FORMOSA.

The subsequent headline in the local paper was breathless: "Formosa
Building 'World's Cleanest' Plant."

Wilson called up Blackburn. If they couldn't prevent Formosa from
building the new plant, could they find a way to slow it down, at least?

# 35

# Stop Plant No. 6 or Die

A N ENVIRONMENTAL IMPACT STATEMENT," BLACKBURN TOLD
her on the phone. "I'm already filling out the paperwork."

"A what?" Wilson asked.

Formosa's bulldozers were already turning dirt while workers raised
scaffolding across the thousand-acre compound overlooking Lavaca Bay,
but Blackburn had a strategy. If they could persuade the EPA to insist
upon an environmental impact statement before granting the permits
allowing Formosa to discharge its wastewater in the bay, it might force
the company to adhere more closely to safety guidelines.

But shortly after filing, they were told by federal authorities that
there would be no demand for an EIS. Formosa's executives were unwilling, and Texas wasn't about to buck the company bringing thousands of
jobs into the state by insisting on one.

As construction continued, goodwill was bought for cheap. Coloring
books for the kids. Free corsages for the school dance. A free roof for the
church and free folding chairs for the auditorium. On Earth Day 1990,
Jack Wu, a vice president at the plant, posed with a young girl alongside
a newly planted sapling outside Point Comfort Elementary School: Formosa had given 102 ash, mesquite, and live oak trees, one for each stu-

dent. The local paper touted the $5,200 spent by the chemical plant for the trees.

NOBODY WAS TOUTING WILSON'S EFFORTS. HER OWN SISTER, A teacher whose husband worked at Formosa, was embarrassed by her suddenly controversial sibling. Her older brother told her she'd be better off if she just went back to shrimping. Her husband made no effort to conceal his resentment. Her children were angry over how preoccupied she was with the chemical plants.

Wally Morgan, who was married to her first cousin, ran a competing fish house in town, but he started dropping by more regularly to shoot the breeze with her. He was a fin-fisherman who'd been rendered an outlaw overnight by the ban on commercial fishing for redfish. His gill nets were confiscated, but he couldn't resist keeping a small but illegal stash of redfish in an ancient refrigerator truck behind his fish house. When asked if he'd join her in taking on the plants, he demurred and said he was tired of fighting and losing.

"Why don'tcha do what Howdy wants?" he asked her one day, his hands fumbling with loose change in his pockets.

"I ain't got no idea what yore talkin' about, Wally." Wilson sighed.

"Sure you do. Howdy wants you to quit messin' with those plants. Says he can get something for the fishermen if you'd just settle down."

"A *banker* is gonna do all that?" she asked incredulously.

"Sure! . . . Howdy's talkin' to big industry. . . . So just let 'em alone! Give 'em a little breathin' room!"

She liked talking to Wally. She trusted him and felt free thinking out loud with him, even if he didn't see things the same way. But she had no intention of having a friendly sit-down with Howdy or anyone from Formosa. She had something more ambitious in mind.

AS NEWS OF HER STUBBORN OPPOSITION TO FORMOSA SPREAD throughout the world, a group of environmental activists in Taiwan asked her if she wanted to come see what the future held for the Texas coastline if Formosa got its way. She applied for her first passport, packed a wheeling suitcase with a Texas Longhorns team logo on it, and boarded her first international flight for a ten-day trip in January 1991.

After decades of explosive industrialization with little regard for the environment, the tiny island—the second most densely populated country on earth—was wheezing. As they made their way to school amid ninety thousand factories and ten million cars, children wore masks to filter out pollution; sulfur dioxide and nitrogen oxide rendered it dangerous to breathe for two full months of the year. A third of the rivers were dangerously contaminated, pushing aquatic life to the brink of extirpation. Toxic water had conferred upon Taiwan the status of the highest hepatitis rate on earth, and trimmed the average life expectancy.

Such destruction gave rise to a broad movement to protect the land, driven largely by farmers, workers, and fishermen. Six years earlier, environmentalists had blocked DuPont from erecting a titanium dioxide plant. In 1988, fishermen had waged such a fierce protest that they managed to temporarily shut down eighteen petrochemical plants that had fouled their fishing grounds. Activists threatened a mass suicide to prevent the China Petrochemical Corporation from building a naphtha cracker plant, which produced a toxic petroleum distillate. In 1989, the year of Wilson's awakening, these same groups halted Formosa's plans to construct yet another naphtha cracker on the island, which is why Chairman Wang decided to start building in Texas. One of the activists gave her a banner they'd used in their fight against Formosa's plant; in bright red Chinese characters, it read: STOP PLANT NO. 6 OR DIE.

Wilson spent ten days in bewilderment as her hosts secretly toured her throughout the island to show her one Formosa facility after another. They sneaked her into a mountaintop hideout to meet with an activist who had gone into hiding. She met a man whose wife and children had been stabbed to death by unknown assailants after he became a leader in the fight to stop building new nuclear power plants on the island. She stepped into the shack of a fisherman who had gathered thousands of water samples from the nearby river into tiny glass jars each morning for years. His collection, each jar labeled with the date and time of the sampling, covered every square inch of shelving and spread onto the floors and in the corners. He was too poor to have them tested for anything, but he was certain they contained the truth of what had happened to his water.

Every stop on her tour focused on the rivers. The Keelung struck her as more cesspool than river, fishless and full of pig carcasses, its water oily and yellow with an acrid smoke rising off it. The Er-Jen was foul with mercury and copper. Farmers living alongside the lifeless Houchin were forced to use its black water to irrigate their rice fields. They told her about acid rain and vapor clouds filled with a yellow oil that spattered their fields and foreheads. She watched a Formosa truck drive out onto a sandbar, dump a five-foot heap of something into the river, and chug off.

Surrounded by activists who were willing to die to protect the land and water, she felt something radical germinating inside her and sensed that she was being too polite back home. Holding meetings and firing off press releases wasn't going to change a thing. What she saw in Taiwan was a glimpse into the dystopian future that awaited her fellow Texans. If Formosa was given enough time and permits to dump, her beloved home waters would meet the same toxic fate.

WHEN SHE RETURNED, HER HUSBAND WAS BARELY SPEAKING TO her. He was drinking heavily and breaking things in the house. Her children were upset with her for being gone, but she told herself it was more important to give them an example of moral courage than to fold their laundry and bake sheet cakes.

"I think I'm going to go on a hunger strike," she told her husband, surprised by her own words. Blackburn had tried and failed to force the plant to agree to an environmental impact statement, and Formosa showed no sign of slowing its construction. Where court filings failed, she would borrow a page from Gandhi and her fearless Taiwanese brethren and put her own life on the line.

"The kids ain't comin' down to see you, and I hope you die!" her husband shouted as she drove off, headed for the docks in Port Lavaca, just across the bay from where the new smokestacks of the Formosa plant were starting to tower over the shoreline.

# 36

# Hunger

D OWN AT THE DOCKS, WILSON FOUND A DECREPIT SHRIMP BOAT whose owner didn't mind her starving herself to death in it. She carried an armful of water jugs onto the trawler and stared across the bay at the plant. Five hundred feet from the shoreline was Alcoa's Dredge Island, where mercury and other toxic wastewater had been dumped before being discharged through an outfall into the bay, which first alerted Billy Joe Aplin to the dangers of the plants.

Nearby, a Texas Department of Health sign warned: FISH AND CRABS MAY BE CONTAMINATED BY MERCURY. CONSUMPTION OF FISH OR CRABS FROM THE PROHIBITED AREA MAY BE DANGEROUS TO YOUR HEALTH. Fishermen usually heeded the signs, but there was no way to know whether fish caught in nearby bays had fed in Lavaca—it wasn't as though they spent their entire lives in one spot.

The first two days of the hunger strike were the worst. Beyond the aching hunger, Wilson was suffering the consequences of caffeine withdrawal. She sipped from a thermos of hot water, trying to imagine it was coffee, and waited.

Her strike brought a significant amount of attention, most of it critical. "Her ideas are good and she has done some good," Point Comfort mayor Theresa Tanner told the local paper. "I just think the way she's going about this is wrong." The mayor of Port Lavaca called her "just a little bit radical." Calhoun County judge Alex Hernandez was less constrained: "I don't like people running from county to county or state to state trying to force their beliefs on us . . . if they push too hard, Formosa could say it's not worth it and conceivably we could lose this whole thing."

"I don't get any feeling that everybody's gung ho behind her," said a teacher at Point Comfort Elementary School, just a block from the plant. "In my opinion she's just tootin' her own horn."

"Why she has this vendetta, I really don't know," griped another local resident.

WILSON KNEW SHE WAS MAKING MORE ENEMIES THAN FRIENDS; plenty of locals were excited about Formosa. When a community college announced classes, like Introduction to Chemical Process, that could improve chances of landing a job at the new plant—many of which would pay nearly double the median income in Texas at that time—hundreds of residents lined up. The college's director of vocational programs said that people "had crawled out of bed sick" in order to register.

Blackburn hated the idea of a hunger strike, and he told Wilson he wanted nothing to do with it. But around the twelfth day, it seemed as though it was working: EPA officials told her they wanted to look into the potential environmental consequences of the plant. Not long thereafter, Formosa volunteered to submit to an environmental impact statement.

She broke her fast with a slice of pizza, but as she drove home to her family, she had the gnawing sense that she was being played, just to get her out of the media's spotlight. Formosa was spending billions of dollars to build the plant, with the full-throated backing of senators, congressmen, and the governor. Was some regulatory document really going to stop anything?

After all, Senator Phil Gramm, one of the largest boosters of Formosa's plant, appointed Robert Layton, one of his campaign county chairmen, to the role of EPA administrator for the region covering Calhoun County and the plant. Joe Wyatt, the former congressman who had represented the area during the worst of the tensions between White and Vietnamese fishermen, was now on Formosa's payroll as a public relations consultant. His wife, Mary Anne, served on the Texas Air Control Board, which had direct regulatory oversight of the plant. When newly elected governor Ann Richards asked her to step down from the board, citing "the strong appearance of a conflict of interest," she declined. State senator Ken Armbrister was the managing partner of a company that provided security services to the plant.

When toxic discharges from Formosa's original plant at Point Comfort led the EPA to slap a record-setting $8.3 million fine, Jack Wu, the vice president who'd gifted trees to Point Comfort Elementary School, maxed out contributions to Senator Gramm and Governor Richards. The fine was soon reduced to $3.3 million.

WHEN WILSON PULLED UP THE RUTTED DIRT ROAD TO HER HOME, she found David sitting by the front windows. The house didn't have air-conditioning, so on muggy days, he liked to feel the breeze and run his finger up and down the screen. He had just turned four but still hadn't said a word. He was a happy boy, and he had a painfully acute sense of hearing; the quiet zipping sound of his nail filing against the mesh of the screen was pleasing to his ears.

She smothered him with a kiss. After noticing a tear in the screen, she smirked and said, "Now who made that hole in the screen, David?" not expecting a reply.

She was halfway to the kitchen when he spoke his first words: "Formosa did it."

It wasn't the happiest welcome home. Her fifteen-year-old daughter, Ramona, upset that she'd been gone for so long, proclaimed that she was going to work for Formosa when she was old enough. Wilson remembered something her mom had once told her: If you give your kids the choice of you being alive in the next town or dead in the next room, they'll pick the latter. She felt a pang of guilt, but not nearly enough to persuade her to give up her fight.

THE CONSTRUCTION OF THE FORMOSA PLANT WAS SUPPOSED TO be a boon for thousands of contractors, but within a year of the groundbreaking ceremony, the *Houston Chronicle* ran a shocking exposé: some thirty lawsuits had already been filed by construction companies and their employees alleging fraud, gross negligence, breach of contract, violations of worker safety, and a tawdry kickback scheme.

One Formosa official involved in doling out contracts received tens of thousands of dollars in bribes, including free flights to Atlantic City and a room at the Trump Plaza Hotel and Casino. Another contractor left thousands of dollars in a hotel refrigerator to be picked up by Formosa officials. A construction company owner, desperate to be paid the $2.8 million owed by Formosa for the work he'd already completed on the plant, shelled out $3,000 to fix the car of a Formosa purchasing agent. When the agent spoke about the lavish birthday party he wanted to throw for his wife, the owner responded by giving him a cashier's check for another $5,000.

Wilson was more concerned about reports of shoddy construction practices and previously unreported toxic leaks at the original Formosa plant than the kickback schemes. A worker who discovered a chlorine gas leak reported it immediately to his supervisor, urging him to shut down the process because the gas was deadly, but as a green cloud of gas plumed over the plant, no actions were taken until a week later, when the worker was fired. In another event, a supervisor discovered that the company was knowingly shipping polyvinyl chloride powder contaminated with illegal and dangerous concentrations of vinyl chloride monomer, a cancer-causing agent. Soon after he reported it, he too was fired.

The *Houston Chronicle* outlined dozens of previously unreported spills and environmental violations, but the EPA was prepared to ignore them and grant the crucial wastewater discharge permit that would allow the newly expanded plant to dump 9.7 million gallons of chemical waste—benzene, naphthalene, fluorine, phenol, and chloroethane, among other toxic substances—directly into Lavaca Bay each day. State health officials were already planning on shutting down the oyster industry in the area as soon as the discharges commenced.

Domino slept at Wilson's feet while she read the *Houston Chronicle* exposé, sipping coffee and trying to process the news. In addition to what would be dumped into the bay, Formosa was set to receive permits for discharging millions of pounds of pollutants into the air: 4.5 million pounds of nitrous oxide, an anesthetic, authorized each year; 2 million pounds of poisonous carbon monoxide; and 46,000 pounds of sulfur dioxide, which posed a risk of suffocation.

Louann Morris, whose three children walked to Point Comfort Elementary School, was terrified about the nauseating smells coming from the plant. The stench frequently gave her headaches, but she was more concerned about an explosion at the plant, which was immediately next to the school. She was part of a group of homeowners asking Formosa to buy them out so that they could move somewhere safer. "They have taken away our property values and now we live in fear," she told a *Houston Chronicle* reporter.

FORMOSA HAD SUBMITTED TO AN ENVIRONMENTAL IMPACT STATE-ment, but freakish amounts of rain during the assessment caused Wilson and other activists to suspect that the "flushing capacities" of the bay were grievously exaggerated. It wasn't long before Wilson set out on her second hunger strike. This time, she had three demands for Formosa: do no harm to the community, do no harm to the workers, and do no harm to the bay.

Blackburn visited his fasting client, who was attracting both local and national coverage. He knew that by the second week she would no longer be coherent, so he wanted to talk over strategy in case her fast compelled Formosa to negotiate. He had an idea for an outside committee, to be funded by Formosa, with the authority to audit air quality and hazardous waste at the plant. She told him that sounded fine, but reminded him that there were two other goals: she wanted the company to buy out the homeowners in Point Comfort who wished to leave, and for workers at the plant to have the right to organize for better conditions.

SOMEWHERE AROUND THE FIFTEENTH DAY, HER HUSBAND SENT word for her to call home. When she reached a pay phone, he was beside himself. At eight thirty on the morning of April 9, 1992, his mother, who lived in a trailer behind their home, was walking toward the mailbox when she heard three gunshots, which struck the dirt around her. The following morning, a helicopter landed on the property and deposited a man with a gun, who opened fire on the house. Domino was shot twice, in his leg and neck. By the time her husband emerged, the helicopter had disappeared.

When he brought the blood-covered dog to the veterinary clinic and explained what had happened, the vet brushed aside his claims and said its injuries looked more typical of a dogfight. It wasn't until her husband insisted on an X-ray that the vet discovered the bullets. Astonishingly, the dog survived.

When Wilson arrived, her husband stormed off. He had a two-week job escorting workers to an oil rig in the gulf and was glad to be getting out of town. She was still on her hunger strike, but each night after getting the kids to sleep, she grabbed a shotgun and climbed up to the roof to keep watch for helicopters.

HER HUNGER STRIKE WAS APPROACHING A FULL MONTH, COMMANDing so much attention that Formosa officials came by and pleaded with her to eat. By then, she had shed dozens of pounds, and she was able to answer only in simple sentences.

On the thirtieth day, Blackburn called with news: Formosa was ready to negotiate. Over a several-hour meeting, they hammered out a twenty-four-page document agreeing to her three demands, to be finessed in the coming days before a signing ceremony. Formosa's attorney extended her hand to secure the deal, after which Wilson raced off to find a burger.

Two days later, with Wilson's hunger strike concluded and the media attention gone, Formosa reneged on two parts of the deal: they would not buy out any of the Point Comfort homeowners, and they refused to permit any union organizing among their workforce. When the *Texas Observer* caught wind of it, Formosa's attorney denied that they had reneged, for the simple fact that "there never was any agreement." Joe Wyatt, the ex-congressman now working as a Formosa PR consultant, suggested that Wilson's proposal had just been a ploy to "shove the union down our workers' throats."

But the company was still willing to agree to Blackburn's outside review panel. The environmental lawyer drove back down to Seadrift and sat with Wilson on a pair of folding chairs at Froggie's, looking out onto the bay as gulls perched like sentries on the pilings of the rotting pier.

He knew she was furious with Formosa, but he implored her to sign the agreement setting up the review panel, arguing that she was letting the perfect be the enemy of the good. She was upset that he'd hammered something out with the company's lawyers without her being present—now he was asking her to sign on to something, the details of which were unclear. This was an unprecedented arrangement, he stressed, an end run around regulatory agencies that were too lax to conduct meaningful oversight on Formosa.

He told her that the signing ceremony was to be held in the Speaker's conference room in the state capitol the following morning. There was sure to be a horde of news crews present, as Formosa was eager to publicize that Wilson was ending her fight. But she also understood that Blackburn would sign the agreement with or without her.

Wilson didn't know what to do. Her closest advisers and mentors in the environmental movement had urged her not to sign. She was mostly quiet as her lawyer invoked principles of Jungian psychology and spoke of Joseph Campbell's writings about the hero's journey and why she should put her signature to the agreement. He told her that his law firm was struggling to make ends meet, that the Formosa case had become "a black pit," and that he had to stop.

Blackburn pleaded with her to meet him in the rotunda of the capitol early the next morning, a three-hour drive up from Seadrift. As he climbed into his truck and drove up the oystershell road, he had no idea whether she'd show.

# 37

# Losing It

L ATER THAT NIGHT, WILSON SLIPPED OUT OF BED AND TIPTOED down the hallway, the floorboards creaking faintly. She lingered for a moment outside her children's rooms, breathing shallowly as her thoughts writhed and squirmed to get free of the merciless question: *What else can you possibly do?* After her meeting with Blackburn, she'd taken them to the Victoria Mall to ride the merry-go-round and eat whatever they wanted. She gave each of them a kiss and tiptoed out of the house.

She was still suffering the effects of her thirty-day hunger strike, exhausted and frail, but she could think clearly enough to decide that Blackburn had sold her out by negotiating an agreement on his own.

She felt like a zombie as she drove under a waxing crescent moon. She was headed for the bay, but first she stopped at the Pic-Pac grocery store, a few blocks east of Verlon Davis's crab-picking plant and the Vietnamese trailer park. It was nearly closing time as she wandered the aisles, finally stopping in the pharmacy section.

She grabbed a container of sleeping pills and went over to the liquor section for two bottles of Boone's Farm Strawberry Hill wine. *If you're going to do this*, she thought, *why not go out like Marilyn Monroe?*

———

IT WAS STILL OVER EIGHTY DEGREES IN THE DARKNESS AS SHE crept past Froggie's out to the docks and untied the *SeaBee*, her beloved forty-two-foot trawler. There was no wind or chop as she motored out into the heart of the bay.

She killed the engine, dropped anchor, and swallowed a fistful of pills. After chasing it down with the sugary wine, she lay down on the engine hatch where the wood was warm and tried to will herself to stop breathing.

But death did not come. Frustrated, she swallowed more pills, stumbled over to the stern, and draped herself on the edge. Her breath felt like a small pearl. As she sipped air, she thought about what a perfect way to die it would be, rolling off her boat and sinking into the cool embrace of the bay, the old gray lady she had seen ever since she was a little girl.

THE MORNING OF AUGUST 14, 1992, JIM BLACKBURN, DRESSED IN A black suit and crisp white button-down, anxiously paced the polished marble mosaic of the state seal in the capitol rotunda, waiting for Wilson to show. They had already delayed the ceremony an hour to give her time to arrive. He checked his watch, sighed, and made his way up to the Speaker's conference room, where Susan Wang, the daughter of Formosa's chairman, was seated next to Joe Wyatt.

As soon as the signing ceremony began, Greenpeace demonstrators paraded in, dressed as Chairman Wang, Governor Ann Richards, and Blackburn. He cringed as he watched "Slick Jim the Lawyer" prance about with dollar bills pasted to his suit.

The agreement prevented Blackburn from representing anyone else against Formosa, but he assured those present that the agreement was historic: it was the "first time ever that a company has allowed an outside party to have some say and control over its environmental and safety audits."

Blackburn, who had committed some $150,000 worth of pro bono assistance representing Wilson, announced that he was not signing the agreement as Wilson's attorney, but as an individual, rendering it the "Formosa-Blackburn Agreement." "I have three years of my life invested in this and I want to see it done," he said. He would become one of the three board members appointed to an outside oversight committee. Blackburn stressed that he'd received only $10 to make the agreement binding, and would not join Formosa's official payroll, but he didn't disclose that Formosa would pay him some $200,000, routing the corporate payments through some of the other environmental groups he'd represented on a pro bono basis. Formosa could make tax-deductible contributions to environmental organizations, burnishing their image while enriching the lawyer who had until that morning been representing their single greatest antagonist. Blackburn boasted that it was "the best agreement of its sort that has ever been negotiated in the United States."

Formosa was thrilled; their attorney announced that they'd "like to see this agreement become a prototype."

Wilson's absence from the ceremony was not lost on all the reporters who had covered her battle with Formosa over the previous few years. When a reporter asked where she was, Blackburn was circumspect: "I have to assume that she chose not to sign the agreement."


THE SLIVER OF MOON WAS STILL HIGH WHEN WILSON, IN HER PILL-induced stupor, realized that she couldn't surrender to death. She rolled over and clumsily steadied herself, trying to fill her lungs as she reached for the anchor chain. The sound of the *SeaBee*'s engine echoed across the still bay as she headed back to the docks. When she returned home, she crawled back into bed next to her snoring husband. As she drifted to sleep she knew she wanted nothing to do with Blackburn's deal. It would be years before she realized he'd made hundreds of thousands of dollars off it: when pressed by a journalist about why he didn't continue handling the case, he offered a blunt response: "I was broke. There are limits to pro bono. That was the whole reason."

———

IT HAD BEEN THREE YEARS OF BATTLE SINCE BILL BAILEY WALKED in with the newspaper article that awoke her to the true problems in the bay, but what had she won? The plant's expansion was nearly complete. Despite her efforts, the EPA and Texas regulatory bodies had granted Formosa all the permits they needed to discharge into the air, water, and soil. And that was just Formosa. After all, Union Carbide, Alcoa, Dow, DuPont, and a slew of other petrochemical companies were still polluting away along the entire coastline.

It was hard to find a new reservoir from which she could draw new courage or stamina. People who didn't know her asked why she wasn't home with her kids, calling her a bad mother. They called her a socialist for wanting Formosa's workers to have the right to unionize.

The people once closest to her were pulling back. Her sister, whose husband worked at Formosa, told her she needed mental counseling. Her younger brother, who owned Froggie's, fired her as fish house manager. In a particularly bitter blow, her older brother Leslie went to work for Formosa.

The first word out of her son's mouth was "Formosa." Ever since the helicopter descended and Domino was shot, he'd been drawing pictures in which the sky was raining bullets.

She knew her marriage was on the brink, but it wasn't until she came home one day and found a loaded pistol sitting on her side of the bed, left there by her husband, that she sensed it was no longer safe to stay, so she gathered the kids and cleared out until they could sort through the divorce.

SHE RECEIVED A CALL FROM A PRIVATE INVESTIGATOR ALLIED WITH several national environmental organizations. The PI gave her advice about minimizing risk and sent her a document with forty-four tips on improving her own security. Keep a log of threatening phone calls. Get a PO box. If you receive death threats by mail, give the original to the police only if they intend to search for fingerprints. Keep your car clean and locked at all times. Report thefts of materials from your office to the police.

It was hard to reconcile such counsel with the reality of her life in a town where half the residents were kin. Plenty of people out on county roads didn't even have street addresses. She was pretty sure the two-man Seadrift police force didn't know the first thing about pulling finger-prints off an envelope. The driver's-side window on her trash-filled truck had a nasty habit of slipping down on its own; when it rained, she'd peel off strips of duct tape to hold it in place. Her "office" in Froggie's hadn't had windows that closed or locked for as long as she'd worked there.

"If you feel something is wrong, trust the feeling," was about the only advice she took to heart.

In the fall of 1992, two months after she tried taking her own life, she was out on the *SeaBee* dragging for shrimp when she realized the boat was listing. She threw the hatch open to find the engine nearly submerged in water; all the wires had been yanked from the pump.

Wilson had spent her life out on the water but never learned how to swim. She frantically pumped water out by hand until she had removed enough to repair the pump. She might've radioed for help, but someone had stolen the CB from the *SeaBee* months earlier.

IN EARLY 1993, NEARLY A YEAR AFTER THE HELICOPTER INCIDENT, she was sitting on her front porch, taking in the quiet of the evening, when she heard what sounded like a police scanner in the dark of the forest. She froze.

She heard a rustling sound. Moments later, Domino ambled out, lay down in front of her, and died. She had no money to bring the dog in for testing, but she was convinced he had been poisoned. She dug a grave in the sandy soil and tried to figure out what to tell the kids.

SIX MONTHS LATER, THE NEW FORMOSA PLANT FINALLY WENT ON-line. Wilson, fired from the fish house, was shrimping as much as she could, but her nets kept coming up light.

One day, she drifted in the *SeaBee* over the newly constructed 2,100-

foot-long pipe that ran from the plant into the bay, thinking about the nine million gallons of contaminated wastewater sloshing into the estuary each day through a diffuser at the end of the pipe, just north of where Alcoa's mercury was interred in sediment.

That was just the legal discharge, allowed by the plant's state and federal permits. What spilled accidentally—those she knew about—was even more concerning. A faulty flange leaked twenty-seven hundred gallons of ethylene dichloride into the water. Seven hundred gallons of hydrochloric acid were spilled when bolts sprung loose from a valve. The Texas Water Commission filed a suit against the company after an inspection found a host of violations in how Formosa was storing wastewater, which had contaminated the groundwater. When news leaked that the plant also exceeded its permitted limits on discharging copper into the bay, Formosa claimed it was harmless, prompting Wilson to dig up a 1956 study by a pair of scientists in England demonstrating that copper mixed with mercury rendered water lethal for crustaceans.

By then, she had learned of a then-obscure concept codified in the Clean Water Act known as "zero discharge"—the goal of capturing and treating all waste before any of it was discharged into the environment. She knew a firm in Texas with effective technology that could help Formosa achieve zero discharge, but it was a long shot. The technology was expensive, she had little leverage against the company, and Blackburn was out of the picture.

She was out of allies to help push zero discharge. Apart from her cousin Wally, who kept dropping by to chat, the White shrimpers and crabbers were too worried about blowing their chance at a job in the off-season to stand with her. Even her brothers and uncles groaned when they saw her, ducking behind a net or pretending not to have seen her.

So she went to the Vietnamese.

SHE WALKED INTO THE NET SHOP OF A VIETNAMESE FISHERMAN named Joe Nguyễn, who had been a young man when he arrived in Texas after the fall of Saigon in 1975. He found a job patching shrimp nets up the coast in Palacios for an elderly White owner of a net shop. When the owner died, Joe took over the business. Just up the way, Bằng "Cherry" Nguyễn, the first Vietnamese crabber of Seadrift, was running a shop of his own.

Wilson asked whether he thought the Vietnamese shrimpers would support her.

"Support on what?" Joe asked.

"Keeping the bay clean."

Joe thought they might go for it; they didn't like Formosa, and they respected Wilson as a fellow shrimper.

"Do you think they'd demonstrate?" she asked.

"Be a hippie?" Joe asked, a twinkle in his eye.

"Sure," she said, laughing. "Something like that . . . out on the water."

Joe showed up at Wilson's with three other shrimpers, the elders of the community, who agreed to help. The following morning, at four a.m., the Vietnamese shrimpers were out on their boats, tuned to the VHF channel through which Catholic prayers were transmitted out into the bay. After the benediction, Wilson's plea was put forward.

SHE WAS SHOCKED BY THE RESPONSE. SHE SOON HAD TWO HUN-dred Vietnamese shrimpers and crabbers and their families marching with signs protesting Formosa's pollution of the bay. They marched outside Formosa in T-shirts and white rubber fishing boots, South Vietnamese and American flags waving amid posters demanding zero discharge. Formosa corporate officers in suits glowered at them.

The company soon agreed to meet with the Vietnamese at their community center in Palacios to explain why zero discharge was an unreasonable ask.

THE NIGHT OF THE MEETING, ON JULY 27, 1993, HUNDREDS OF VIET-namese filed into the community center. News crews came down from

Houston to film interviews while Wilson's children raced around the auditorium alongside Vietnamese kids, all wired on soda.

Jack Wu, Formosa's vice president, looked out over the audience and professed surprise. For ten years, he said, Formosa hadn't had any bad experiences with Vietnamese shrimpers. Suddenly, they were protesting about pollution. Why? Joe Wyatt took to the podium. Back when he was a congressman, he had instructed his staff to "tell me the truth. I'll do the lying." In front of the Vietnamese, he exclaimed that zero discharge was a myth: "We know there is this woman in Calhoun County, Diane Wilson, who claims there is a method of treating water with zero-discharge technology. I am here to tell you there is *no such system!*"

At this Joe Nguyễn stood up and silenced Wyatt with a raised hand. He gestured to Wilson and asked her to address the audience. As she approached the microphone, she saw Jack Wu jump to his feet, and wondered if he was going to start a fight.

As she spoke, Formosa's boosters shouted out, "Lies!" and the meeting devolved into chaos.

She was thrilled to have new allies in the Vietnamese community, but she knew that Formosa would weather the bad press. The company had allies of its own, after all. That same month, a group of six hundred— many of them fishermen—had gathered in Port Lavaca to voice their support for the corporation. "We were in such bad shape we didn't know where we were going to get our next meal," said Howdy Hartzog, who had moved on from his role at the bank to become county judge. Now, he added, the county was even thinking about building a golf course. "I would rather eat the shrimp, oysters and redfish out of Lavaca Bay than have to digest the *Houston Chronicle*'s pro-union articles," blasted Port Lavaca mayor Tiney Browning, clearly referring to Wilson's efforts to support Formosa's workers in her negotiations with the company.

A month later, Wilson and a number of Vietnamese shrimpers drove up to Austin to protest the dumping, calling for the revocation of the plant's permits. They hauled a coffin filled with shrimp nets to the office of Governor Ann Richards, asking for a meeting. Denied, they abandoned the coffin in the capitol hallway.

Soon, Wilson was summoned for a meeting with Chairman Wang at a house owned by Formosa near the plant. For three hours, they sparred. When Wang spoke to her, he locked eyes with her. When she fought back, he turned away.

"I can tell you this," she told a reporter after the unproductive meeting, "I have seen the eye of the dragon and it is green."

IN MARCH 1994, TWO MONTHS BEFORE THE OPENING OF SHRIMP-ing season, and nearly five years after first reading about the Toxic Release Inventory and Calhoun County's perch atop the list of America's most polluted places, Wilson decided that she was done following the rules. For all her actions—filing lawsuits against the plants, starving herself to compel them to negotiate, drafting press releases, and strategizing with her lawyer—she had nothing to show for it other than a wasteland of broken relationships. She didn't put faith in Blackburn's agreement with Formosa, she had become an outcast in her own town, and her livelihood of shrimping was more imperiled than ever.

Two quotes beckoned. The first came from Henry David Thoreau, writing in *Walden*: "If I repent of anything, it is very likely to be my good behavior. What demon possessed me that I behaved so well?"

The second, from Edward Abbey, was clipped to a lampshade in her home office: "At some point we must draw a line across the ground of our home and our being, drive a spear into the land, and say to the bulldozers, earth-movers, government and corporations, *thus far and no farther.*"

With no other tools at her disposal, she pulled the *SeaBee* out of the water. So long as she could pull it off before law enforcement found out, she had a plan to turn her trawler into a great weapon, one that might finally do to the plants what they deserved.

## 38

# The *SeaBee*

THE *SEABEE* HAD GIVEN DIANE WILSON A LIVELIHOOD, HELPING her feed her five children. It was her only way of escaping the mess of people and problems on land, if only for a few hours. It was how she communed with the four generations of shrimpers in her family who preceded her, working the same waters.

She dipped a broad brush into a can of white epoxy paint and spent the day applying a fresh coat, like giving the boat a new dress.

"So what are you gonna do?" asked Donna Sue, her best friend, who had worked in the fish house with her for more than a decade, as she painted the back side of the boat. "Go down with the boat or get off first?"

Wilson glanced over her shoulder. She didn't want anyone else overhearing their conversation, but down at the docks, there were no strangers.

"Well," Donna Sue pressed, "you don't swim, so how 'bout [a life] jacket?"

"Nah," Wilson responded after giving it some thought. "Don't see hanging on to any safety net."

"Oh, hell," muttered Donna Sue. "Just drown then. Formosa's gonna be tickled to death."

Wilson could feel a blue norther coming, so she worked quickly. She wanted to get this done before a storm made it impossible.

She asked Donna Sue's husband to hoist the engine from the *SeaBee*. She didn't want a single drop of oil or gas inside, lest her critics accuse *her* of polluting the bay.

Next, he rigged a large wrench on the propeller shaft. When she was ready, all she'd have to do was give it a turn and water would gush into the *SeaBee*.

WITH EDWARD ABBEY'S QUOTE IN MIND, WILSON CONCLUDED THAT the only spear she possessed was her boat. She planned to sink it in the shipping channel directly over Formosa's discharge pipe, figuring it would be her final, desperate act of protest. If she succeeded, she would jam up their ability to move raw materials in and ship out their toxic products. The idea was outrageous, and it made her nearly vomit when it first formed in her head; sinking it was akin to a farmer burning his fields. The *SeaBee* was such a part of her identity that she thought she would probably die soon after it was over.

As soon as Donna Sue's husband finished removing the engine, Wilson asked him if he would tow her in his boat from Seadrift to the plant in Lavaca Bay.

"No ma'am!" He chuckled. Nothing illegal about removing an engine, but he wasn't going to run afoul of the feds. The penalty for deliberately obstructing a waterway was eighteen years in prison and a $500,000 fine. But he'd keep her engine, if she didn't mind.

She started making calls, first to a shrimper who she knew had trafficked his share of drugs along the coast. *Nope.* Same for his brother.

She called a shrimper swimming in debt after a horrible season, offering $500 if he'd tow her to Formosa, but he laughed and talked about the norther: "Ain't worth it!"

She tried Wally Morgan, figuring that since he'd married into the family he'd be sympathetic, but he wanted nothing to do with it.

She asked her ex-husband and got an angry earful about how valuable the boat was.

At last, she called Formosa and asked for her older brother Leslie, the Vietnam War hero who was now working at the plant.

"What are you doin'?" he asked.

"Lookin' for you . . . need you for a little job. I need your boat, too."

"Whaddya want my boat for?"

When she started talking about her plan, he started howling. "You better shut up! Jack Wu's probably got his ear pasted to this phone!"

"I'll shut up after you say yes," she said.

"Don't talk anymore," her brother said.

After a long pause, he said, "I'll see you at the docks."


THEY HEADED OUT IN THE DEAD OF NIGHT, WILSON IN THE *SEABEE*, which was tethered by a thirty-five-foot towline to her big brother's trawler, the *Pee Wee*. She figured it would take about three hours to get to Formosa, but as soon as they maneuvered up the intracoastal waterway toward Lavaca Bay, the fierce norther picked up. Wilson, in a heavy rain slicker and rubber boots, had been anxiously scanning for signs of the Coast Guard, but her mind soon turned to more immediate worries, like submerged reefs or whether the towline would snap. The visibility was so poor that she couldn't even see her brother's boat.

As the storm grew, wind howling over rolling waves like a fast-approaching train, her brother threw his boat into neutral, tugged on the towline, and helped Wilson clamber aboard. No matter what happened, they might as well be together.

"Thinkin' you better thank your lucky stars I'm your brother, 'cause only a big brother would do this for you. And nobody else!" He grinned. Whatever rift had formed between them as a result of her activism closed back up within moments, as rain pounded down on their tiny cabin.

On they motored in pitch black, through submerged marsh, cotton fields to port, the Espiritu Santo Bay to starboard, and beyond that the rolling gulf. After another hour, they made the turn past Port O'Connor north into Lavaca Bay.

The Formosa plant loomed before them, only a mile off. Wilson, exhilarated, squinted through the back cabin window and froze.

"There they are!"

"Holy shit! The Coast Guard? The Coast Guard?" he exclaimed almost giddily.

"More than likely," she said. "They've got flashin' lights . . . three boats."

"Oh hell!" he shouted as rain and waves sprayed the windows. "Turn off that cabin light!" He'd had an infamous run-in with the Texas game wardens a few years back, outrunning them in a shrimp boat when he thought they were about to give him a ticket; he ended up in court on attempted capital murder charges, which were eventually reduced to a misdemeanor. Something about being a navy test pilot with nearly one hundred combat missions under his belt made things like this in his postwar years amusing. He revved the engine, keeping his sights on the Formosa plant, the towline whip-tight as the *SeaBee* bobbed behind them. She never saw him so happy in her life.

Five gnawing minutes passed before a Coast Guard cutter roared alongside them.

A voice boomed through its loudspeaker: "Is Miz Wilson aboard? Do you have a Miz Wilson aboard?"

Wilson stormed out onto the back deck and into the bright flood lights of the Coast Guard's boats. Her brother began making sharp turns, trying to shake them as the *SeaBee* listed behind, but his trawler was no match for their cutters.

They were only a half mile away from Formosa's discharge pipes when one of the Coast Guard boats drew close enough to nearly touch her brother's boat.

"You're tearing up my boat, you moron!" he shouted. "Keep your damn boat off!"

"We are boarding your boat, sir," shouted a young officer.

The officer jumped aboard the boat and stood directly in front of Wilson.

"Ma'am, are you Miz Wilson?"

"I don't recall."

"You don't recall? You don't know if your name is Miz Wilson?"

The officer threw his hands up, stepped into the cabin, and ordered her brother to bring the boat to the docks at Point Comfort: "We have reason to believe you are carrying Miz Wilson, who we believe has terrorist intentions."

On the docks, she was interrogated, threatened with imprisonment, and informed that the *SeaBee* would be confiscated. After a grilling, they sent her brother home in his boat. She would need to spend the night on her boat. Even though it was engineless, three Coast Guard boats were tied up around it, keeping guard.

Sometime around three a.m., she rustled up an oily life jacket as a pillow and stretched out on the floor of the cabin, as old smells of shrimp and diesel wafted up. Her family had pulled thousands of pounds of shrimp, redfish, and crabs up from the depths of these bays for more than a century. The first in her line used sails on a small skiff and hoisted the nets up by hand, just around the time that oil was discovered in Texas. The next generation had the luxury of an engine and a winch. Around the time the third generation set out in trawlers capable of dragging expansive nets, the farmland along the coast yielded to the chemical plants.

As she tried to sleep, her boat surrounded by government forces that viewed her as a terrorist, she gazed out at the chemical plants of Point Comfort. The Alcoa plant had been built the same year she was born. For most of her forty-six years, she had done the only work she knew how to do, trying to wrest from the waters what her ancestors had, but the nets were light and the catch was often sickly. She knew she was the last generation who would fish the water. Something was gone, and it felt permanent.

A FEW HOURS LATER, THE STORM PASSED AND A GRAY DAWN BROKE, and she made out a number of government trucks at the end of the docks. She counted nearly a dozen Coast Guard officers milling about, several with clipboards. She could see the smokestacks of Formosa in the distance and grew irritated.

"Ain't y'all tired just sittin' around, waitin' on me for somethin'? Ain't y'all got nothing better to do?"

"Just making sure you don't go anywhere, Miz Wilson," shouted one of the ensigns.

"Y'all see me standing here with another boat? Where am I goin'?"

She spun around and returned to her cabin, furious at the absurdity of all these officers monitoring her while the plants illegally discharging poison into the bays hummed along.

Just then, a shrimp boat roared up alongside the docks. As it motored past, a White shrimper raised his fist through the port window in solidarity. She thought it was a mirage, until she heard the engine of another trawler approaching, with another shrimper pumping his fist.

The smell of their diesel would never fade from her memory. More and more trawlers appeared on the horizon, nets swaying in the wind as they jammed the channel. There was her brother, back in the *Pee Wee* with a broad smile on his face. Moments later, an armada of Vietnamese shrimpers from Palacios made the turn into the bay, joining their White counterparts in support of the lone female shrimper of Seadrift.

She watched alarmed Coast Guard officers scramble aboard their boats and shove off to break apart the blockade. They darted back and forth, boarding boats and writing citations, but the shrimpers refused to leave.

Soon, a helicopter landed on a bluff overlooking the bay and a news crew scrambled out. TV news trucks arrived and cameramen crowded onto the docks.

Had the Vietnamese and White shrimpers not shown up to block the shipping channel, making it a juicy enough story for the press, Wilson probably would've been arrested that day.

Instead, she got a call from her old lawyer, Jim Blackburn, who said Formosa wanted to talk. They were sick of the endless rounds of bad press wrought by her antics.

Before long, she was sitting in a corporate conference room across from Jack Wu, who asked her what she wanted.

## 39

# The Whistleblower

ZERO DISCHARGE. WHAT ELSE WAS THERE TO DEMAND? WILSON brought Jack Matson, an engineer who had pioneered the technology, and fixed her eyes on the Formosa executives as he laid out the process. She'd been the burr in their saddle for five years now, but it was the first time she felt they were listening.

Jack Wu turned to her with his own set of demands. If they embraced the technology, would she drop the various lawsuits and petitions she'd filed? Would she put an end to the hunger strikes, the marches, the meetings, the speeches?

It seemed like a fair enough trade. She wasn't going to fast the plant out of existence, but forcing them to invest in zero discharge felt like something resembling victory.

The Wilson-Formosa Zero Discharge Agreement soon led to the recycling of three of the plant's waste streams, removing 32 percent of the discharge in the bay.

A month later, she walked into Alcoa with a question: "Will you sign a zero discharge agreement with me or do we do the whole thing over?" Alcoa's plant manager stared out the window at Formosa next door and, after a pregnant pause, said, "I believe that's doable."

———

WALLY MORGAN CALLED HER UP WITH SOMETHING HEAVY IN HIS voice, asking if they could meet. As soon as she sat down across from her cousin, he confessed that Formosa had been paying him $65,000 a year to spy on her and report back to them.

It was Wally who had tipped off Formosa about her plans to sink the *SeaBee*. It was Wally who told them when she was planning marches, and who else was expected to show.

She was shocked, but she understood it. She couldn't keep from laughing when he asked her if she would take on Union Carbide next— he wanted to pitch his services to them.

At some point, unable to afford a new engine or the harbor space, she had the *SeaBee* towed out to an artificial reef and sunk alongside other ancient boats. After that, she could only afford a little skiff, which she used to trotline for black drum. Every time she motored past her old trawler, there was a little bit less of it. Each norther took it down a bit more. Boards were breaking off, paint blistering on those that remained.

But she didn't quit her fight for the bays. She sneaked into the Union Carbide plant, climbed a seventy-foot tower, and chained herself to it in protest of its pollution. After they cut the chains, the police threw her in a squad car; she spent the next four months in the county jail where Sáu and Chính Văn Nguyễn had once slept, after the district attorney called her a "dangerous woman." When she got out, she flew to Delaware and did another thirty-day hunger strike, in front of DuPont's headquarters.

Five years after signing it, she pulled out of her agreement with Formosa: a 32 percent reduction was nice, but it sure wasn't the same as zero discharge.

It wasn't until a decade later that she got the call that would finally deliver her first real taste of justice.

LATE ONE MORNING IN THE WINTER OF 2009, WILSON CLIMBED into her cherry-red Chevy pickup and drove out of town, passing Union

Carbide and the Seadrift Coke smelters before taking the country road down to Rockport, a hardscrabble fishing town an hour to the south. She'd received a phone call from someone who wanted to speak with her about Formosa, but only in the privacy of a run-down bar called the Hideout.

She drove past Veterans Memorial Park, once the site of the "world's largest crab," a twenty-two-foot-wide blue crab made of papier-mâché and chicken wire erected in the sixties, ravaged by hurricanes over the next decade, and finally torn down after authorities discovered that the hollowed innards of the crustacean were a favorite stash site for drug dealers.

She passed one RV park after another until she eased into the parking lot of the Hideout, a low-slung bar with faded smoke-blue paint a block from the water's edge. She was sixty-one, and awfully tired of these meetings. Over the decades, her activism had led scores of informants, current and former plant workers, to call her with tips about what they'd seen, but more often than not these rendezvous were dead ends. Workers wanted to vent about the sloppy way chemicals were disposed of, but when she asked them to stick their necks out, they vanished.

But this guy sounded different.

Her eyes struggled for a moment to adjust to the darkness of the bar, which was seemingly lit only by neon Budweiser and Miller Lite signs. Behind the bartender hung a sign: WILD HOGS FOR SALE: CONTACT JESSIE. The tip jar was wrapped in Mardi Gras beads, the tables had peeling paint, and the chairs looked painfully uncomfortable. She smiled: if a hurricane hit a bar like this, they'd probably just open the doors, wait for the water to drain back out to the bay, and fire up the jukebox.

A man in a cowboy hat sitting by himself in the corner waved her over. He had a horseshoe mustache, weather-cracked skin, and deep-set, wary-looking eyes. When she sat down, he asked her to open her purse so that he could check for a wire. She laughed and handed it over with a "Hop to it."

The man introduced himself as Dale Jurasek. He had started working as a chemical technician operator at Formosa's original plant in 1983, shortly after graduating from Calhoun High. He worked on the plant's expansion in the early nineties, and graduated up the ranks to lead operator. When something bad happened at the plant, he told her, he was the first one they called to take over.

For most of his career, he'd worried about the exposure to chemicals he knew caused cancer, and frequently saw fellow employees throw up just from being hit with a gas, but he accepted the stark trade-off of the job: "Go in there, do what you gotta do, and keep your mouth shut about it."

Despite the great salary, there were things that pricked his conscience. The plant was obligated to sample streams of water for twenty-four hours, which would then be assessed by the Texas Water Commission. When Jurasek went to gather the five-gallon bottle one morning, the bottom quarter was sludge. His superiors told him to "dump it out and refill it with good water."

When Jurasek refused, saying, "That's against the law . . . I'm not going to jail for Formosa," his superior grabbed the bottle, dumped it onto the concrete, and refilled it with clean water.

Other days, he saw chemicals washed down through the storm sewer, shot straight down to the bay.

He told Formosa that they had problems, but what was he going to do? Every worker at the plant knew just how replaceable they were: hundreds of people in the county would jump at the chance to take their jobs.

"When you start breaking laws," he said, "you start to wonder what's right and what's wrong."

A series of explosions at the plant just four years earlier, in 2005, had shut down the entire town of Point Comfort. As the fires reached 150 feet into the sky, kicking black smoke over the town, alarms blared and workers fled from the site. Residents a block away could feel the heat from the fires as ambulances sped off with severely burned workers. Students at Point Comfort Elementary School waiting for the buses when the explosion occurred had to shelter in place; terrified parents were unable to get through roadblocks.

The Formosa plant in Point Comfort, Texas, on fire in 2005.

The local paper reported that there were "no signs of hazardous materials produced" by the explosions, but Jurasek knew better; he'd seen vinyl chloride monomer readings at the school well over the threshold limit. He was a father himself, and it enraged him to think that these schoolkids were sitting in the middle of it for eight hours a day.

He began researching the chemicals that were being dumped into the bay and read that it could cause deformities and cancer in children, but that it would likely affect the next generation down.

"They have no right!" he exclaimed. "None whatsoever. Especially when you're talking children. You don't *ever* fuck with children. That's the rule!"

He had called the Environmental Protection Agency, and within a couple of days, agents from both the EPA and the FBI knocked on his front door. After he told them what he knew, they asked him to start clipping a pager on his hip. Cell phones weren't permitted at the plant, but nobody minded a worker with a pager. Formosa didn't realize that the pager had a miniature recorder inside.

He felt terrible feeding information to the feds, recording his friends talking about what they were seeing at the plant, but he wanted things to be run properly, and he was racked with guilt for putting the children of Calhoun County in jeopardy.

"These people need to be dealt with, and dealt with severe," he said. "You walk in with and gun a rob a place, they put your ass in jail. These men are dumping chemicals into the bay and killing people—what's the difference?"

After three years, the FBI built a substantial case against Formosa, but they didn't prosecute. Experts believed that the case lost momentum because a similar case brought against Koch Industries had recently foundered.

He was furious that the feds dropped the case, but toward the end of his career at Formosa, his anger was replaced by pain. He was aching all over, and sores and boils began to emerge on his neck. After six months of tests, his doctor rattled off a list of chemicals and asked if Jurasek was familiar with any of them. "Yeah," he muttered, "I work with every one of them." He was diagnosed with "chronic exposure to neurotoxic solvents."

When word eventually got out that he had blown the whistle on Formosa, albeit unsuccessfully, he began receiving threats: loosened lug nuts on his truck, menacing phone calls from anonymous people, shots fired at his home. Once, when he was out fishing on the river, four other fishermen beat the hell out of him. He started carrying a .45 in the back of his britches, and kept a sawed-off shotgun within reach. He was living in constant fear.

Wilson had heard stories like this for years, but it wasn't until well into their hushed conversation at the Hideout that winter morning that Jurasek told her something that shocked her. He asked her what she knew about "nurdles," the tiny pellets that serve as the building blocks of most products made of plastic. Compared with the liquid and gaseous chemicals dumped by the plant, they seemed insignificant, but they accounted for some 85 percent of all plastic pollution on the shorelines. Early research showed that nurdles eventually grow porous, absorbing industrial chemicals, pesticides, toxins, and dangerous bacteria like *E. coli*. It wasn't hard to see how they might enter the food chain.

After leaving Formosa, Jurasek spent much of his free time fishing in Cox Creek, a stream running behind the plant into Lavaca Bay. Twelve outfall points ran directly from the plant into the brackish water of the creek. He noticed that every time one of his kids waded into the water, they emerged with nurdles clinging to their feet and ankles.

Jurasek knew that Formosa wasn't reporting these spills. Having been let down by the FBI and the EPA, he approached Wilson for her help. With his health deteriorating, he wanted to see some kind of justice done before he died.

Jurasek took her to Cox Creek and the two poked around, quickly finding the plastic pellets in the muck, clinging to blades of grass, baking in the sun on the banks. She thought of the fisherman she'd met in Taiwan, surrounded in his tiny shack by thousands of water samples sealed in little glass jars. A plan formed in her mind.

Wilson and Jurasek recruited and trained other volunteers to gather evidence. By this point in her activism, she knew enough about the law and how regulators functioned that a simple he-said-she-said argument would never survive Formosa's lawyers.

Nearly every week for the next seven years, she went out to gather

Diane Wilson with a handful of nurdles dumped in the bay by Formosa.

nurdles, walking the shoreline and running her hand through the grass, plucking out the bits of plastic like crime scene evidence. Alongside Jurasek and other volunteers, she kayaked into channels past lurking alligators with a pocket full of Ziploc bags to collect more nurdles, marking down the date and time of capture.

By 2016, Wilson had filled a barn on her property with nearly thirty million nurdles. As she walked past the bins filled with tens of thousands of little baggies, she thought of her old attorney Blackburn's 1992 agreement with Formosa. No wonder they'd been so thrilled to sign it—it was toothless. Sinking the *SeaBee* nearly twenty years earlier had produced a similarly hollow pledge for zero discharge.

This time, though, she had more than the mere threat of bad press. She had evidence. She found a new lawyer, who was shocked by what she and Jurasek had painstakingly gathered, and filed a new suit.

# 40

# Justice

IN JULY 2017, DIANE WILSON FILED A SUIT AGAINST FORMOSA UN-der an unusual provision in the Clean Water Act allowing private citizens to sue for compliance when state regulators fail to do so. It would take another two years before her day in court.

The weekend before the trial, Vietnamese and White fishermen protested outside the plant, waving American and South Vietnamese flags and signs emblazoned with the word STOP.

On the first day of the trial, Wilson pulled up to the courthouse with a trailer piled high with bins containing the thirty million nurdles. Kenneth Hoyt, the federal judge overseeing the trial, allowed them to store the bins in the basement of the courthouse.

At the outset, Wilson's attorneys made clear that even though many were ill from what they suspected was exposure to Formosa's toxins, the plaintiffs were not seeking any monetary damages for themselves. They wanted Formosa to pay to clean up the bays, and figured $184 million was an appropriate figure.

Jurasek testified about his two decades of work at the plant and his disabled nervous system. Oceanographers testified about how nurdles were capable of carrying toxic mercury. Lawyers for Formosa argued that the pellets were "inert" and released only in "trace amounts."

But Formosa's assurances weren't worth as much as they used to be. Just a year earlier, a Formosa steel plant in Hà Tĩnh province along the north-central coast of Vietnam used three hundred tons of chemicals—among them, cyanide—to clean a wastewater pipe running into the sea. Several days later, a mass fish die-off occurred as millions of fish washed ashore along 120 miles of beaches. Hundreds of people fell ill from eating poisoned fish. Fishing grounds were closed and fishing communities were devastated.

Two months after the disaster, the Vietnamese government still hadn't identified the source of the poison, although everyone suspected Formosa. As the scope of the disaster grew, protesters demanded action: thousands began marching in cities and fishing villages. The government responded with mass arrests and beatings before finally acknowledging that aquatic life had been poisoned, warning people not to eat fish, and banning fishing altogether. In compensation, they gave fishermen bags of rice and a cash gift of 50,000 dong: $2.20.

"You have to decide whether to catch fish and shrimp or to build a modern steel industry," a Formosa representative told reporters after the spill. "Even if you are the prime minister, you cannot choose both." The company finally admitted its responsibility in Vietnam and pledged $500 million to clean up the area, promising to start adopting cleaner methods in its plant.

Three years later, the bodies of thirty-nine Vietnamese people were discovered in the back of a refrigerated truck in an industrial park in Essex, England. Many of the deceased, who had hired a "snakehead" to smuggle them to the UK, hailed from Hà Tĩnh province, which was economically ravaged by the Formosa disaster.

Wilson could tell Formosa was squirming. She felt proud about the case being laid out, but there was one testimony that stood out.


IN THE LATE 1980s, RICHARD HAIGHT WAS DRIVING THE SEADRIFT garbage truck in the Vietnamese part of town when he saw two Vietnamese men framing out a shrimp boat on their front lawn. He felt bad for them; they had only hand axes and hammers.

When he got off his shift, he loaded up an industrial saw that had been sitting in his garage for years and drove it over to them. They were thrilled at the gesture, and quickly put it to work.

Haight never mentioned that he recognized the older man measuring cuts for his new boat as one of the Vietnamese who'd fled the home he'd firebombed the night Billy Joe Aplin was killed a decade earlier. They didn't seem to recognize him as the arsonist; he was just a nice White guy helping them out. It made him feel good. That, and the fact that nobody ever talked about what they'd done that night within the ten-year window of the state's statute of limitations governing arson. Some White residents of Seadrift subsequently shunned him for helping the Vietnamese, but he didn't mind. For years after that, whenever he passed by that family's home, they would run out with a meal of fried fish or shrimp.

The feelings of guilt kept bubbling up, though, and eventually he found a therapist. He told him what he'd done, how it had felt to see the Vietnamese children running out of the burning home after he and the others let their Molotov cocktails fly. His therapist told him to make a list of all the good things that had happened in his life, and then all the bad things he'd done. When he finished, he was to stick the paper in a bottle, set it afire, say a prayer, and he'd be all right.

He began writing it all down, storing it in a roll-top desk in his apartment, but before he had a chance to burn it, an electrical fire started in the floor above him. The fire department sprayed so much water into the building that it flooded his apartment, taking his confession with it.

IN JULY 2018, HAIGHT HAD A CRAVING FOR FISH. SINCE RETIRING, he'd moved up to Port Lavaca, on the western edge of the bay where Wilson had staged her first hunger strike. He didn't fish very often; his boat and crab traps were all things of the shadowy past. He went into his garage and found a rod and reel shrouded in cobwebs, and headed down to Magnolia Beach on the southern shore of the bay, across from the Formosa plant.

He reeled in a twenty-six-inch redfish and a twenty-one-inch trout. The redfish looked fine, but the trout was in bad shape, sluggish and without any fight. Haight wasn't about to make a meal of a sick fish, but before throwing it back in, he realized he'd run out of bait. He grabbed a knife and cut the trout open to see if it had any usable bait in its guts.

His eyes bulged. The trout was full of plastic pellets a little smaller than a pencil eraser, some of them white, some of them green. Along with the plastic, the trout's belly was full something that looked like white sawdust. He tamped the pellets and sawdust into a water bottle and gave Diane Wilson a call.

A year later, he provided sworn testimony about what he'd found in his trout. Wilson, who had seen Haight and so many of her fellow Sea-drifters go mad over the arrival of the Vietnamese shrimpers, was proud of him. It was nice to see him fighting the right villain.

AT THE END OF THE TRIAL, JUDGE HOYT TOLD FORMOSA'S ATTOR-neys that if he found the company guilty, the penalty phase of the trial would be held in public hearings so that the community could attend.

"I'm just warning you right now if you're going to settle the case, call me right away," the judge said.

"Not much chance of that, Judge," Formosa's lawyer responded.

In late 2019, thirty years after she first became aware of the extent of the toxic dumping in Seadrift and along the Gulf Coast, Diane Wilson was awarded $50 million in a settlement with Formosa Plastics. In approving the agreement, Judge Hoyt described Formosa as a "serial offender," with over a thousand days of accidents.

"I know what justice feels like," Wilson exclaimed. "It's Christmas in July!"

The agreement was historic: the largest in US history stemming from a private citizen's lawsuit against an industrial polluter. The money would go toward mitigating pollution, habitat restoration, and other environmental efforts.

Formosa released a statement promising to "implement a range of improvements to the wastewater and stormwater discharge facilities." An executive vice president said that the conditions of the settlement agreement "demonstrate Formosa's commitment to manufacturing our products in a safe and environmentally friendly manner."

Some of the trees in front of Point Comfort Elementary School that Formosa vice president Jack Wu planted on Earth Day in 1990 are still there, but the kids are gone. Facing a loss of tax revenue created in large part by all the tax abatements granted to Formosa, the district closed the school. Formosa soon bought the school and subsumed it into its operations. The company also bought all the homes in Point Comfort, where it is now the landlord to those who have spent their entire lives there.

Many in town believed that Wilson was suddenly a multimillionaire, but she didn't receive a penny of the settlement. She still lives on $425 a month from Social Security and, now that she's in her seventies, finally has health insurance through Medicare.

The shrimpers and others who bad-mouthed her over the decades now look to her as the only person capable of saving the bays. Every few weeks, she gathers White and Vietnamese fishermen to discuss how the settlement money can revitalize their beleaguered industry. After a lifetime of condemning the idea as communist, they're finally forming a co-op, pooling their catches to barter for higher prices rather than competing against one another. They are getting a new fish house and a new icehouse, and replacing much of the infrastructure that has collapsed or rotted away over the years.

Even though the suit is long over, Wilson and Jurasek still meet by the boat ramp at Cox Creek to paddle off in search of more pellets.

CHAIRMAN WANG DIED AT NINETY-ONE IN 2008, WITH A PERSONAL fortune of $5.5 billion. At his funeral, a deathbed letter was read to a crowd of thousands: "My children . . . although wealth is something everyone loves to have, nobody is born with it, nor can it be taken with them when they leave this earth. My conviction has grown that the greatest meaning and value in life lies in giving your all to contribute to the beauty and betterment of society. I hope that all of my sons and daughters can fully understand the true meaning of life . . . to leave my wealth for all of society. I hope the company I've founded in this lifetime will be managed with sustainability in mind, and be a blessing for employees and society in the long run." Upon his death, some $20 billion in assets was discovered to have been hidden in foreign tax shelters.

In April 2021, Wilson began yet another thirty-day hunger strike at the mouth of Lavaca Bay, in an appeal to the Biden administration to halt the dredging of the bay for a new shipping channel that would allow for deeper-draft oil tankers to enter. Nearly fifty years after Billy Joe Aplin wrote to his fellow shrimpers begging them to confront the mercury dumped into the bay by Alcoa in the 1960s, Wilson was doing everything possible to keep the dredgers from stirring up the toxic waste. She lowered herself into a coffin on a boat trailer and warned that the bay would ruin their fledgling efforts to revive the local fishing industry.

The day after she was arrested and spent a night in jail, Wilson emerged, her voice frail.

"I got a new mugshot," she said. "They're not going to take the bay from me."

IN JUNE 2021, FORMOSA VICE PRESIDENT JACK WU ASKED CALHOUN County for a new round of tax abatements for another massive expansion to its Point Comfort plant.

With the White and Vietnamese fishermen at her back, Wilson is preparing for another fight.

# Epilogue

I N AUGUST 1981, JUST A FEW MONTHS AFTER JUDGE McDONALD'S injunction, *The Thunderbolt*, the newsletter of the National States Rights Party, ran two articles on its front page. The first was a call to stop legal immigration, focusing on Vietnamese refugees and the economic threat they posed. The second, titled "Keep Refugees Out—Build the American Wall," included an elaborate schematic for a border wall design, with electrified fences, antipersonnel mines, pressure-trigger mines, floodlights, and runways for guard dogs. Ever since the Immigration and Nationality Act of 1965 ended the lawful cyclical immigration of hundreds of thousands of Mexican agricultural workers, turning those who stayed into "illegal immigrants" overnight, the issue had become a potent rallying cry for the extreme right wing. "The Berlin Wall keeps people in, but we desperately need an American Wall to keep Mexicans out...."

From his hideout in the Aryan Nations compound in Idaho, Louis Beam was at work on publications of his own. "Fellow patriots," he wrote in the months after bolting from Texas in 1982, "we have for the first time in many years, been able to take an active hand in the affairs of the state." He claimed credit for the legislation capping new shrimping permits, and described the ninety-day deadline he issued at the Klan rally at Jody Collins's ranch as "the speech that churned the gulf."

Beam characterized the campaign of violence and harassment of the Vietnamese as "guerrilla theater," capable of being replicated anywhere: "The 'plot' must be carefully planned; each actor must know his part, and the 'scenes' carefully rehearsed." He heralded "White Victory," but outlined the substantial legal fees his battle with the "anti-Christ communist jew" Morris Dees had produced, and got to the point: "The heavens do not open and rain money into my hands. That is not god's duty. It is yours." He asked his supporters to "call forth the courage and strength that flows through your veins," and donate the financial equivalent of one hour a week of their labor to him.

In between fundraising appeals, Beam put out the *Inter-Klan Newsletter & Survival Alert*. "Being sued by the anti-Christ Morris Dees?" one newsletter asked. "Give us the complete background and case history so we can pass it on to other Klansmen." At the end of each newsletter was an order form. A cassette of "the speech that churned the gulf" could be had for just $4. For $7.50, subscribers could lay their hands on the thing Beam had dedicated so much of his time to since being run out of Texas: his first book, titled *Essays of a Klansman*.

Beam wrote about the betrayal he felt from his government after the loss of the Vietnam War and the constant threat of FBI infiltration, but he couldn't resist devoting a chapter to Dees, quoting from a recent publication of the Southern Poverty Law Center's Klanwatch program, which described the "dangerous alliances . . . being formed between the Aryan Nations, the Canadian Klan, and the Texas Klan of Louis Beam."

"Does Morris Dees perceive something that perhaps you do not?" Beam challenged his reader. "Soon once again, a home, a place of refuge, a state for our people will exist. . . . Are you ready to fight for your Nation? If so, become part of the 'Dangerous Alliance.'"

Dees was a useful foil to solicit money from Beam's followers, but Beam had loftier ambitions. His writings offered an ideological framework and tactical guidance to White supremacists, who were increasingly turning their sights on the federal government. "It is becoming clear . . .

that the greatest threat to freedom and liberty in America is the Washington D.C. government," Beam's *Inter-Klan Newsletter & Survival Alert* warned. "For those of us who truly love this country it is time to give the politicians in Washington what they gave the veterans of Vietnam—WAR." Among the features of Beam's book: "a graph that outlines who the enemy is and . . . a 'proposed point system' for their execution." Each murder counted for a fraction of a point; killing a Jew earned one-sixth. Only one assassination— of the president of the United States—was worth a full point. A "true Aryan warrior" had to kill enough people to earn a full point.

SHORTLY AFTER BEAM ARRIVED AT THE ARYAN NATIONS COMPOUND, a small group of men formed an offshoot cell dedicated to revolution against the federal government and to the creation of a separate state in the Pacific Northwest exclusively for Whites. The group, known as the Order, was led by a neo-Nazi rancher from Washington state named Robert Mathews.

Mathews gave each member *Essays of a Klansmen*, along with an essay of Beam's, titled "Leaderless Resistance," which argued that the best way to evade the grip of the law was to operate in a lone-wolf fashion. In Mathews's grand vision, Beam, with the nom de guerre Lone Star, would be the future civilian leader of the "Western district" of America after the government was overthrown by White supremacists.

The Order began casting about for ways to bankroll its forthcoming war. Mathews robbed a bank in Seattle and made off with $26,000 in cash, most of it ruined by an exploding dye pack slipped into the bag by the teller. Then he stole $230,000 from an armored truck; then $3.6 million from a Brink's truck in Ukiah, California.

Mathews had a dream of unifying the disparate White supremacist groups into one terrifying force, invulnerable to government crackdown— and the Brink's haul was the glue. He directed $100,000 to finance a vision of Louis Beam's about the potential of an emerging technology.

"It may very well be that American know-how has provided the technology which will allow those who love this country to save it," Beam wrote in the opening pages of the 1984 *Inter-Klan Newsletter & Survival Alert.* "Computers, once solely the domain and possession of governments and large corporations, are now bringing their power and capabilities to the average American. . . . A computer, when connected to a modem (a telephone for computers) possesses the ability to access virtually unlimited amounts of information.

"Imagine . . . a single computer to which all leaders and strategists of the patriotic movement are connected. Imagine further that any patriot in the country is able to tap into this computer at will in order to reap the benefit of all accumulative knowledge and wisdom of the leaders. 'Someday,' you may say? How about *today?* . . . We hereby announce Aryan Nation Liberty Net."

Beam's bulletin board system had a five-dollar fee for joining. When new users dialed in, they could choose from various sections. In the "Know Your Enemy" section, the names and addresses were posted of members of the Anti-Defamation League identified as "informers" and "race traitors." Pressing 8 would pull up "MORRIS DEES QUEER," which retrieved the following message: "According to the word of our God, Morris Dees has earned two (2) death sentences."

The Order kept a hit list of its highest-value targets for assassination. Morris Dees was in first place, but Alan Berg, a Denver talk-show host who frequently mocked the extreme right wing, was the first to be assassinated: staked outside his home in June 1984, Mathews flung the door for one of his deputies to rake him with a MAC-10.

For Dees, though, the Order's plan was more elaborate than a driveway shooting: "We've gathered good intelligence on him . . . we're going to kidnap him and then we'll torture him and get as much information out of him as we can," Mathews told his followers. "And when we have that, we'll kill him, and bury him and pour lye over him."

DEES KNEW HE HAD KICKED THE HORNET'S NEST WITH THE VIETnamese shrimpers' suit. In early 1983, he received a letter from Beam challenging him to "a duel to the death. You against me. No federal judges, no federal marshals, no F.B.I. agents, not anyone except yourself and I. We go into the woods (your state or mine) and settle once and for all the enmity that exists between us. Two go in—one comes out."

Dees was momentarily tempted by the challenge. But there were far better—and more profitable—ways to fight him. After a US attorney concluded that the letter wasn't a clear-cut expression of intent to injure, Dees shared the letter with potential donors to the Southern Poverty Law Center as a way of underscoring the danger he was in as a result of taking on the Klan.

A few months later, in the middle of the night of July 28, 1983, a pickup truck eased to a stop on South McDonough Street in Montgomery. Two twenty-one-year-old men, shouldering worn canvas bags holding flashlights, brown gloves, duct tape, a small garden sprayer, and a container of gasoline, dismounted from the truck and slipped down into the city's sewer system.

As the two men made their way through the sewer lines, they marked their path with spray paint, emerging just behind the Southern Poverty Law Center. One of the men stuck a piece of duct tape against a window and tapped it gently with a tire iron, breaking the glass quietly, before darting back to a nearby bush to wait for an alarm. Hearing none, they crept inside the center, filled the garden sprayer with gas, and began to spray.

Just before four a.m., Dees was startled awake by a ringing telephone.

"Hello?" he mumbled, his stomach already tightening. Nothing good ever came from a call at that hour.

"This is the Montgomery Fire Department, Mr. Dees. The Law Center is on fire."

In the thirteen years since they'd been in operation, the center had already accumulated a mountain of pleadings, depositions, newspaper clippings, and case notes, all jammed into cardboard boxes and stored in a wood-and-brick building that had once been a dentist's office. Even without their roster of arson-inclined enemies, the center was a natural fire hazard.

In the months leading up to that phone call, they had begun storing their sensitive documents in fireproof cabinets, and had hired a security guard to watch the building at night. As Dees raced to get dressed, he wondered whether the guard had flicked a cigarette and inadvertently started the fire. Could it have been the result of faulty wiring?

He jammed a revolver into his back pocket and sped a hundred miles per hour from his farm into Montgomery. Before he even got into town, he had ruled out any possibility of an accident. *This was arson*, he thought, and he even had a suspect in mind: Joe Garner, a volunteer fire chief and Klansman he'd deposed two months earlier.

By the time Dees arrived at the center, there was a low-hanging blanket of smoke over the building. As much as he pleaded, the firefighters would not let him enter. He sat down on a nearby curb and planted his face on his knees. The building was still standing, but he felt sick. He quickly learned that the security guard had skipped work that night to work another job.

When the fire was finally extinguished, law enforcement allowed Dees and his team to enter. The fire's point of origin was Randall Williams's office, over which a large sign hung: KLANWATCH. The heat was so intense that the ceiling had collapsed onto the floor. Williams's venetian blinds melted. Of all the posters hanging on the wall, the only one that had been ripped down was a blown-up photo of the Klan boat patrol, taken on the morning it churned along the Seabrook waterfront to Colonel Nam's house.

The arsonists had doused several file folders in gasoline and torched them, but failed to destroy several filing cabinets filled with thousands of KKK photographs, videotapes, and computer disks holding the names and addresses of thousands of Klansmen and neo-Nazis. If they had knocked out a few windows for ventilation, the whole building would have burned to the ground.

The large banker's box holding all the depositions and case files for *Vietnamese Fishermen's Association v. Knights of the Ku Klux Klan* survived, narrowly, but as Dees waded through the wreckage, his eyes fell upon the large clock in the shape of Vietnam that Nam and the other shrimpers had given to him after their victory in court. It was charred but still recognizable. Dees picked it up and set it on a desk covered in soot.

*The New York Times* ran a story on the fire, and checks began pouring in to help the center rebuild. A $25,000 reward for any information leading to the arrest of the arsonists was offered. Before long, the center announced plans for a million-dollar building, with an electronic security gate, a high-pressure sprinkler system, and a state-of-the-art security vault for its files.

A YEAR LATER, IN 1984, ROBERT MATHEWS GAVE $75,000 FROM THE Brink's haul to Frazier Glenn Miller, a forty-two-year-old former Green Beret and then–Grand Dragon of the North Carolina Ku Klux Klan, with instructions to kill Dees.

A couple of weeks after that, Bill Stanton, head of investigations for the center, received a call from the receptionist. There was an unexpected television crew in the lobby.

Stanton couldn't mask his alarm at the sight of Louis Beam in the lobby of the Southern Poverty Law Center.

"I can see by the look on your face you know who I am," said Beam, who wore a gray pin-striped suit and a lavalier microphone clipped to his blue tie.

"I'd like to interview Mr. Dees." The camera was rolling. Stanton looked at the crew and recognized Thom Robb, the national chaplain of the Klan who'd been among those who spoke at the Billy Joe Aplin memorial rally in Seabrook. Stanton couldn't see any sign of weapons on the men, but he slipped off to call the police.

When he returned, Beam's cameraman was focused on an artist's rendering of the new building the organization was planning to build in the wake of the arson.

"You're going to have to leave here immediately," Stanton said to Beam.

Beam continued to film outside the building. When Stanton approached him again, Beam said, "Sir, we will no longer be intimidated.

We are bringing the war to you." He hopped into a red Lincoln Continental and drove off.

Dees sensed something closing in rapidly on his personal freedom. One of the center's paid Klan informants confirmed that Beam had filmed outside Dees's property during his time in Montgomery, and that a Canadian neo-Nazi cocaine smuggler had been asking all kinds of questions about his car and the route he took to work. And then an agent from the FBI called Dees with an urgent message: "We have information of a serious threat on your life. I'm not authorized to tell you more."

The center made the decision to provide "wall-to-wall" security for Dees and his family. Protective fencing and floodlights would be mounted around his ranch; for the foreseeable future, he would make no movements without an armed guard. Starting at $20,000 a month, his security would become the organization's single largest expense.

In something of a farewell before the guard detail began, Dees mounted his motorcycle and tore off down country roads. He opened up the throttle, bringing the bike to 120 miles per hour. In the past, he savored the cocktail of fear and exhilaration that such a speed served up, but on his last solo run, he felt no fear. Now he felt as though riding his bike solo was the last time he'd be in total control—the true fear would come from living with the knowledge that people were actively planning to assassinate him.

By October 1984, the center had been transformed into a bunker. There were armed guards out front at every hour of the day. The doors could only be electronically unlocked from the inside. Panic buttons and strategically placed shotguns proliferated throughout the building. Randall Williams, considered one of the most likely targets after Dees, was issued a weapon. Stanton called Dees into his office to show him the latest posting on Louis Beam's bulletin board system. On top of other death threats against Dees, Beam was now selling copies of a one-hour video of his trip to Montgomery for $10. In the Montgomery heat, Dees, Williams, and others began squeezing into body armor.

On December 3, one of the new guards patrolling the perimeter of Dees's ranch spotted two men wading through the high grass of the back pasture with small flashlights. They bolted before the guard could apprehend them.

On December 12, the Montgomery County district attorney announced indictments against several Alabama Klansmen in connection to the burning of the Southern Poverty Law Center a year and a half earlier, among them Joe Garner, the man Dees had suspected all along. As it turned out, Louis Beam had paid Garner a visit during his trip to Montgomery. Dees told reporters that while he welcomed the indictments, he was certain that the arson order went "far beyond" Alabama, referencing the Vietnamese shrimpers case.

Four days after the press conference, on December 16, Dees cut a cedar down from a grove on his ranch and hauled it into the house. That evening, his fourteen-year-old daughter, Ellie, unpacked the Christmas ornaments as E.T., a heavily armed security guard with a two-way radio, stood in the corner. Dees tried to lighten the mood by talking about the holly wreaths he'd once sold in college, when the voice of a guard outside crackled through the radio.

"Jesus Christ, there's someone out here! Do you read me? There's someone on the property!"

Dees raced over to the bookcase and grabbed a Beretta. He gave a Browning .22 pistol to his daughter. E.T., a former police officer, rushed them into the pantry, the house's designated safe room. "Stay on the floor and don't come out until I tell you," he barked.

"There were two of them," the outside guard reported. "I think I see one in the bushes."

"Shoot the bastard," E.T. radioed back.

"Shoot the motherfucker!" Dees shouted as he huddled with his daughter, but the guard outside was reluctant. Over the radio, they heard him addressing one of the gunmen. "Sir, would you please step out so I can escort you off the property?"

"What's this escort bullshit?" E.T. radioed. "Shoot him fast before he moves."

"I don't want to shoot," the guard outside responded. "What if it's a hunter?"

"It's almost midnight. That's no hunter!" cried Dees.

When the FBI and sheriff arrived, a deputy found a piece of camouflage cloth on the road. The officers fanned out in search of the gunmen, but they had long since vanished into a thousand acres of forest.

After that, a guard building was erected on the property, along with a gun range for the team of guards, four-wheel vehicles, and even more floodlights and security cameras.

The center needed more money.

In 1985, the Southern Poverty Law Center moved into its gleaming new headquarters, a futuristic bunker in the heart of Montgomery on the same block as Martin Luther King Jr.'s Dexter Avenue Baptist Church.

"I see a very bright future," wrote Dees in an internal memo, but the staff's morale was dispiritingly low, and it had to with his obsession with fundraising off the specter of an ever-expanding Klan. Donations were pouring in, tens of thousands of dollars a day and climbing fast, in great big stacks just like during the glory days of Fuller and Dees. But instead of hyping tractor cushions and rat poison, he was selling an idea to donors—most of them from the north and the coasts—that their money could help knock racists on their heels.

One woman in need of a new overcoat for winter decided to contribute her meager savings to the center instead, not realizing that it was already sitting on millions of dollars. Dees wrote about her sacrifice in a fundraising appeal that spurred more donations. The center worked with aging donors to ensure that a portion of their estate was donated upon their death. Each year the list of donors grew, as Dees tinkered with mailings and studied which drew the greatest response rates.

The center soon had $12 million in reserves and was raising far more than it could figure out how to spend. It spent money to raise even more money, sending glossy publications and mailers with frightening pictures of Klansmen and contribution forms. Critics of the center began referring to it as the "Poverty Palace."

In its early years, the center had focused on fighting the death penalty, employment discrimination, and voting rights constraints, and confronting the structural bases for poverty. For the first four years, Dees drew no salary, but in time, he began paying himself comfortably. Yet when staff attorneys proposed taking on cases confronting discrimination in housing, Dees often said no. "Our attention is on the Klan," one staff attorney recalled him saying. "Let some other lawyers—some do-good lawyers—come through and file a suit."

In 1986, the original team of lawyers Dees had recruited resigned en masse, frustrated by his obsession with a Klan they regarded as fragmented and feckless—not the grave and gathering threat that the center's fundraising appeals made it out to be. "The fund-raising letters would make it seem to people who didn't really know the South as if the Klan was out of control," said one of the attorneys who resigned.

Randall Williams, the Klanwatch head who'd played such an important role in the Vietnamese shrimpers case, joined the lawyers in submitting his resignation letter. "I thought we had done what we set out to do," he told a reporter after leaving, "but Morris was still firing away with all the guns and still writing to donors about the Klan menace and the money was flowing in."

In 1988, Louis Ray Beam Jr. was charged, alongside Aryan Nations leader Richard Butler and senior White supremacists, with seditious conspiracy. He snatched his daughter and fled with his new wife to Mexico, where he holed up in a neighborhood of American expats south of Guadalajara. The FBI put him on its most wanted list; months later he was seized in a shoot-out with Mexican federales. When he eventually stood trial in Fort Smith, Arkansas, he represented himself and was acquitted. A juror married one of his White supremacist co-conspirators months after the trial. Another juror said he admired Beam and agreed with his stance against race mixing.

Beam gave the occasional speech—in an Aryan Nations summit in Idaho that prompted a march of one thousand antiracist protesters to "smash the fascists" and at a neo-Nazi rally in Pulaski, Tennessee, where a Confederate statue was under consideration for being scrapped—but he otherwise receded from public view.

By the end of the 1980s, the national membership of the Klan was down to roughly five thousand; in Texas, there were fewer than a hundred active Klansmen, according to the Anti-Defamation League. "There hasn't been any Klan without Beam," an ADL staffer said. "You can really chart the decline when Beam left the Klan." That said, the staffer added, "it only takes two guys to create havoc."


IN 1989, THE SOUTHERN POVERTY LAW CENTER'S ANNUAL BUDGET was $3 million, a significant amount of which went to providing security; their endowment was $27 million. In the early 1990s, one of Dees's mailers urged donors to write a check for an upgraded security system: "Your gift is needed now so we could set up this new system as soon as possible." Their financial reserves were over $33 million.

By 1994, the endowment was at $52 million.

That year, after a three-year investigation, the *Montgomery Advertiser* ran a series of investigative reports about how the center raised its money; how it was seeking to build a massive endowment even though it spent only as little as 18 percent of the funds it raised on programs each year; how the board members were all Dees's friends; and how ferociously Dees curated his image and thwarted detractors.

In the preceding four years, the center had reaped over $40 million from mailings touting its legal prowess in cases like *Vietnamese Fishermen's Association v. Knights of the Ku Klux Klan*, but it had not filed a single suit against the Klan or any other hate group. Despite tens of millions in reserves, it brought only twelve additional suits, including one against the Alabama High School Athletic Association for barring foreign exchange students from participating in sports. The paper quoted Dees as saying that he was now considering dropping "Law" from the name of the organization.

The series also painted an alarming picture of the organization's history with its Black employees, none of whom had reached the highest positions at the center. Twelve of thirteen Black current or former employees told *Advertiser* reporters of "racial problems" at the center. Some described it as akin to working at a plantation; others recounted hearing slurs. In twenty-three years, the center had hired only two Black staff attorneys, both of whom left in disappointment. In response, Dees denied that there were "black slots and white slots," before complaining that "probably the most discriminated people in America today are white men when it comes to jobs because there are more of those who had more education opportunities and who the test scores show are scoring better and on paper look more qualified. That's why you have so many reverse discrimination cases around."

The *Advertiser* ran no anonymous quotes. Many of them were unsparing, the most surprising of which came from Millard Fuller, the man with whom Dees had made his millions. Since selling his half of the company to Dees and renouncing a money-driven life, Fuller had gone on to found Habitat for Humanity, which was at that time building tens of thousands of homes for lower-income families in forty-one countries.

"Morris has a real flair for knowing what will sell and what won't sell . . . I think he realized that jumping on the Klan was very popular with a lot of people," Fuller said, echoing a comment from Gloria Browne, one of the only two Black legal staffers, who said, "The market is still wide open for the product, which is black pain and white guilt." While it was indeed easier to raise money to confront the Klan than it was to fight a death penalty conviction, the center could have diverted the tens of millions it had in surplus to fund less popular work. But they just weren't filing many suits at all.

Of the many disgruntled former center employees, Fuller was acidic about his former partner: "He does not know how to treat people . . . he leaves a trail of bodies behind, of broken relationships. It's just how he treats people."

In the run-up to the *Advertiser*'s series, the center hired an outside attorney, who routinely threatened a suit against the publisher, citing libel laws, and refused to share financial records with the paper. When it ran, though, the series didn't break into the national news cycle; its impact was confined mostly to Montgomery. That changed, though, when it was named as a finalist for the Pulitzer Prize.

Dees mobilized a number of the best-known liberal politicians for whom he'd raised money over the years, who lobbied the Pulitzer Board against awarding the prize to the *Montgomery Advertiser*. According to Jim Tharpe, then managing editor at the paper, it was "the first lobbying that I know of of that kind." The series did not win.

"That's just the way he deals with [critics]," Millard Fuller said of Dees. "Rather than looking at himself and thinking that he may be part of the problem, he dismisses the people who don't like him as if something were wrong with them."

In 1994, in the wake of the *Advertiser*'s series, Dees announced that the Southern Poverty Law Center would stop fundraising after its endowment hit $100 million, which, invested properly, would ensure the long-term stability of the organization. (In 1978, the center had announced it would stop fundraising when it hit $5 million.)

Dees also announced that he planned to step down from the center within five years. "I want to go back to farming," he told the *Montgomery Advertiser*.

THE KLAN'S NUMBERS HAD DECLINED, BUT THE WHITE SUPREMAcist movement charged ahead. Louis Beam emerged from the shadows to crash a press conference during the ATF siege of the Branch Davidian compound near Waco, Texas, in 1993, decrying the emergence of a "police state." Two years later, the right-wing militia movement's seething hatred of a "tyrannical" federal government culminated in the 1995 bombing of the Alfred P. Murrah Federal Building in Oklahoma City by Timothy McVeigh and Terry Nichols, two White supremacists operating according to the "lone wolf" strategy Beam had advanced in "Leaderless Resistance." McVeigh timed the bombing to coincide with the anniversary of the Waco siege. A total of 168 were killed, 19 of them babies and young children, and more than 680 were injured. Many suspected Beam was a co-conspirator, but he insisted he couldn't be held accountable for the ways his writings were interpreted.

In October 1996, Beam wrote a letter to his followers, talking about the work he had done for the extremist right in the decade since his acquittal at Fort Smith. "Since 1969, I have been in the struggle. . . . I intend to give my family the next years of my life. They need me and have borne so much on my account. Additionally, as a result of exposure to Agent Orange while in Vietnam, my health declines. I have concealed this for years but now find myself less than fit to continue as in days before.

"I have for 30 years given my all. I pray others will do the same."

BY 2001, THE SPLC'S ENDOWMENT WAS AT $98 MILLION; THE CEN-ter's assets had shot to $136 million. Dees had said he'd retire, but he remained, and the five years became ten, and the ten became twenty.

By 2010, the endowment was at $175 million.

By 2014, $302 million.

By 2017, the endowment was at $432 million—on top of $44 million in annual contributions and other gifts.

In 2019, the center announced assets and contributions of $581 million, making it among the wealthiest nonprofits in the United States.

That spring, Dees was fired from the Southern Poverty Law Center amid allegations of inappropriate "sexualized" banter with staffers, and racially insensitive comments. At a 2017 fundraiser in Atlanta, he put his hand on the shoulder of a younger female staffer and asked about a tattoo on her arm. When she asked if he had any tattoos, he pointed to the front of his right, clothed thigh, where he apparently had one. "No one has ever suggested that you harassed someone," Richard Cohen, the organization's president, wrote in an email to Dees. "But the reality is that you made a young woman feel uncomfortable, and she complained to a supervisor."

"Why is he still here?" a senior staffer complained to the president. "People see him as racist and sexist."

"Or an anachronism," replied Cohen. "That would be kinder."

In the media firestorm, the 1994 *Montgomery Advertiser* series re-surfaced, and the twenty-five-year-old indictments held up: there were still few Black staffers in senior positions, and the center still seemed far more focused on fundraising than on its programs. After Cohen fired Dees, more than a dozen staffers signed an email to the senior executives applauding the firing and insisting that "those individuals in leadership and on the Board of Directors who, for years, were aware of and covered up and ignored" allegations of Dees's misconduct be brought to account. Cohen resigned shortly thereafter.

In an interview with *The Washington Post*, Dees insisted that he never made any advances toward female staffers, but this seems improbable. Two center employees who worked with him for many years smirked when I relayed his claim. The second of his six wives was a center employee.

The SPLC deleted any reference to Morris Dees from its website. The postcards featuring a pensive Dees were removed from the gift shop at the Civil Rights Memorial across the street. The fundraising continues.

So, too, does the round-the-clock security of his home. At eighty-three, Dees sits in his home office, which is piled high with trophies and awards, among them the 2016 Martin Luther King Jr. Nonviolent Peace Prize, the American Trial Lawyer Hall of Fame, the 1994 Clarence Darrow Public Interest Advocate Award, the 2000 Freedom Keeper Award from Planned Parenthood, the 1955 Star Farmer of Alabama, and, perhaps his most cherished, the 1998 Direct Marketing Association's Hall of Fame award. "I'm not ashamed to say I'm a salesman," Dees told the association at the time. "I've used other talents at the center, but without my direct-marketing skills, I wouldn't have the money to do it with."

His old partner, Millard Fuller, was fired from his perch atop Habitat for Humanity after multiple allegations of sexual harassment, several of which were settled internally.

"The South is a complex place, and I admit—indeed, I hope—that I am a complex fellow," Dees once wrote. While he can still rattle off return and yield rates on mailings with great specificity, he pleads confusion over his ouster. He said he's considering suing for wrongful termination.

His enemy Louis Beam is still alive, an icon to many on the extreme right. After sitting in on some classes in the anthropology department at Texas State University, he began writing papers arguing that the first settlers of America were not migrants from North Asia, but mysterious "bearded men with red, blonde, and light brown hair."

IN 1983, JIM STANFIELD RESIGNED HIS POSITION IN THE KU KLUX Klan after "falling in love with a Mexican girl," according to his former attorney, Sam Adamo. "Faced with the choice of a sexless life with his beloved or leaving the Klan, love won the day and Jim resigned," Adamo relayed in a mirthful letter to Dees, before reporting a bombshell: "Last weekend, Jim Stanfield's shrimp boat was burned to the waterline. A TOTAL LOSS! Authorities strongly suspect the Klan was responsible because Stanfield had accepted a deposit for sale of the boat to a Vietnamese family."

In early 1988, Gene Fisher, then working as a contractor, agreed to an on-camera interview with Ginger Casey, a TV reporter from KUHT in Houston. They filmed along the Seabrook waterfront under a milk-colored sky, as shrimp boats churned through the channel the Klan boat patrol had menaced seven years earlier.

"Might've been wrong," he said, shrugging his shoulders. "But you can't go back and change it. I didn't sit in a beer joint and talk about it. I didn't sit in a coffee shop and bitch about it. I went and tried to do something about it. And now, I have no regrets, other than the losing. I don't have any guilt complexes."

Fisher still sported a thick mustache and sideburns, but he was no longer posing in a Klan T-shirt. "I was trying to stop something that this country was built on and based on, and it wasn't going to happen, it's not gonna happen," referencing the American tradition of welcoming refugees. "Things kinda escalated, maybe more or less on their own . . . and with a lot of shove from the media. It was almost like they were more bloodthirsty than I was. *They* wanted a confrontation."

"Well, don't you think seeing the robes and crosses kinda incites people?" Casey asked.

"Oh, I *know* it does! Sure. But that wasn't the primary purpose. The primary purpose was to get the attention to tell our side of the story."

"Do you ever find yourself grudgingly respecting what these people have done?" Casey asked, referring to the Vietnamese American shrimpers, as the two walked down a pier thronged with trawlers.

"No!" Fisher snapped. "What have they done?! Do you respect an army of ants because they can devour a tree?"

"Is that what you think is going on?"

"Sure," he replied, his tone shifting. "I love my people. My people are all white . . . I love them above and beyond anyone else's race. Doesn't mean I hate anyone else's race."

"What about the boat burnings?" she asked quietly. Fisher looked down at the planks of the dock for a moment as he considered his response.

"Well at the time, like I said, it's too bad. . . ." He looked at Casey and smirked. "Not too bad there's a boat burnt, but too bad that they didn't all burn! Doesn't disturb me one way or another. I was in it to win."

He gazed out over the Vietnamese boats tied along the piers. "I still don't care! If all these boats right now was to burn it wouldn't bother me one bit! So, I'm not ashamed of anything I've done, or the way I went about it."

"Are you bitter?" Casey asked.

"Bitter? Yeah. Anyone who loses has got to be bitter. . . . People who grow accustomed to losing, that's what they are . . . losers."

When he died, a couple of years later, the morgue had a difficult time finding anyone willing to pick up his body.

JUDY APLIN, WIDOW OF BILLY JOE AND ONETIME GIRLFRIEND OF Gene Fisher, lives with her daughter, Beth, on a tract of farmland outside Seguin, Texas, where an all-White jury acquitted Sáu and Chính Văn Nguyễn. As with so many others from Seadrift and the Gulf Coast, Judy has been diagnosed with lung cancer.

In 2019, after decades of struggling against the legacy of her family and what had happened to her father, Beth felt compelled to formally apologize to the Vietnamese community in Seadrift. One of her aunts told her Billy Joe would be ashamed of her.

COLONEL NAM VĂN NGUYỄN NEVER RETURNED TO SHRIMPING. After selling off his boat and property in Seabrook, he opened a laundromat, then launched the Vietnamese-language *United Times*, a newspaper for the Houston community. He and An raised three daughters, who all went on to earn advanced degrees. His daughter Judy, who was whisked as an infant from the house when the Klan boat patrol pulled up behind it, became a licensed family counselor.

Now in his eighties, the Colonel drives around Houston in a spotless black Jeep Wrangler with a general's star on the driver's side door. He always wears a pin showing the crossed flags of the United States of America and the Republic of Vietnam. The dock that once jutted from his home in Seabrook is gone, washed away by the most recent hurricane. He keeps the ashes of his parents in the Buddhist Phật Quang Pagoda in South Houston, determined to return them to Vietnam if the Communists are ever driven out.

His son, Michael, was visiting Vietnam in July 2018 when he was arrested by Vietnamese authorities and charged with "attempting to overthrow the people's government." The fifty-four-year-old father of four young daughters was blindfolded, given a sham trial, and thrown into prison on a twelve-year sentence. While in prison, he cherished the occasional dried fish smuggled in and shared among inmates. Each day, he was required to assemble wicker chairs that are sold online through major retailers. His imprisonment wasn't helped by the fact that his guards knew that his father was once a great colonel for the Republic of Vietnam. Two years into his sentence, he was released after extensive lobbying by the US State Department and his congresswoman, Katie Porter.

In 2018, Sáu Văn Nguyễn died in Morgan City, Louisiana, of vibrio, a bacterial infection most commonly afflicting people who work in the seafood industry.

Bằng "Cherry" Nguyễn's health is flagging, but he still works as a fisherman in Palacios, just up the road from Seadrift. Most other Vietnamese who resettled to the Gulf Coast in the mid-1970s worked the waters for a couple of decades before they sent their kids off to college and moved to the Vietnamese neighborhoods of Houston. One Vietnamese family opened a seafood market on 1619 Red Bluff Drive in Pasadena for a while, not realizing that the building was once the headquarters of the Knights of the Ku Klux Klan.

JODY AND DAVID COLLINS, GENE FISHER, JAMES STANFIELD, LOUIS Beam, and others repeatedly claimed they were fighting communism, but they were lashing out against capitalism all along. The Vietnamese weren't receiving secret government support; they were just willing to work harder, for longer hours and less pay, while spending less. The White shrimpers and crabbers of the Texas Gulf Coast might have tried working more closely together like the Vietnamese, loaning each other money, using family members as deckhands, driving cheaper cars, and eating free fish caught from the bay, but it seemed as though they were in a race to the bottom of the free market. The only way to win was to make less and live with less.

Jody was several hours late for our meeting in Kemah, just a couple of blocks away from where the Dutch Kettle café—where they'd all given so many interviews about the "Vietnamese problem"—once stood. His truck was a beat-up Dodge with prescription pill bottles in the ashtray and a pile of unopened medical bills caked in dirt and clay on the floor mats. A bright orange plastic snake was coiled around his rearview mirror.

His face was leathery, his hair long, whitish-yellow, and pulled into a thin ponytail. As he drove, he kept scratching his leg, which was besieged by a rash that had broken out ever since he'd started on a new medication for his chronic obstructive pulmonary disease. He was wracked with asbestosis, a consequence of all the asbestos he was required to knock off of generators back in the 1960s when he was a grunt in the army.

He set his portable breathing machine on the seat between us. In the bed of his truck was a pile of spent oxygen tanks, bungeed up next to empty coolers he'd hoped to fill with shrimp that day. It was May 15, the opening day of shrimping season, and we had made plans to go out on the water and drop some nets.

But there was "fuck-all" to do that day, he told me. Three days earlier, an outbound tanker had collided with two barges in the channel, capsizing one and splitting open the hull of the other. Officials estimated the initial leak at twenty-five thousand barrels' worth of reformate, an extremely flammable liquid blended with gasoline to boost octane, and toxic to marine life.

The air reeked of gasoline. City officials urged people indoors not to run their air conditioners, to keep the noxious odor from entering their homes. Collins had come down to the waterfront to shrimp, smelled the air, and decided it was pointless. He knew everything was dying off because the crabs and bottom-feeders had already started clawing onto dry land in their final moments. Nobody sees shrimp when they die; they're heavier than water, so when there's a die-off, they all sink to the bottom.

We went over to his brother's trailer, where David admitted that he'd burned Jody's, John's, and his own boat and house six months after the trial, as part of an "insurance job." Alternating between lighting cigarettes and eating Starbursts he kept in a bowl by his recliner, he talked about burning crosses, denying that he was a Klansman while rattling off jokes riddled with the N-word.

"Why'd you do it, then?" I asked, meaning all of it—the Klan boat patrol, the burning crosses, the rallies, the rattlesnakes he'd dropped into Vietnamese boats.

"Just for mischief," he said with a smile. "I was wild and crazy when I was young."

The brothers spoke of Freddie "Bean." Now that he was dead, they said, people might as well know about who'd burned the boats. Jody sat next to me on the couch, struggling to breathe in the smoke-filled room.

Even though Freddie had told both of them he'd burned the *Trudy B*,
Jody had publicly accused the Vietnamese of burning their own boats as
a plot to win sympathy. He scrunched his face up and stepped outside,
where the air was cleaner.

I told David about the Vietnamese who had sought shelter in Father
John's church, who had put their boats up for sale while angry White
Americans aimed their guns at them.

"Wasn't that bad?" I asked. "The Vietnamese were scared. . . ."

"Yeah, that was," he acknowledged. "None of it was a good thing
from the beginning. . . ."

We sat in silence, the air in the tiny trailer thick with smoke. A black-
and-white western played on a flat-screen mounted in a corner. David
took a call from his doctor regarding some spots detected on his lungs
after a recent examination. I stood up to go, but he held his hand up.

"Make sure you spell my name right," he whispered, a twinkle in his
eye. "That's Mr. C-O-L-L-I-N-S."

Months later, he was dead.

Jody and I drove down an unpaved road beneath the Kemah-
Seabrook bridge. He pointed to where all the fish houses had once stood;
now there was nothing but ghost piers running out into the bay. We came
to a stop ten feet from the water's edge, at the same spot on the channel
he'd been tying up his boat since 1959. It was here that David had loaded
up the Klansmen onto the *Cherry Betty*, nearly four decades earlier.

It wasn't the first time our plans to go shrimping were scotched at
the last second. A few months earlier, the bay had been fouled by a massive explosion at the Intercontinental Terminals Company, a chemical
storage facility in Deer Park along the Houston Ship Channel. A days-
long chemical fire kicked up a plume of black smoke visible for miles; it
took nearly a week for firefighters to put it out, by spraying a chemical
foam. An emergency dike wall meant to keep it all from seeping out of
the ship channel into the bay then failed, and tens of thousands of gallons
of slurry headed on its way. By the end of the year, researchers would
report the presence of "forever chemicals" in the waterways, but little was
known about their impact on aquatic life.

Jody's older brother, John, who had died years earlier, gave him his current boat, the *Captain Chris*. It looked half sunk, its outriggers rusted, nets all bunched up, more rot than paint on the wood.

Even without the chemicals swirling in the bay, Jody was too frail to shrimp effectively, but he wouldn't give it up. When the *Captain Chris* sank three times in about as many months, he hauled it up to try plugging the leaks; at one point his oxygen levels ran so low that Marilyn had to speed over with a fresh tank. She was resigned to the fact that he would die on the boat.

We stayed in the cab of his truck; there was no point even boarding his boat. He took a hit of oxygen and stared out his cracked windshield. He gestured to a marina jam-packed with pristine sailboats and yachts.

"See them sailboats over there? That's where all the Vietnamese used to tie up. That was Saigon Harbor."

A lot had changed since he first started working these waters sixty years earlier. There were hardly any shrimp left in the bays. Jody didn't believe in climate change, but he cared about the environment, and it pissed him off whenever another spill shut the bay down. There was a place nicknamed "DuPont Channel," where he had to wrap his face up because the air was so foul from the smell of chemicals; the shrimping was good, but he would never eat them himself. Kemah, once home to a

Ghost piers running from where Colonel Nam's fish house once stood in Seabrook, 2019.

sizable shrimping fleet, had been turned into an amusement park by a billionaire restaurateur, Tilman Fertitta. Across the channel, Seabrook had only a few fish houses left—after the most recent hurricane wiped away most of the structures, the billionaire Taub family, who owned the land, decided it wasn't worth their time to lease the property, so most of it was now overrun with weeds and stray cats. Most of the larger gulf trawlers were idling along the coast, their owners desperate for seasonal workers from Mexico who'd once come in through the H-2B short-term visa program dismantled by the Trump administration; they couldn't find American citizens willing to do the work. Ninety percent of all shrimp consumed in America was now imported. All the restaurants within sight served up prebreaded shrimp that had been raised on a farm in Vietnam or Thailand in conditions often described as slave labor. Even if Jody had a miracle day on the water, he'd have a difficult time finding someone to buy it.

Bubbling beneath it all was climate change. The most recent National Climate Assessment described the Texas coastline as especially vulnerable to climate catastrophe, including rising sea levels, increased intensity of storms, and flooding. Shortly before I arrived, a shrimper complained that they were "getting drowned in freshwater," as pesticides washed into the bays, altering salinity content to levels inhospitable for aquatic life. "These storms are getting crazy," the shrimper told a journalist. "They're getting bigger and bigger . . ."

Just across the channel was a small pier with a half-dozen shrimp boats, all of them owned by Vietnamese American fishermen. They were all fresh-painted, high on the water, their nets neatly hung.

"It's like I told 'em. I was here before they come, and I'll be here when they leave. And I only got six more to outlive." Jody laughed, started coughing, and took a long drag off his oxygen tank. "Then I'll have it back to myself again."

A year later, he was dead.

Given the limited number of permits available, his half-sunk boat was worth a small fortune because of the license that came with it. Marilyn, his wife, sold his boat to a Vietnamese shrimper.

# Acknowledgments

Right out of the gate, I'll reject the custom of saving a couple of lines at the end of an acknowledgments section for one's partner (although I'll return to her then, too). Everything I have in this world that means anything comes from my wife, Marie-Josée. Since the day we met, I am convinced that the sun rises, that words carry meaning, that music brings joy, that hardship can be endured, only because she is here. I could not have written this book or achieved anything in my life had it not been for her.

Second, I owe an unexpected debt to Bruce Springsteen, of all people, for writing his song "Galveston Bay." On December 3, 2018, my dad passed away from a slew of cancers that he had been stoically ignoring until he retired, only six months earlier. I felt a compulsion to escape the noise and smoke of Los Angeles and be on a river, to fling my gear into the trunk and speed up into the frosted southern Sierra Nevada mountains. Along the drive, my senses numb to all around me, I barely noticed the music playing through the radio. And then a Springsteen song came on, about a White shrimper planning to kill a Vietnamese refugee in Galveston Bay over turf. It was such a strange premise for a song that it stuck with me as I waded up the Kern River that day, chasing for trout in frigid water and mourning the loss of my father, who'd served in Vietnam and taught me to fish. Not knowing anything of the true story, I figured Springsteen had spun his ballad out of whole cloth. It wasn't until I eventually looked up the origin of the song that I realized I might have my next book.

This book is the result of a staggering amount of help from others, who endured years' worth of phone calls, texts, emails, and visits as I burrowed deeper into the investigation.

In reporting out the events of Seadrift in 1979, I am indebted to Beth Aplin Martin; Judy Aplin; Diane Wilson; Verlon Davis; Pat, Michael, and Trish Maloney; Josie Reid; Leonard Bermea of the Seadrift Police Department; and the Guadalupe County District Clerk's Office. I am especially grateful to Richard Haight for sharing his account of the torching of the Vietnamese home and boats the night Billy Joe was killed.

A very special thanks to Tim Tsai, director of the profound documentary *Seadrift*, for sharing the transcripts of his interviews with Bằng "Cherry" Nguyễn and facilitating other introductions. Mark Brice's 1980 documentary, *Vietnam in Texas*, was also useful in reconstructing the events of the killing of Billy Joe Aplin and the trial of Sáu and Chính Văn Nguyễn.

In investigating what happened in the Seabrook-Kemah area of Galveston Bay from 1980 to 1982, I must first convey my gratitude to Colonel Nam Văn Nguyễn, who was exceedingly generous with his time and recollections. More than once, I asked him to rehash uncomfortable memories, but he was always gracious and patient, as was his family; I owe special thanks to his daughter Judy and his son, Michael, for helping me piece together their story.

The Southern Poverty Law Center has been extremely helpful over the years, despite great organizational turmoil. Morris Dees made himself available for extensive interviews on numerous occasions. Thanks to the center's staff, specifically Judy Bruno, for making the case files of *Vietnamese Fishermen's Association v. Knights of the Ku Klux Klan* available to me on multiple visits. These records nearly went up in smoke after the torching of the center by Klansmen in 1983—without them, it's hard to imagine this book existing.

I am indebted to David Berg and Sam Adamo for their generosity of spirit, time, and recollections, and for helping me understand both sides of the suit. Thanks, too, to Philip Zelikow, Randall Williams, and Mike Vahala for all of the time they gave me.

But this book was not simply a reconstruction from faded transcripts and clippings. It also depended on lengthy, challenging, and frequent interviews with many of those who lived through it—on all sides. Louis Beam and I will never agree on what this sordid story meant, but my thanks for the courtesy of his replies to my inquiries. Jody and David Collins were both admirably open in admitting their involvement and their motives, forty years after the fact. A very special thanks to Marilyn Collins for her repeated willingness to reexamine the past (and her husband's role in it). For their time, I'm grateful to Carl "Buddy" Richardson, Joe Nowalk, Captain Ronnie Galloway, Tom Hults, Bob Rosenberry, Allen Clark, Glenda Joe, Bill Shields, Barry Freece of the Bureau of Alcohol, Tobacco and Firearms, and Paul Kelly of the US Secret Service. Karl Rove was a great help in helping me to understand the landscape of Texas politics in the late 1970s and early 1980s.

For giving me several hours of her valuable time, I'm indebted to Judge Gabrielle Kirk McDonald, who has never spoken at length about her perspective on this lawsuit. Judge Mark Wolf has my thanks, again, for his friendship, but also for taking the time to recount his own role in efforts to resettle Vietnamese refugees as Saigon was falling.

Thanks to Father John Toàn Minh Hoàng, not only for sharing his story, but for introducing me to parishioners throughout Houston who lived through the events of this book. My gratitude to Lisa May at the Archdiocese of Galveston-Houston and John Descant at St. Dominic Village for facilitating my meetings with Father John.

Police Chief R. W. "Bill" Kerber has my thanks for exhuming a box full of clippings, surveillance photographs, and other crucial documents from the time.

John Van Beekum's photographs of the fateful Klan boat patrol hung in my office throughout this investigation. Thanks to him for recounting his memories of that day. I am also grateful to Ginger Casey for making available her documentary *"Made" in America*, which included an important conversation with Gene Fisher. Dan Molina and John Treadgold were also helpful in sharing their recollections and clippings from their own coverage of the Klan's activities in Galveston Bay. Wayne Derrick and Brad Walker's 1981 *Portrait of a Klansman* and Robert Hillman's 1982 *Fire on the Water* were both valuable documentary records of portions of this story. Thanks to Tish Stringer and Baird Campbell at Rice University's Department of Visual and Dramatic Arts for arranging a screening of *Portrait*.

For making sense of the environmental and ecological destruction of the bays, my fervent thanks goes (again) to Diane Wilson, who answered hundreds of texts, emails, and phone calls, to say nothing of giving me a tour of Seadrift and sitting for a lengthy interview. Bill Balboa, formerly of Texas Parks and Wildlife and currently of the Matagorda Bay Foundation, was also very helpful. Thanks, too, to Jim Blackburn for his work.

Thanks to Lucy Turoff at the Pasadena Historical Society, Tanya Parlet and Bruce Tabb at the University of Oregon's Keith Stimely collection on revisionist history and neo-Fascist movements. Thanks to the staff at the University of Texas at Austin's Dolph Briscoe Center for American History, which maintains the Clements Texas Papers Project. For sending undercover audio from Louis Beam's 1979 KKK speech, I'm grateful to the staff at the Texas State Library and Archives Commission.

One of the first interviews I conducted for this book was with Viet Thanh Nguyen, whose work—particularly *Nothing Ever Dies: Vietnam and the Memory of War*—has helped me immensely.

A very special thanks to Dr. Thao Ha for all the time, wisdom, and insight she shared over the years I've reported this book, and for her close read of it (along with help on diacriticals). I'm very much looking forward to seeing her book one day. I'm also grateful to her father, Phat Ha, for all the time he gave me during one of my visits to Houston and over subsequent phone calls.

We seem to be in a mass-extinction event when it comes to local newspapers, which compels me to say that I can't imagine writing this book without the luxury of dipping into the archives of papers such as the *Victoria Advocate* and the *Galveston Daily News*. Thanks to Greg Jaffe for confirming details about his reporting on the SPLC in the *Montgomery Advertiser*. Stories like this are happening throughout the country, but consolidation and conglomeration is forcing papers to shed the reporters who should be out capturing them. If you still have one, subscribe to your local paper.

Dr. Kathleen Belew's *Bring the War Home: The White Power Movement and Paramilitary America* was a font of knowledge, particularly in helping me understand the Vietnam War's role in revitalizing the White Power movement. Thanks to Dan T. Carter, for taking the time with me to illuminate parts of George Wallace's career beyond what is covered in his masterful *The Politics of Rage*. Taylor Branch, author of the invaluable America in the King Years trilogy, sent encouragement at a crucial moment, for which I'm grateful. Thank you to Ansil Saunders, who guided Martin Luther King Jr. on his boat in Bimini days before King's assassination, for sharing his account; I only wish I could've worked it into this book as originally envisioned.

Thanks to David M. Hardy, section chief of the Record/Information Dissemination Section at the FBI, for his timely response to my Freedom of Information Act request.

I remain indebted to Geoff Cowan for his friendship, mentorship, and the honor of being a Senior Fellow at the USC Annenberg Center on Communication Leadership and Policy, which enabled invaluable access to USC's library and online archives.

I can scarcely understand how it came to be that I can call upon these authors for advice and friendship, but I hope they understand I realize my good fortune. Thanks to Jonathan Franzen for helping me figure out the book's title (while sitting in a sweltering bird blind in Thailand waiting for a rare pheasant to wander by) with John Wray, who slogged through early drafts and jammed with me whenever he passed through L.A. Thanks to George Packer for counsel along the way, and to A. Scott Berg for his help in navigating book launches and the pitfalls of Tinseltown. Thanks to Liaquat and Meena Ahamed for their friendship and support over the years.

For enduring the early draft of this book, helping me think through cover design and subtitles, and being an all-around great friend, thanks to Jordan Goldenberg. Thanks to Matt King, too, for sharing his artistic insights when it came to cover art.

For friendship in a time of isolation, I am grateful to Max Weiss, Jordan and Lauren Goldenberg, Jakke and Maria Erixson, Tom and Christen Hadfield, Peter and Lisa Noah, Eddie Patel, Justin Sadauskas, Arie Toporovsky, Kevin Brewer, Jesse Dailey, Andy Rafter, Sherine Hamdy, Jon Staff, Shawn and Elizabeth Peterson, Tim Hoekstra and Fatimah Rony, Jonathan and Tara Tucker, Julie Schlosser and Rajiv Chandrasekaran, Gahl Burt, Yanic Truesdale, Henrik and Victoria Björklund, Ezra Strausberg and Enrique Gutierrez, Philip Wareborn, Cory Baskin, Serim Çetin, Jason Francis, Nancy Updike, Tim and Annette Nelson, Sharon Yang, Garret Price, Mary Haft, Marc Skvirsky, Camille Duhbreuil and Ed Shea, Deb and Hannah VanDerMolen, Jennie Paigen, Usman Khan, Tona Rashad, Roger Frappier and Caroline Dumas, Yaghdan and Ghada Hameid, Amélie Cantin, Matt King and Sarah Cunningham, Lela Hutchinson and Mark Smrecek, Harlan and Christine Werner, Yazen Joudeh, Mélanie Joly, David Attenborough, Spencer Seim, Josh Gad and Ida Darvish, George Packer and Laura Secor, and Samuel Dubé.

The peerless Katherine Flynn. What else is there to say? Without her, I'd still be flailing around with muddled proposals and unanswered questions. I am so grateful for her wisdom and friendship. Thanks, too, to the entire Kneerim and Williams family (can't wait until you add Flynn to your masthead!), as well as Heather Baror-Shapiro of Baror International, for coordinating foreign rights.

I never could have imagined the honor of publishing my books with Viking. For that, I am forever grateful to Kathryn Court, who helped bring my previous book into the world and got this one started before embarking upon a well-earned retirement. When the time came to discuss who would take over this project, I had only one person in mind: Wendy Wolf. She is tough, demanding, precise, and funny—all the qualities I could hope for as I develop as a writer. Thanks, too, to Brian Tart, Terezia Cicel, and Ben Petrone, and Kate Berner and Rachel Horowitz at the Penguin Random House Speakers Bureau. Similar thanks to Christie Hinrichs at Authors Unbound for handling my speaking engagements.

My gratitude to David Rohde and Carla Blumenkranz for publishing my work at *The New Yorker*, a dream ever since my first subscription as a thirteen-year-old.

I am forever thrilled to be able to collaborate with Nancy Updike, Ira Glass, Miki Meek, Diane Wu, and Sean Cole at *This American Life* in rendering my stories into something worthy enough for their airwaves.

Thanks to Michelle Kroes and Jiah Shin at CAA. I feel very lucky to call Rebecca Arzoian at Smokehouse Pictures a friend, and remain grateful to her for her stewardship in adapting this book for television. To place ugly, early drafts of one's work in the hands of such wonderful authors like Dave Eggers and Thi Bui was excruciatingly humbling; my thanks to them for their patience as I searched for the signal in the noise. Thanks, too, to Paramount for backing.

I wish my dad was still here. His map of Vietnam that he deployed with as a grunt in the 101st Airborne hangs on my wall next to two photos: In one, I stand next to him on a riverbank as a five-year-old, watching him fish. In the other, he has wasted away from cancer—spurred in part by his repeated exposure to Agent Orange during the war. He raised me to not look away from the ills of the world, to approach complicated social problems with humility, and to fight for change.

It often feels as though this wretched virus has conspired to keep us apart from those we love at the moment we need them the most. This painful passage of time and distance has only reinforced my awareness of what an extraordinary family I have. Mom, Soren, and Derek, I love you. Ever and Carolyn, thank you for being such wonderful sisters-in-law, and for raising the inspiring Ever-Therese, Owen, Berend, Virginia, Charlie, Vivian, and Anders. Thank you to my belle-maman Suzanne Ladouceur for bringing the love of my life into this world.

Janine Cantin, my aunt, landed in Los Angeles to watch our two young children for a long weekend. When the pandemic shut their schools down, she stayed for six months. Without her, we would've had a vastly different, darker experience of the pandemic, and I am quite certain I wouldn't have been able to tackle this book in time.

I work with words, but there is no sequence of them that can even hint at the expanding universe of love I have for August, Isidora, and Marie-Josée. I started this book when Isi still fit in the baby harness, and I wrote vast stretches parked in front of the house while August napped in the backseat. They tolerated a sleepy, stressed-out father for three years, all while sustaining me with their laughter and curiosity. I hope the world they grow into looks nothing like the one described in these pages.

In the end, everything returns to Marie-Josée, my first reader, my best friend, my partner in life, my infinite love.

# Photo Credits

# Notes

**AUTHOR'S NOTE**

xii **I have similarly capitalized:** Kwame Anthony Appiah, "The Case for Capitalizing the *B* in Black," *The Atlantic*, June 18, 2020.

xii **"objectifying and dehumanizing":** Author interview with Dr. Viet Thanh Nguyen, Los Angeles, March 20, 2019.

**1. THE DEFORMED CRAB**

10 **Beth whispered to a classmate:** Author interview with Beth Aplin Martin, Seguin, TX, May 14, 2019.

11 **The bays were filled with debris:** Pat White, "Quail Season Opens Here with Record Crop Seen," *Victoria Advocate*, November 27, 1966, 19A.

11 **a gun deal gone bad:** Author phone interview with Joe Nowalk, July 5, 2021.

13 **Amid the junk fish:** Author interview with Judy Aplin, Seguin, TX, August 30, 2019.

**2. THE LONE FISHERWOMAN OF SEADRIFT**

14 **extermination of the Karankawas:** Kelly Frank Himmel, "Anglo-Texans, Karankawas, and Tonkawas, 1821–1859: A Sociological Analysis of Conquest" (PhD dissertation, University of Texas at Austin, 1995), 95, ProQuest.

14 **Diane's grandpa, who went by "Chief":** Interview with Robert W. Sanders and Mildred Lester, "The Institute of Texan Cultures, Oral History Program," May 13, 1987.

15 **only a few hundred Seadrifters remained:** Rebecca Rubert, "Seadrift TX," Texas State Historical Association, https://www.tshaonline.org/handbook/entries/seadrift-tx.

15 **knowing in a matter of seconds:** Diane Wilson, *An Unreasonable Woman: A True Story of Shrimpers, Politicos, Polluters, and the Fight for Seadrift, Texas* (Chelsea Green, 2005), 49.

16 **the most highly decorated veteran:** Wilson, *An Unreasonable Woman*, 52.

17 **When she eventually returned:** Author interview with Diane Wilson, Seadrift, TX, August 29, 2019.

17 **"brown as a turd":** Wilson, *An Unreasonable Woman*, 52.

18 **had it been a rooster:** Diane Wilson, *Diary of an Eco-Outlaw: An Unreasonable Woman Breaks the Law for Mother Earth* (Chelsea Green, 2011), 8.

18 **one ring of Seadrift fishermen was busted:** "Heroin Ring Cracked," *Victoria Advocate*, May 21, 1977, 1.

19 **pickers were paid a third:** Michael J. Oesterling and Charles Petrocci, "The Crab Industry in Venezuela, Ecuador, and Mexico: Implications for the Chesapeake Bay Blue Crab Industry," Virginia Sea Grant Marine Resource Advisory no. 56, VSG-95-01 (1994), 26.

## 3. A HURRICANE WARNING

20 **By midcentury, two hundred plants:** "Petrochemical Industry," *Handbook of Texas Online*, Texas State Historical Association, https://www.tshaonline.org/handbook/entries/petrochemical-industry.

20 **"I see no reason why this shouldn't be":** "Victoria Area Praised by President of Alcoa," *Victoria Advocate*, February 22, 1950, 1.

20 **A reception was thrown in his honor:** "Industrialist Is Visitor at Port Lavaca," *Victoria Advocate*, February 22, 1950, 1.

21 **By the early 1960s:** "'64 Banner Year for Alcoa Plant," *Victoria Advocate*, December 31, 1964, 16.

21 **"We cannot come into a community":** "Ground Broken at Point Plant," *Victoria Advocate*, July 15, 1964, 1.

21 **"virtually unchanged":** AP, "Union Carbide Gets Water Okay," *Victoria Advocate*, February 27, 1952, 1.

22 **She quit after three weeks:** Diane Wilson, *An Unreasonable Woman: A True Story of Shrimpers, Politicos, Polluters, and the Fight for Seadrift, Texas* (Chelsea Green, 2005), 32.

22 **A friend trotlining for black drum:** Author interview with Diane Wilson, Seadrift, TX, August 29, 2019.

22 **When mysterious brown algae bloomed:** Wilson, *An Unreasonable Woman*, 37.

23 **"My name is Billy Aplin":** Billy Joe Aplin letter to fellow fishermen. Provided by Aplin family.

24 **Bit by bit, the overflow was dumped:** "Five-Year Review Report: Alcoa (Point Comfort)/ Lavaca Bay Superfund Site Point Comfort, Calhoun County, Texas," United States Environmental Protection Agency, June 2, 2011, 5.

24 **An emergency order was issued:** Diana Claitor, "Letter from Lavaca Bay," *Texas Observer*, July 8, 2005.

## 4. ONE DAY IN JUNE, 1979

27 **coloring books for kindergartners:** Diane Wilson, *Diary of an Eco-Outlaw: An Unreasonable Woman Breaks the Law for Mother Earth* (Chelsea Green, 2011), 17.

27 **"oysters had cleansed themselves":** "Alcoa Representative Calls Lavaca Bay One of the Cleanest," *Corpus Christi Caller-Times*, April 25, 1971, 14B.

27 **"Every man, woman and child":** "Leaders Praise Plant," *Victoria Advocate*, May 13, 1979, 9.

28 **Dow Chemical poached:** Bob Rosenberry, "History of the Galveston Laboratory," Shrimp News International, March 15, 2017.

28 **Union Carbide opened a shrimp-farming operation:** George Chamberlain, "History of Shrimp Farming," in *The Shrimp Book*, ed. M. V. Alday-Sanz (Nottingham University Press, 2010), 7.

28 **Upon coming into contact:** Linda Garmon, "Autopsy of an Oil Spill," *Science News* 118, no. 17 (1980), 267–70.

28 **Pemex workers sprayed a chemical dispersant:** Jay Rosser, "U.S. Asks Pemex to Stop Using Chemical on Oil," *Corpus Christi Caller-Times*, August 24, 1979, B1.

29 **"there is not very much danger":** AP, "Mexican Oil Well Spills at Gulf Site," *Victoria Advocate*, June 9, 1979, 7A.

29 **Forty-eight hours later:** UPI, "Geyser Spreads 60-Mile Oil Slick," *Galveston Daily News*, June 10, 1979, 1.

29 **Local Mexican fishermen:** Julian Miglierini, "Mexicans Still Haunted by 1979 Ixtoc Spill," *BBC News*, June 14, 2010.

29 **fifteen-thousand-pound floating booms:** Ken Herman, "Oil Spill Control Operations Begin," *Longview News-Journal*, August 2, 1979, 1.

29 **Researchers tested the toxicity:** AP, "Tests of Oil Spill Encouraging," *The Paris News*, August 10, 1979, 18.

30 **"Every dollar I've ever made":** AP, "Oil Slick Inches toward Texas Coast," *Odessa American*, August 1, 1979, 5A; AP, "Oil Spill Presents Slick Irony to Texans," *El Paso Times*, August 5, 1979, 1.

30 **The neighbor's young daughter:** Author phone interview with Beth Aplin Martin, May 20, 2020.

30 **two days after Billy Joe received a not-guilty verdict:** "Defendant Vindicated," *Victoria Advocate*, June 27, 1979, 12A.

30 **"I'll bet you understand *that!*":** Author interview with Beth Aplin Martin, Seguin, TX, May 14, 2019.

## 5. NEWCOMERS

33 **There were eighty-two members of his family:** Interview with Bảng "Cherry" Nguyễn by Tim Tsai.

33 **hundreds of thousands of others were fleeing:** Office of the United Nations High Commissioner for Refugees and M. Cutts, *The State of the World's Refugees, 2000: Fifty Years of Humanitarian Action* (UNHCR and Oxford University Press, 2000), 90.

33 **a Gallup poll:** Lewis M. Stern, "Response to Vietnamese Refugees: Surveys of Public Opinion," *Social Work* 26, no. 4 (1981), 306–11.

33 **"to do less would have added moral shame to humiliation":** Quang X. Pham, "Ford's Finest Legacy," *The Washington Post*, December 30, 2006.

34 **they'd rather spend their days behind bars:** Frank Randol, "Seafood Industry Safety Standards," testimony before the US Senate Committee on Small Business and Entrepreneurship, May 6, 2015.

34 **More often than not, he was met:** Interview with Bảng "Cherry" Nguyễn by Tim Tsai.

35 **White townspeople began referring to by various names:** Author phone interview with Richard Haight, September 27, 2019.

36 **No paperwork or lawyers were required:** Thao Le-Thanh Ha, "Immigrant Business and the Racialization of Work: A Tale of Two Niches in Texas' Vietnamese Communities" (PhD dissertation, University of Texas at Austin, 2012), 86.

36 **By 1978, two years after Bằng's arrival:** Marine Advisory Service, "Strangers in a Strange Land—a Delicate Balance" (Texas A&M University, November 1979), 5.

36 **Verlon was flying so much crabmeat:** Frank A. DeFilippo, "The Real Threat to National Security," *Maryland Matters*, July 8, 2018.

36 **He'd been conscripted into the South Vietnamese marines:** Ross Milloy, "Vietnam Fallout in a Texas Town," *The New York Times Magazine*, April 6, 1980, 39.

37 **"I got a problem!":** Interview with Bằng "Cherry" Nguyễn by Tim Tsai.

37 **But even when he went out early:** *Seadrift*, directed by Tim Tsai (Title 8 Productions, 2019).

37 **one Vietnamese family was missing 86:** "Resentment Seen Cause of Viet Crabbing Hassle," *Victoria Advocate*, February 19, 1977, 8B.

37 **"Wait right here!":** Interview with Bằng "Cherry" Nguyễn by Tim Tsai.

38 **"Oh yeah?! I've got a knife, too!":** Author interview with Beth Aplin Martin, Seguin, TX, May 14, 2019.

## 6. COLLISION COURSE

39 **Billy Joe wandered past:** Author interview with Judy Aplin, Seguin, TX, August 30, 2019.

39 **she had even driven around their part of town:** Author interview with Judy Aplin, Seguin, TX, August 30, 2019.

39 **Aplin started chopping at it:** Interview with Bằng "Cherry" Nguyễn by Tim Tsai.

40 **When a Vietnamese crabber pulled up:** Author phone interview with Richard Haight, October 2, 2019.

40 **When Billy Joe raised a rifle:** "Aplin Shooting Recounted by Vietnamese Defendant," *Victoria Advocate*, November 2, 1979, 10A.

40 **The two had a similar build and haircut:** Testimony of Sáu Văn Nguyễn, November 1, 1979. The State of Texas v. Sau Van Nguyen and Chinh Van Nguyen, 21.

40 **The Vietnamese were buying guns of their own:** *Seadrift*, directed by Tim Tsai (Title 8 Productions, 2019).

40 **Bằng had received threats:** Interview with Bằng "Cherry" Nguyễn by Tim Tsai.

40 **a photojournalist published a bombshell series of photos:** Ron Laytner, "I Infiltrated the Ku Klux Klan . . . and Lived!," *Argosy*, August 1978.

41 **"Fuck you! I ain't moving nowhere!":** Interview with Bằng "Cherry" Nguyễn by Tim Tsai.

41 **a forty-mile-long "tongue":** AP, "Spill Less Toxic Than First Feared," *Kilgore News Herald*, August 10, 1979, 1.

41 **Those who swam in the water:** Jim Baker, "Giant Vacuums Used to Clean Up Padre's Oil," *Austin American-Statesman*, August 8, 1979, 1.

41 **"The Vietnamese are gonna ruin the bays!":** Author interview with Diane Wilson, Seadrift, TX, August 29, 2019.

42 **Forty times a day:** Diane Wilson, *An Unreasonable Woman: A True Story of Shrimpers, Politicos, Polluters, and the Fight for Seadrift, Texas* (Chelsea Green, 2005), 360.

42 **Late one Saturday night:** Ross Milloy, "Vietnam Fallout in a Texas Town," *The New York Times Magazine*, April 6, 1980, 39.

42 **Sáu told his brothers that trouble:** Milloy, "Vietnam Fallout in a Texas Town."

43 **He slashed its tires:** Interview with Bằng "Cherry" Nguyễn by Tim Tsai.

43 **It felt as though his eye was filled:** Author interview with Judy Aplin, Seguin, TX, August 30, 2019.

43 **he fell into a deep sleep:** John Bloom, "A Delicate Balance," *Texas Monthly*, October 1979, 257.

43 **Police Chief Bill Lindsey added a chat:** "Testimony to Resume in Brothers' Trial," *Victoria Advocate*, November 1, 1979, 12A.

43 **he trudged out the door:** Author interview with Beth Aplin Martin, Seguin, TX, May 14, 2019.

44 **"Who is this guy?":** "Aplin Shooting Recounted by Vietnamese Defendant," *Victoria Advocate*, November 2, 1979, 10A.

44 **"If you don't move out of Seadrift":** "Aplin Shooting Recounted by Vietnamese Defendant."

44 **Sáu stood up and folded his arms:** Testimony of Sáu Văn Nguyễn, November 1, 1979. *The State of Texas v. Sau Van Nguyen and Chinh Van Nguyen*, 37.

44 **Sáu managed to pry himself free:** "Testimony to Resume in Brothers' Trial."

44 **"This town is my town!":** "Witnesses Reconstruct Aplin Slaying," *Victoria Advocate*, October 31, 1979, 12A.

44 **"Where's my gun?":** Interview with Bằng "Cherry" Nguyễn by Tim Tsai.

## 7. "NO, MAN . . . NO!"

46 **"No, man . . . No!":** Author interview with Beth Aplin Martin, Seguin, TX, May 14, 2019.

46 **"There's going to be trouble at the docks!":** Interview with Bằng "Cherry" Nguyễn by Tim Tsai.

46 **Bằng sped off in search of Sáu:** "Testimony to Resume in Brothers' Trial," *Victoria Advocate*, November 1, 1979, 12A.

46 **she went numb:** Author interview with Judy Aplin, Seguin, TX, August 30, 2019.

47 **the car erupted with screams:** Author interview with Beth Aplin Martin, Seguin, TX, May 14, 2019.

47 **"What happened?":** Interview with Bằng "Cherry" Nguyễn by Tim Tsai.

47 **Bằng was worried that the Klan might show up:** Interview with Bằng "Cherry" Nguyễn by Tim Tsai.

47 **Chief Lindsey pulled up to the trailer park:** "Testimony to Resume in Brothers' Trial."

47 **Chính was arrested as a probable accomplice:** Clifford Cain, "Rifle Said Lost After Arrest," *Victoria Advocate*, November 1, 1979, 1.

## 8. SEADRIFT AWAKES TO ASHES

48 **Bằng pulled up to the bus station:** "Testimony to Resume in Brothers' Trial," *Victoria Advocate*, November 1, 1979, 12A.

48 **When Beth walked through the living room:** Author interview with Beth Aplin Martin, Seguin, TX, May 14, 2019.

49 **The police were waiting for him:** Interview with Bằng "Cherry" Nguyễn by Tim Tsai.

49 **Across town, in a small mesquite grove:** Author phone interview with Richard Haight, October 2, 2019.

49 **They rustled up several empty liquor bottles:** Author phone interview with Richard Haight, September 25, 2019.

49 **They all shook on it:** Author phone interview with Richard Haight, October 15, 2019.

50 **"Go fuck yourselves, you sonsofbitches!":** Author phone interview with Richard Haight, September 25, 2019.

51 **"Ray Mooney's house is burning down!":** Author phone interview with Richard Haight, September 25, 2019.

51 **As he drifted off:** Author phone interview with Richard Haight, October 15, 2019.

51 **One of her high school classmates:** Author interview with Diane Wilson, Seadrift, TX, August 29, 2019.

51 **"There's going to be war":** Warren Brown, "Fishermen's Feud Now a Town's War," *The Washington Post*, August 11, 1979.

51 **"You killed my brother":** Linda Gillan, "Seadrift Violence Could Haunt Coast," *Fort Worth Star-Telegram*, August 21, 1979, 12A.

52 **"I don't have the power to protect them":** Lucius Lomax, "Vietnamese Refugees Embroiled in Coastal Town Controversy," *Austin American-Statesman*, August 8, 1979, A1.

52 **They pulled their crab traps out of the water:** Stephanie Kiesel, "Seadrift Quiet, but Still Tense," *Victoria Advocate*, August 19, 1979, 9.

52 **A photographer from the Associated Press:** Molly Ivins, "Violent Texas Feud Makes Vietnamese Refugees Once More," *The New York Times*, August 11, 1979, A8.

53 **Rumors swirled that Verlon Davis's crab-picking plant:** Gillan, "Seadrift Violence Could Haunt Coast."

53 **Some 120 of the 150 Vietnamese:** Linda Gillan, "Texan-Viet Clashes Kill One and Frighten Many," *Los Angeles Times*, August 26, 1979, 3.

53 **"They're so *different*":** Lomax, "Vietnamese Refugees Embroiled in Coastal Town Controversy."

53 **"They're the hardest-working people here":** Lucius Lomax, "Diverse Cultures Fuel Seadrift Feud," *Austin American-Statesman*, August 12, 1979, A8.

53 **When they brought him into an interrogation room:** Bằng Nguyễn interview with Tim Tsai.

53 **"My son died standing up for his rights":** *Seadrift*, directed by Tim Tsai (Title 8 Productions, 2019).

53 **"These people . . . they don't think like us!":** *Seadrift*.

54 **His brother Doc:** Ivins, "Violent Texas Feud Makes Vietnamese Refugees Once More," A8.

54 **He was wearing the white shirt:** Author interview with Beth Aplin Martin, Seguin, TX, May 14, 2019.

54 **The bewildered officer:** AP, "Refugees, Texans in Fish Fight," *The Independent-Record*, August 9, 1979, 10.

54 **"Somebody's gonna take care of those Vietnamese":** *Vietnam in Texas*, directed by Mark Brice (1980).

54 **He started carrying a snub-nosed .38:** Author phone interview with Verlon Davis, October 28, 2019.

54 **Chief Lindsey burst inside:** "Men Arrested for Explosives," *Victoria Advocate*, August 9, 1979, 1.

## 9. THE KLAN COMES TO SEADRIFT

57 **He knew the wheels of justice:** "Pat Maloney Sr.," *San Antonio Express-News*, September 13, 2005.

57 **"redneck" and a "plaintiff's purgatory":** "Venue Change Sought Again," *Victoria Advocate*, October 19, 1979, 12.

57 **Maloney thrashed through the voir dire:** Voir Dire Examination of the Jury Panel, October 29, 1979. The State of Texas v. Sau Van Nguyen and Chinh Van Nguyen.

57 **"If those boys don't get a reasonable sentence":** AP, "Jury Quiz Begins for Viets," *Fort Worth Star-Telegram*, October 29, 1979, 17A.

57 **On the first day:** Author interview with Pat Maloney Jr., San Antonio, August 30, 2019.

58 **"a big ole fighter with a bad reputation":** Guillermo Garcia, "Seadrift Official Says Rifts Were Rumors," *Austin American-Statesman*, November 1, 1979, B1.

58 **According to the constable:** AP, "Witnesses Say Fisherman Made Threats," *Odessa American*, November 1, 1979, 10A.

58 **Verlon Davis's wife, Georgia Ann:** AP, "Witnesses Say Fisherman Made Threats."

58 **Maloney even managed to get the prosecution's eyewitnesses:** AP, "Witnesses Describe Seadrift Slaying," *Fort Worth Star-Telegram*, October 31, 1979, 11C.

59 **Speaking in a quiet voice:** "Aplin Shooting Recounted by Vietnamese Defendant," *Victoria Advocate*, November 2, 1979, 10A.

59 **"As little as they are":** Guillermo Garcia, "Refugee Acquitted in Seadrift Slaying," *Austin American-Statesman*, November 3, 1979, 9.

59 **He'd hoped all along to be acquitted:** Clifford Cain, "Vietnamese Acquitted in Slaying," *Victoria Advocate*, November 3, 1979, 12A.

59 **proclaiming that Sáu's acquittal:** Cain, "Vietnamese Acquitted," 1.

59 **"The Vietnamese just declared war":** "Seadrift Apprehensive," *Victoria Advocate*, November 3, 1979, 1.

60 **Bằng drove Sáu and Chính up to Houston:** Interview with Bằng "Cherry" Nguyễn by Tim Tsai.

60 **"We're getting ready for the worst":** AP, "Second Refugee Acquitted in Seadrift Killing," *El Paso Times*, November 3, 1979, 5-B.

60 **lead the charge to "burn 'em out":** *Seadrift*, directed by Tim Tsai (Title 8 Productions, 2019).

61 **Someone from Seadrift:** Felix Sanchez, "6 Klansmen Come to Seadrift," *Corpus Christi Caller-Times*, November 25, 1979, 4E.

61 **Junior high schools were pulling out:** Clifford Cain, "Seadrift Resolution Condemns Violence," *Victoria Advocate*, November 21, 1979, 1.

61 **"All we're after is truth and justice":** AP, "Seadrift Officials Want KKK Out," *The Marshall News Messenger*, November 22, 1979, 8A.

61 **By a unanimous vote:** *Vietnam in Texas*, directed by Mark Brice (1980).

62 **But to Beam, it suggested a cover-up:** "Klan Leader, Officials Meet," *Victoria Advocate*, November 25, 1979, 3A.

62 **If he wasn't pleased, he warned:** AP, "Klan Seeks Trial Evidence," *Fort Worth Star-Telegram*, November 26, 1979, 8C.

62 **"Would the Klan be here today":** *Vietnam in Texas*.

62 **"There will be no peace on the bay":** Patrick Oster, "Texas Town Turns Against Viet Refugees," *Los Angeles Times*, November 23, 1979, 10.

63 **"I got news for them":** Bill Douthat, "Seadrift Ready to Forget Tragedy," *Austin American-Statesman*, January 27, 1980, B4.

63 **The Vietnamese trailer park:** Douthat, "Seadrift Ready to Forget Tragedy."

63 **She felt "dumb as a hammer":** Diane Wilson, *Diary of an Eco-Outlaw: An Unreasonable Woman Breaks the Law for Mother Earth* (Chelsea Green, 2005), 12.

63 **As millions of gallons seeped into Galveston Bay:** Shelly Henley Kelly, "1970–1979: Bringing the Past Alive," *Galveston Daily News*, December 12, 1999, C6.

63 **And on land, the Formosa Plastics Group:** "Bond Issue for Formosa Plant OK'd," *Victoria Advocate*, December 15, 1979, 1C.

64 **She might have told them about the ceremony:** Author interview with Judy Aplin, Seguin, TX, August 30, 2019.

64 **After checking out the John Birch Society:** *Portrait of a Klansman*, directed by Wayne Derrick and Brad Walker (1981).

64 **He was arrested on charges:** "4 Indicted in Crosby School Bus Bombing," *The Baytown Sun*, June 11, 1971, 1; and http://www.bbsdocumentary.com/library/CONTROVERSY/EVIL/RACISTBBSES/sampletext.txt.

65 **The initiation ceremony:** Douthat, "Seadrift Ready to Forget Tragedy."

## 10. THE AMERICAN FISHERMEN'S ASSOCIATION

71 **As dawn broke over 1980:** Greg Cantrell, "Attempt to Put Out Burmah Fire Fails," *Galveston Daily News*, January 8, 1980, 1.

71 **Fishermen reported a heavy "rainbow sheen":** "Light Sheen of Oil Leaks from Tanker," *Galveston Daily News*, January 4, 1980, 2-A.

71 **along its seabed ran 247 miles:** Stephen Harrigan, "Worked to Death," *Texas Monthly*, October 1988, 192.

72 **By the dawn of the 1980s:** L. Handley, D. Altsman, and R. DeMay, eds., *Seagrass Status and Trends in the Northern Gulf of Mexico: 1940–2002*, US Geological Survey Scientific Investigations Report 2006-5287 (2007), 17.

72 **"I think you would have to say":** Cantrell, "Attempt to Put Out Burmah Fire Fails."

72 **That same week:** AP, "Pemex Denies Oil Well Leak Is Threat to Coast of Texas," *Fort Worth Star-Telegram*, January 3, 1980, 7B.

72 **"If the oil happens to be out there":** AP, "Further Gulf Oil Spill Losses Predicted," *Fort Worth Star-Telegram*, January 4, 1980, 1C.

73 **Fisher, who'd spent a portion of his childhood:** Author phone interview with Marilyn Collins, February 11, 2020.

73 **A handful of years later:** Paul Sweeney, "Texas Fishing Town Struggling with Influx of Vietnamese," *Boston Globe*, August 29, 1982, 78.

73 **After coming home:** Sweeney, "Texas Fishing Town Struggling."

73 **The National Marine Fisheries Service:** AP, "Clements Requests SBA Loans for Ailing Texas Shrimpers," *El Paso Times*, November 21, 1979, 9-A.

73 **But Gene viewed Galveston Bay like an ATM:** Author interview with Joseph "Jody" Collins, Kemah, TX, May 15, 2019.

73 **"He's a real redneck":** Sweeney, "Texas Fishing Town Struggling," 78.

74 **But Gene never took his counsel:** Sweeney, "Texas Fishing Town Struggling."

74 **"Nobody realizes the hell I go through":** Mark Smith, "The Resurging Texas Klan," *Houston Chronicle*, July 1, 1990, 2.

74 **"This is not their country":** Leon Daniel, "Klansmen vs. Viet Refugees on Galveston Bay," UPI, June 11, 1981.

75 **"We cannot compete with these people":** J. Michael Kennedy, "Gulf Violence on Threshold?," *Los Angeles Times*, March 13, 1981, 1D.

75 **"We know this money can't replace her husband":** Darla Morgan, "Refusal of Gifts Dampens U.S.-Viet Shrimper Meeting," *Galveston Daily News*, December 20, 1979, 8A.

75 **Mediators looked on nervously:** UPI, "Relocating Vietnamese Proposed," *Galveston Daily News*, October 19, 1979, 16-B.

75 **"This is a fight for survival!":** Morgan, "Refusal of Gifts Dampens U.S.-Viet Shrimper Meeting."

76 **"The solution is no more refugees!":** Max Rizley Jr., "Tension Continues in Viet Shrimper Dispute," *Galveston Daily News*, May 15, 1980, 2-A.

## 11. THE COLONEL

77 **He was the Colonel's firstborn son:** Author interview with Michael Phương Minh Nguyễn, Orange, CA, May 19, 2021.

78 **Hồ Chí Minh returned from exile:** Fredrik Logevall, *Embers of War* (Random House, 2012), 34.

78 **For nearly a century:** Logevall, *Embers of War*, 74.

78 **Days later, the French claimed:** Interview with Nam Văn Nguyễn by Nancy Bui, March 1, 2011. Vietnamese American Heritage Foundation oral history interviews, 2011, MS 647, Woodson Research Center, Fondren Library, Rice University. Translation by Steve Pham, USA Vietnamese Translation Services.

78 **After another classmate was shot:** Interview with Nam Văn Nguyễn by Nancy Bui, March 1, 2011. Vietnamese American Heritage Foundation oral history interviews, 2011, MS 647, Woodson Research Center, Fondren Library, Rice University. Translation by Steve Pham, USA Vietnamese Translation Services.

79 **US destroyers ferried matériel:** Thomas A. Bass, *The Spy Who Loved Us: The Vietnam War and Pham Xuan An's Dangerous Game* (PublicAffairs, 2009), 46.

79 **Fourteen thousand men and women:** Charles R. Shrader, *A War of Logistics: Parachutes and Porters in Indochina, 1945–1954* (University Press of Kentucky, 2015), 344.

79 **the first two American pilots were killed:** Bernard Fall, *Hell in a Very Small Place: The Siege of Dien Bien Phu* (Lippincott, 1967), 327–28.

79 **In the forests of Khe Sanh:** Author interview with Nam Văn Nguyễn, Houston, August 28, 2019.

81 **others paid small fortunes for a sip of water:** Malcolm W. Browne, "A Refugee Barge Yields 50 Dead at Vietnam Pier," *The New York Times*, April 7, 1975.

81 **There were more than eight thousand refugees:** Andrew H. Malcolm, "48,000 Refugees Jammed on Guam," *The New York Times*, May 10, 1975, 1.

## 12. THE SEABROOK AGREEMENT

85 **After the payment was made:** Darla Morgan, "Refusal of Gifts Dampen U.S.-Viet Shrimper Meeting," *Galveston Daily News*, December 20, 1979, 1.

86 **The Vietnamese called themselves "thầy trọc":** Nam Văn Nguyễn, "Remarks at a General Meeting Convened at Seabrook Between Texas State Officials and American and Vietnamese Fishermen," February 23, 1981.

87 **"Some people don't like us":** Darla Morgan, "New Life for Vietnamese Means New Struggles," *Galveston Daily News*, November 8, 1979, 1-D.

87 **"they don't want Vietnamese fishing":** Morgan, "New Life for Vietnamese Means New Struggles."

87 **They were chatting too much:** Max Rizley Jr., "Tension Continues in Viet Shrimper Dispute," *Galveston Daily News*, May 15, 1980, 1.

87 **"If a man's working for me":** *Fire on the Water*, directed by Robert Hillmann (1982).

88 **"The Vietnamese still have the togetherness":** *Fire on the Water*.

88 **"I just think it's unfair competition":** Glenn Lewis, "Troubled Waters," *Houston Post*, November 11, 1979, 1.

88 **"The Americans are jealous":** Lewis, "Troubled Waters."

88 **"When it is raining":** Morgan, "New Life for Vietnamese Means New Struggles."

89 "All it's going to take": Morgan, "New Life for Vietnamese Means New Struggles."

89 "The government thinks more of them": Rizley, "Tension Continues in Viet Shrimper Dispute," 2-A.

89 "I'm talking, running off at the mouth": Rizley, "Tension Continues in Viet Shrimper Dispute," 2-A.

90 In the ten months since the deep-water well ruptured: Linda Garmon, "Autopsy of an Oil Spill," *Science News* 118, no. 17 (1980), 267–70.

90 They claimed there was "improper or incomplete screening": UPI, "Shrimpers Warning Refugees," *Tyler Courier-Times*, March 30, 1980, 8.

90 "All the ingredients are here": UPI, "Shrimpers Warning Refugees."

91 "The current situation, if it is not to explode": "Report on Meeting with Shrimp Fishermen at Seabrook, Texas," March 28, 1980, box 21, folder 5, Governor William P. Clements, Jr. Official State Papers, 1st Term, 1979–1983, William P. Clements, Jr. Collection, Cushing Memorial Library and Archives, Texas A&M University.

91 One week before the start: Ken Herman, "Tension Up over Viet Shrimpers," *Fort Worth Star-Telegram*, May 9, 1980, 23A.

91 Martinez was hopeful: "Vietnamese Find Ally in Texas: Time," *The New York Times*, September 29, 1986, 12.

91 The number of boats working Galveston Bay: AP, "American, Vietnamese Fishermen Keep Feuding Despite Agreement," *El Paso Times*, December 31, 1980, 3-A.

92 After Southern California: Fred R. von der Mehden, "Vietnamese," *Handbook of Texas Online*, Texas State Historical Association, http://www.tshaonline.org/handbook/online/articles/pjv01.

92 "I discourage other Vietnamese": Rizley, "Tension Continues in Viet Shrimper Dispute," 1.

92 "Given time, I think the programs will work": Rizley, "Tension Continues in Viet Shrimper Dispute," 1.

## 13. A FRAGILE PEACE, TORCHED

93 "Nam! Why are you letting your people": Deposition of Nam Văn Nguyễn, May 5, 1981, Vietnamese Fishermen's Association v. Knights of the Ku Klux Klan, Civ. A, no. H-81-895, United States District Court for the Southern District of Texas, 543 F. Supp. 198 (S.D. Tex. 1982), 36.

94 "If I catch anyone burning boats here": AP, "Witness Tells of Threats," *Victoria Advocate*, May 12, 1981, 3A.

94 The Vietnamese shrimper was alarmed: Deposition of Nam Văn Nguyễn, 51.

94 The sixth was registered in Louisiana: AP, "Seabrook Groups OK Pact," *Fort Worth Star-Telegram*, January 9, 1981, 7C.

95 "We hope the American shrimpers": AP, "Vietnamese Shrimpers Agree to Boat Limit," *Odessa American*, January 10, 1981, 10A.

95 "Better to burn them": AP, "Vietnamese Shrimpers Agree to Boat Limit."

95 On January 10: AP, "Viet, Texas Shrimpers Find Accord," *Fort Worth Star-Telegram*, 8-B.

95 She owned the boat: Seabrook Police Department Arson Report no. 81-0149, January 11, 1981. Freedom of Information Act (hereafter FOIA).

95 Someone had severed the boat's fuel line: Seabrook Police Department Arson report no. 81-0149.

96 The Opel had been at the Stardust: Kemah Police Department Arson Report no. 81-6, January 12, 1981. FOIA.

96 **"With the current Vietnamese fishing problems"**: Kemah Police Department Arson Report no. 81-6.

96 **"There's no doubt in anyone's mind"**: AP, "Fires Fan Shrimp Feud," *Longview News-Journal*, January 13, 1981, 3-A.

96 **After midnight, a white-and-blue 1971 Oldsmobile**: Memorandum of Houston Arson Intelligence Division, Bureau of Alcohol, Tobacco and Firearms, Department of the Treasury, "Vietnamese Shrimp Boat Fires," January 20, 1981. FOIA.

97 **Then, as quietly as they'd come**: Memorandum of Houston Arson Intelligence Division, "Vietnamese Shrimp Boat Fires."

## 14. ESCALATIONS

98 **He'd done three tours in Vietnam**: Author phone interview with Barry Freece, March 26, 2020.

98 **When the Klansmen realized his training**: Author phone interview with Barry Freece, March 26, 2020.

99 **"We have no way of proving it"**: AP, "Tension Blamed on Press," *Fort Worth Star-Telegram*, January 14, 1981, 8A.

99 **Even though he was privately skeptical**: AP, "Vietnamese Problems Grow on Coast," *Victoria Advocate*, January 14, 1981, 7B.

99 **As part of his investigation**: Memorandum of Houston Arson Intelligence Division, Bureau of Alcohol, Tobacco and Firearms, Department of the Treasury, "Vietnamese Shrimp Boat Fires," January 20, 1981. FOIA.

99 **"It is interesting"**: Memorandum of Houston Arson Intelligence Division, "Vietnamese Shrimp Boat Fires."

99 **"I feel that the suspects in this case"**: Memorandum of Houston Arson Intelligence Division, "Vietnamese Shrimp Boat Fires."

100 **he'd started describing as "fire ants"**: *"Made" in America: Refugee Dreams, Refugee Nightmares*, KUHT Houston, produced by Ginger Casey, January 27, 1988.

101 **The air was so foul**: Kent Biffle, "No Place Like Pasadena," *Scene: the Dallas Morning News Sunday Magazine*, July 31, 1977.

101 **In the 1970 census**: Biffle, "No Place Like Pasadena."

## 15. LOUIS RAY BEAM JR.

102 **One army helicopter was lost**: John Sotham, "Huey," *Air & Space Magazine*, May 2000.

102 **killing forty-five hundred pilots and crewmen**: Bill Lord, "The Chopper Pilots," *The New York Times*, March 20, 2018.

102 **"the envy of every door gunner"**: Louis Beam, "Body Count," http://www.louisbeam.com/bodyct.htm.

102 **He survived all the "meat runs"**: Louis Beam, "A Card and Cookies," http://www.louisbeam.com/cardcook.htm.

102 **Survived the day a Viet Cong fighter**: Louis Beam, August 29, 2005, email, http://www.louisbeam.com/backgroundlb.htm.

102 **Survived a thousand hours of combat flight time**: Louis Beam, *Essays of a Klansman* (1983), 36.

103 **As Deng and his wife**: Z. Joe Thornton, "Irate Man Lunges at Teng in Houston," *Fort Worth Star-Telegram*, February 3, 1979, 1.

103 **He was only feet away**: Author phone interview with Paul Kelly, July 3, 2019.

103 **As Kelly and the Chinese delegation sped off:** Author phone interview with Paul Kelly, July 3, 2019.

103 **No time served:** AP, "Houston Bombing Probe Grand Jury Declares Recess," *Valley Morning Star*, May 29, 1971, 9.

104 **Freed on bond:** "Police-Klan Link Eyed in Houston," *The New York Times*, March 7, 1972.

104 **Beam couldn't resist bragging:** Ron Laytner, "Vietnam Diary of a Klansman Hero," *Sunday Post-Herald*, October 20, 1974, 13.

104 **"new generation Klansman":** UPI, "Louis Beam Is New Generation Klansman," *The Seymour Tribune*, October 24, 1979, 1.

104 **One credulous profile:** UPI, "Louis Beam Is New Generation Klansman."

104 **due to the rising popularity of David Duke:** Kathleen Belew, *Bring the War Home: The White Power Movement and Paramilitary America* (Harvard University Press, 2018), 35.

105 **the Klan's favorability ratings:** Belew, *Bring the War Home*, 58.

105 **threats to "racial order":** Belew, *Bring the War Home*, 61.

105 **as far back as junior high:** "Friends, Relatives Recall Former State KKK Chief as 'Electrifying' Speaker," *Kerrville Times*, November 18, 1987, 8.

105 **In 1965, the year his mother went on trial:** Casey Edward Greene, "Apostles of Hate: The Ku Klux Klan in and near Houston, Texas, 1920–1982" (master's thesis, University of Houston–Clear Lake, 1995), 60.

105 **"the epitome of what a dedicated Klan leader":** "National Convention, Knights of the KKK, New Orleans, Louisiana, Labor Day Weekend, Presentation of Louis Beam of Texas, Confidential, 1979," audio recording, records of Governor Mark White, Texas State Archives, box 1991/106-38. Beam's comments following are from the same source.

106 **When the cheering subsided:** "National Convention, Knights of the KKK."

106 **Not long after the Klan convention:** *Portrait of a Klansman*, directed by Wayne Derrick and Brad Walker (1981).

107 **killing his father-in-law for an $800 bounty:** AP, "Contract Killer Reportedly Taught 'Survival' at Camp," *Odessa American*, December 7, 1980, 13A.

107 **"There are only two groups I'll battle with":** UPI, "Klansman Teaches Explorers How to Kill," *Longview News-Journal*, November 23, 1980, 6-A.

107 **"We'll set up our own state here":** Daniel Gearino, "Armed Klansmen Taught How to Take Over U.S.," *Billings Gazette*, July 26, 1980, 1.

107 **They taught the boys how to garrote:** "Paramilitary Actions Irk Neighbors of Texas Camp," *The New York Times*, November 30, 1980, 67.

107 **One furious mother reported:** AP, "Woman Asserts Scouts Planned to Hunt Aliens," *The New York Times*, November 26, 1980, B4.

107 **Other parents reported that their kids:** UPI, "Boys Reported Learning to Shoot and Kill at a Klan Camp in Texas," *The New York Times*, November 24, 1980, A21.

107 **At the end of 1980:** *Portrait of a Klansman*.

108 **He took stock of the bookstore:** Dick J. Reavis, "Klan on the Ropes," *Texas Observer*, September 19, 1980, 8.

108 **Klan robes and hoods were on sale:** Kent Biffle, "No Place Like Pasadena," *Scene: The Dallas Morning News Sunday Magazine*, July 31, 1977.

108 **"Well, what are the intentions":** *Portrait of a Klansman*.

## 16. THE COLLINS RANCH

111 **"Do *not* have it on our property!":** Author phone interview with Marilyn Collins, September 4, 2019.

112 **"Haven't you had enough?"** Dan Bradford, "KKK Action Prompts SF Mass Meeting Law," *Galveston Daily News*, February 5, 1981, 1.

112 **"It all boils down to this guy":** Bradford, "KKK Action Prompts SF Mass Meeting Law."

112 **"I *went* to my government":** "1979–81 Special Report: 'Vietnamese vs. Ku Klux Klan,'" YouTube video with CBS News footage, at 4:33, posted by Hezakya Newz & Films, January 28, 2019, https://www.youtube.com/watch?v=6tS7mR8iDL0&t=506s.

113 **The Texas Education Agency:** Mark Toohey, "Refugees to Learn Seafood Processing," *Houston Chronicle*, date unknown.

113 **The legislature was considering a "Limited Entry" bill:** Relating to the Issuance of Commercial Bay Shrimp Boat Licenses and Commercial Bait-Shrimp Boat Licenses, H.B. 828, 67th Cong. (1981).

113 **On February 13, Governor Clements announced:** AP, "Klan Plans Protest of Gulf Vietnamese," *Austin American-Statesman*, February 14, 1981, B5.

113 **"No, I'm not worried":** Transcript of Governor William P. Clements Jr. press conference, February 13, 1981, 11, Governor William P. Clements, Jr. Official State Papers, 1st Term, 1979–1983, William P. Clements, Jr. Collection, Cushing Memorial Library and Archives, Texas A&M University.

## 17. A VALENTINE'S DAY KLAN RALLY

115 **The road leading onto the Collins ranch:** AP, "KKK, Fishermen Protest Viet Refugees," *Fort Worth Star-Telegram*, February 15, 1981, 40A.

115 **The air was thick with the smell:** Bruce Nichols, UPI, "Texas KKK Has Other Fish to Fry: Viets," *The Honolulu Advertiser*, February 15, 1981, J-48.

115 **The Bandidos motorcycle gang:** UPI, "Klansmen Burn 'USS *Viet Cong*,'" *The Billings Gazette*, February 15, 1981, 2-H.

115 **A young boy with a toy rifle:** AP, "KKK, Fishermen Protest Viet Refugees."

115 **The Texas Rangers arrived:** Teri Crook, "Rally Showcase for Media Attention," *Galveston Daily News*, February 15, 1981, 2.

116 **"There's a lot of people that's mad":** Plaintiffs' Exhibit 18, Vietnamese Fishermen's Association v. Knights of the Ku Klux Klan, Civ. A, no. H-81-895, United States District Court for the Southern District of Texas, 543 F. Supp. 198 (S.D. Tex. 1982).

116 **"But I've got a dream":** Nichols, UPI, "Texas KKK Has Other Fish to Fry: Viets."

116 **"I've always thought the Klan stirred up":** Nichols, UPI, "Texas KKK Has Other Fish to Fry."

116 **"support all of the fishermen":** AP, "Klan, Gulf Fishermen Protest Viet Refugees," *Victoria Advocate*, February 15, 1981, 14A.

117 **"They paid us to shoot them":** Nichols, UPI, "Texas KKK Has Other Fish to Fry: Viets."

117 **"merely sympathetic to U.S. fishermen":** Crook, "Rally Showcase for Media Attention."

117 **"show us the right way to burn":** *Portrait of a Klansman*, directed by Wayne Derrick and Brad Walker, 1981.

117 **"Now . . . this is just in case":** Plaintiffs' Exhibit 18, Vietnamese Fishermen's Association v. Knights of the Ku Klux Klan.

117 **With the insurance payment:** Author phone interview with Marilyn Collins, September 4, 2019.

118 **"I'm white and proud":** Dan Bradford, "Klan Gives Officials 90-Day Ultimatum to Solve Conflict," *Galveston Daily News*, February 15, 1981, 2-A.

118 **"I'll be here fishing":** Plaintiffs' Exhibit 19, Vietnamese Fishermen's Association v. Knights of the Ku Klux Klan.

118 **"Your instructions are to apprehend":** Crook, "Rally Showcase for Media Attention."

118 **"you just hit 'em in the head":** *Portrait of a Klansman.*

118 **"Isn't it true that the fishermen asked you all here?":** *Portrait of a Klansman.*

118 **He never read from notes:** Deposition of Louis Beam, vol. II, April 30, 1981, Vietnamese Fishermen's Association v. Knights of the Ku Klux Klan, 26.

118 **"All of you understand, we're not having an anti-Vietnamese rally":** *Portrait of a Klansman.*

119 **"They are your replacements":** UPI, "400 Hear KKK Assail Refugees," *The Arizona Republic,* February 16, 1981, A24.

120 **"If a burned boat doesn't look like that":** Bradford, "Klan Gives Officials 90-Day Ultimatum to Solve Conflict."

121 **"I promise you":** *Portrait of a Klansman.*

121 **The cross, propped up:** Memorandum Opinion and Order, Vietnamese Fishermen's Association v. Knights of the Ku Klux Klan, 5.

## 18. THE BALD-HEADS OF SEABROOK

122 **As Jody picked up the trash:** Deposition of Joseph C. Collins, May 2, 1981, Vietnamese Fishermen's Association v. Knights of the Ku Klux Klan, Civ. A, no. H-81-895, United States District Court for the Southern District of Texas, 543 F. Supp. 198 (S.D. Tex. 1982).

122 **Of the twenty thousand commercial shrimpers:** AP, "Fishing Dispute Attracts Klan," *Victoria Advocate,* February 16, 1981, 8A.

123 **"It cost us $2,000 for the rally":** J. Michael Kennedy, "Gulf Violence on Threshold?," *Los Angeles Times,* March 13, 1981, 1D.

123 **"What we are aiming for is a complete halt":** Bill Douthat, "The Battle Neither Side May Win," *Austin American-Statesman,* February 22, 1981, A10.

123 *Houston Monthly* **posed a question:** Pete Billac, "Right or Wrong?," *Houston Monthly,* April 1981, 36.

124 **Jones himself was born in Alabama:** Douthat, "The Battle Neither Side May Win," 1.

124 **"As soon as he pulled it out of the water":** Douthat, "The Battle Neither Side May Win," A10.

124 **"It's nice they are all grouped together":** Douthat, "The Battle Neither Side May Win."

124 **"You have to find a way":** Interview with Nam Văn Nguyễn by Steven Loyd and Mei Leebron, Houston Asian American Archive, Chao Center for Asian Studies, Rice University, June 11, 2019.

125 **"Ladies and Gentlemen":** "Remarks Made by Mr. Nguyễn Văn Nam," February 28, 1981, Governor William P. Clements, Jr. Official State Papers, 1st Term, 1979–1983, William P. Clements, Jr. Collection, Cushing Memorial Library and Archives, Texas A&M University.

126 **"I personally remained behind":** Dan Bradford, "Vietnamese Shrimper Offers to Depart in Response to Crisis," *Galveston Daily News,* March 4, 1981, 2-A.

126 **sixty of the one hundred Vietnamese fishermen:** Mark Toohey, "Sense of Outrage," *Houston Chronicle,* March 8, 1981.

## 19. THE KLAN BOAT PATROL

127 **"The reason I decided":** J. Michael Kennedy, "Texan-Asian Fishing War Heating Up on Gulf Coast," *Los Angeles Times,* March 12, 1981, 10.

127 **"I guess what it comes down to":** Mark Toohey, "Sense of Outrage," *Houston Chronicle,* March 8, 1981.

128 "The American fisherman is lazy": Toohey, "Sense of Outrage."

128 "they created their own animal": J. Michael Kennedy, "Gulf Violence on Threshold?," *Los Angeles Times*, March 13, 1981, 1D.

128 "There is tension": Kennedy, "Gulf Violence on Threshold?," 1D.

128 "Violence won't accomplish anything": "Bay Shrimping Has Always Been a Highly Competitive Situation," *San Antonio Light*, January 25, 1981.

129 Two weeks after the rally: Kennedy, "Gulf Violence on Threshold?"

129 "Combat-ready fishermen": Kennedy, "Gulf Violence on Threshold?"

130 It would be a display of patriotism: Deposition of David Collins, May 3, 1981, Vietnamese Fishermen's Association v. Knights of the Ku Klux Klan, Civ. A, no. H-81-895, United States District Court for the Southern District of Texas, 543 F. Supp. 198 (S.D. Tex. 1982), 24.

131 "give it a little character": Author interview with David Collins, Kemah, TX, August 29, 2019.

131 Phú started shrimping in late 1977: Deposition of Trần Văn Phú, May 5, 1981, Vietnamese Fishermen's Association v. Knights of the Ku Klux Klan, 16.

131 As it drew close: Deposition of Thi D. Hoàng, May 5, 1981, Vietnamese Fishermen's Association v. Knights of the Ku Klux Klan, 7.

132 The wind was whipping in from the west: Deposition of David Collins.

132 That Sunday, piloted: Author phone interview with John Van Beekum, April 3, 2019.

134 Phạm was in the kitchen: Deposition of Phương Phạm, May 8, 1981. Vietnamese Fishermen's Association v. Knights of the Ku Klux Klan.

134 In a panic, she snatched up the sleeping baby: Memorandum Opinion and Order, Vietnamese Fishermen's Association v. Knights of the Ku Klux Klan, 6.

134 The blast left her momentarily deaf: Memorandum Opinion and Order, Vietnamese Fishermen's Association v. Knights of the Ku Klux Klan, 6.

135 Under the heading: List provided to author by Police Chief R. W. "Bill" Kerber on May 15, 2019.

135 "I cannot argue, because this is not my country": "1979–81 Special Report: 'Vietnamese vs. Ku Klux Klan,'" YouTube video with CBS News footage, at 4:09, posted by Hezakya Newz & Films, January 28, 2019, https://www.youtube.com/watch?v=6tS7mR8iDL0&t=506s.

## 20. THE COOKBOOK SALESMAN FROM MONTGOMERY

141 The Dees family was poor: Morris Dees and Steve Fiffer, *A Season for Justice* (Simon & Schuster, 1991), 54.

141 His uncle Lucien: Author interview with Morris Dees, Montgomery, AL, February 12, 2019.

142 He did the same with chickens: Author interview with Morris Dees, Montgomery, AL, February 12, 2019.

142 he was introduced to George Wallace: Author interview with Morris Dees, Montgomery, AL, February 12, 2019.

142 "Bubba," his dad said: Author interview with Morris Dees, Montgomery, AL, February 12, 2019.

142 the mob swelled to over three thousand: Jessa Reid Bolling and Rebecca Griesbach, "Autherine Lucy Foster's Legacy Honored with Historical Marker," *The Crimson White*, September 18, 2017.

142 That night, while the mob burned a cross: Madison Davis, "First Negro's Entrance Sets Off Chain Reaction; Adams Called into Court," *The Crimson White*, February 7, 1956.

143 **he wasn't remotely interested:** Author interview with Morris Dees, Montgomery, AL, February 12, 2019.

143 **"to get rich":** Millard Fuller, *Beyond the American Dream* (Smyth & Helwys, 2010), 95.

143 **After all, Morris's dad:** Laurence Leamer, *The Lynching* (William Morrow, 2016), 115.

143 **He also mounted his own campaign:** "Dees Affirms Demo Loyalty," *Montgomery Advertiser*, March 4, 1958, 2.

144 **While traveling the state:** "Gallion Presses Vote Drive in Dadeville," *The Dadeville Record*, March 6, 1958, 5.

144 **Millard Fuller also hit the trail:** Fuller, *Beyond the American Dream*, 171–72.

144 **Newspaper advertisements listed Morris:** Advertisement, *The Evergreen Courant*, May 1, 1958, 16.

144 **He appeared in another paid print advertisement:** Advertisement, *Montgomery Advertiser*, May 5, 1958, 5B.

144 **On the first day of sales:** Fuller, *Beyond the American Dream*, 133.

145 **"This was a goal we had set long ago":** Fuller, *Beyond the American Dream*, 137.

145 **"I had to keep it covered up":** Millard Fuller, *Love in the Mortar Joints* (New Century, 1980), 46.

145 **In 1965, Martin Luther King Jr.:** Dees and Fiffer, *A Season for Justice*, 90.

145 **On the way, Dees's license plate was logged:** Author interview with Morris Dees, Montgomery, AL, February 12, 2019.

145 **"I know all about you":** Author interview with Morris Dees, Montgomery, AL, February 12, 2019.

145 **Both men went to the hospital:** Author interview with Morris Dees, Montgomery, AL, February 12, 2019; "Mt. Meigs Men Exchange Shots After Dispute," *Montgomery Advertiser*, March 18, 1946, 5.

146 **Not long thereafter:** Leamer, *The Lynching*, 185.

146 **He wasn't known by anyone:** Dees and Fiffer, *A Season for Justice*, 88–89.

146 **little had changed in the Deep South:** Dees and Fiffer, 97.

147 **"I was a good lawyer wasting my time":** Dees and Fiffer.

147 **After discovering a secret arrangement:** Dees and Fiffer, 125.

147 **By early 1971:** Jack Anderson, "U.S. Funds Help Build All-White Hospital," *Detroit Free Press*, June 28, 1971, 7-A.

147 **"to seek legal remedies":** Reuters, "Julian Bond Heads Poverty Law Unit," *Des Moines Tribune*, September 24, 1971, 5.

147 **Working out of a converted dentist's office:** Bruce Nichols, "Suit Seeks Million," *Montgomery Advertiser*, June 27, 1973, 1.

148 **They successfully sued:** AP, "State Raps Black Ratio on Troopers," *Montgomery Advertiser*, November 16, 1971, 66.

148 **she became the first woman:** Hasan Kwame Jeffries, *Understanding and Teaching the Civil Rights Movement* (University of Wisconsin Press, 2019), 85.

148 **"flowed with the quiet, steady wash":** Howard Romaine, "The Man Behind McGovern's Money," *The Atlanta Constitution*, September 24, 1972, 9.

148 **"honey drawl":** Marcia Kunstel, "Dees' Switch to Ted's Campaign Sends Jolt Through White House," *The Atlanta Constitution*, November 4, 1979, 2-A.

148 **Within a couple of years of its founding:** AP, "Economic Bias Replaces Race as Target of Montgomery Group," *The Selma Times-Journal*, October 15, 1973, 2.

148 **With each mailing:** Leamer, *The Lynching*, 214.

149 **"This verdict makes history":** UPI, "Black Convicted in Klan Attack Given Probation," *The Berkshire Eagle*, October 3, 1980, 16.

## 21. ALLIES AND ENEMIES GATHER

151 **Kỳ Trinh, owner of a fish house:** "Vietnamese Fishermen's Association v. Knights of the Ku Klux Klan. Chronology of Events: Texas Gulf Coast Shrimping Dispute," Southern Poverty Law Center case file.

152 **"You're not the ones causing trouble!":** Morris Dees and Steve Fiffer, *A Season for Justice* (Simon & Schuster, 1991), 23.

153 **"I won't lie to you":** Dees and Fiffer, *A Season for Justice*, 24.

154 **"I promise you will live in peace":** Author interview with Father John Toàn Minh Hoàng, Houston, May 16 and August 28, 2019.

155 **His buddy David Collins:** Author interview with David Collins, Kemah, TX, August 29, 2019.

155 **The boat was valued at $25,000:** AP, "Boat Burned; Probe Begins," *Fort Worth Star-Telegram*, March 31, 1981, 15A.

155 **A northerly wind fed the flames:** AP, "Arson Police Called in Two Boat Burnings," *Tyler Morning Telegraph*, March 31, 1981, 11.

## 22. UNQUIET BEFORE THE STORM

156 **"If we wanted violence":** Mark Toohey, "Seabrook Burning of Two Vietnamese Shrimpers Probed," *Houston Chronicle*, March 30, 1981.

157 **"They got some good training at the rally":** AP, "Arson Police Called in Two Boat Burnings," *Tyler Morning Telegraph*, March 31, 1981, 11.

157 **"Those are unfounded allegations":** Felix Sanchez, "Klan Denies Burning Boats in Seabrook," *Corpus Christi Caller-Times*, March 31, 1981, 3.

157 **"I was surprised as anyone":** Toohey, "Seabrook Burning of Two Vietnamese Shrimpers Probed."

157 **"Why would they burn an American boat?!":** Glenn Lewis, "Shrimp Boat Fire in Seabrook Ruled Arson by Investigators," *Houston Post*, March 31, 1981, 24A.

157 **"It looks like some people are already blaming the Klan":** AP, "Arson Police Called in Two Boat Burnings."

157 **Fisher refused:** "Vietnamese File Lawsuit to Get Federal Protection," *Corpus Christi Caller-Times*, April 17, 1981, 5B.

158 **"Dad, what's going on?":** Author phone interview with Michael Phương Minh Nguyễn, July 9, 2021.

159 **The day after the *Trudy B* was torched:** "Vietnamese Fishermen's Association v. Knights of the Ku Klux Klan. Chronology of Events: Texas Gulf Coast Shrimping Dispute," Southern Poverty Law Center case file.

159 **Randall Williams was born:** Author interview with Randall Williams, Montgomery, AL, August 8, 2019.

159 **When Walter Cronkite delivered the news:** Author interview with Randall Williams, Montgomery, AL, August 8, 2019.

160 **The Klan leader began to speak:** Randall Williams, "Notes of a Klanwatcher," *Southern Changes* 4, no. 2 (1982), 11–13.

161 **They sipped lukewarm coffee:** Author phone interview with Mike Vahala, August 26, 2019.

161 **But Williams didn't tell them:** Author interview with Randall Williams, Montgomery, AL, August 8, 2019.

## 23. THE VIETNAMESE FIGHT BACK

164 **didn't know "whether to shit or go blind":** David Berg, *Run, Brother, Run* (Scribner, 2013), 128.

164 **Berg marched against the Vietnam War:** Author phone interview with David Berg, October 22, 2019.

164 **for no reason "other than [their] long hair":** Berg, *Run, Brother, Run*, 129.

164 **Berg took the case all the way:** Schact v. United States, 398 US 58 (1970).

164 **"When there are strong forces":** Tim Fleck, "Spin Lawyer," *Texas Monthly*, November 1993.

165 **"I know that pressures are heavy":** Letter from Morris S. Dees Jr. to Nam Văn Nguyễn, April 21, 1981, "Vietnamese Fishermen's Association v. Knights of the Ku Klux Klan," Southern Poverty Law Center case file.

165 **"The SPLC Klanwatch project filed suit":** Vietnamese Fishermen's Association v. Knights of the Ku Klux Klan, Civ. A, no. H-81-895, United States District Court for the Southern District of Texas, 543 F. Supp. 198 (S.D. Tex. 1982).

166 **"I have stated in the past":** Statement of Nam Văn Nguyễn, President, Vietnamese Fishermen's Association, Vietnamese Fishermen's Association v. Knights of the Ku Klux Klan. Southern Poverty Law Center case file.

## 24. THE SPEEDBOATING LAWYER AND THE JUDGE

167 **The next day, Louis Beam assailed:** "Viet Fishermen Seek Help of Coast Guard," *Houston Chronicle*, April 17, 1981, 12.

167 **"I'm not a prophet or a seer":** AP, "Viets Seek Help from Court," *New Braunfels Herald-Zeitung*, April 17, 1981, 3A.

167 **"a lot better fight than they got from the Viet Cong":** UPI, "Viets Ask Court to Bar KKK, Shrimpers from Violent Action," *Galveston Daily News*, April 17, 1981, 1.

167 **"expose these Vietnamese":** AP, "Vietnamese Fishermen Seek Legal Safeguards," *Victoria Advocate*, April 17, 1981, 8A.

168 **Producers from 20/20:** Author phone interview with Marilyn Collins, September 4, 2019.

168 **"welcomed the lawsuit":** UPI, "Attorney to Request Protection from Klan," *Galveston Daily News*, April 22, 1981, 2-A.

168 **"You gettin' that boat of his":** Author interview with Sam Adamo Sr., Houston, March 28, 2019.

169 **"Whaddaya mean?":** Author interview with Sam Adamo Sr., Houston, March 28, 2019.

170 **there was no need for the federal government:** Author interview with Sam Adamo Sr., Houston, March 28, 2019.

170 **"Texas citizens will not yield":** "1979–81 Special Report: 'Vietnamese vs. Ku Klux Klan,'" YouTube video with CBS News footage, at 8:01, posted by Hezakya Newz & Films, January 28, 2019, https://www.youtube.com/watch?v=6tS7mR8iDL0&t=506s.

171 **In the spirit of legal bonhomie:** Author interview with Sam Adamo Sr., Houston, March 28, 2019.

## 25. GUNS AND DEPOSITIONS

172 **"You don't have to go out":** Millard Fuller, *Beyond the American Dream* (Smyth & Helwys), 2010, 115; email from Morris Dees, January 27, 2020.

173 **"for posterity":** Deposition of Russell Gregory Thatcher, April 30, 1981, Vietnamese Fishermen's Association v. Knights of the Ku Klux Klan, Civ. A, no. H-81-895, United States District Court for the Southern District of Texas, 543 F. Supp. 198 (S.D. Tex. 1982), 4.

174 **"I respectfully decline to answer":** Deposition of Louis Beam, vol. II, April 30, 1981, Vietnamese Fishermen's Association v. Knights of the Ku Klux Klan, 4.

174 **Beam had every right:** People v. Schultz, 380 Ill. 539, 44 N.E.2d 601 (1942).

175 **"Let the record show Morris Dees is an anti-Christ Jew!":** Deposition of Louis Beam, 7.

175 **Ever since the deposition began:** Author interview with Nam Văn Nguyễn, Houston, March 28, 2019.

175 **Nam leaned over and whispered:** Author interview with Morris Dees, Montgomery, AL, February 12, 2019.

175 **"We'd like counsel at this time":** Deposition of Louis Beam, 7.

176 **"YOU HAVE BEEN PAID A SOCIAL VISIT":** Plaintiff's Exhibits, Vietnamese Fishermen's Association v. Knights of the Ku Klux Klan.

177 **The truck sped off:** Author phone interview with David Berg, October 22, 2019.

177 **As they slept, he thought back:** Email to author from David Berg, July 2, 2020.

## 26. "YOU DIE . . . YOU DIE . . . YOU DIE"

179 **Fisher confessed that he hadn't known anything:** Deposition of Eugene K. Fisher, May 2, 1981, Vietnamese Fishermen's Association v. Knights of the Ku Klux Klan, Civ. A, no. H-81-895, United States District Court for the Southern District of Texas, 543 F. Supp. 198 (S.D. Tex. 1982), 20.

179 **"pay attention":** UPI, "750 Show Up for Peaceful Anti-Vietnamese Klan Rally," *The Monitor*, February 15, 1981, 1.

180 **Stanfield denied that his beloved Klan:** Deposition of James Stanfield, May 2, 1981, Vietnamese Fishermen's Association v. Knights of the Ku Klux Klan.

180 **"Yeah, I heard you did!":** Author interview with Jody Collins, Kemah, TX, May 15, 2019.

180 **"possessed by Satan":** William K. Stevens, "Klan Official Is Accused of Intimidation," *The New York Times*, May 2, 1981, 9.

180 **Alongside his robe was a Bible:** Stevens, "Klan Official Is Accused of Intimidation."

181 **"An act of chivalry and honor":** Continuation of the Deposition of Louis Beam, vol. II, May 3, 1981, Vietnamese Fishermen's Association v. Knights of the Ku Klux Klan, 8.

181 **When Dees turned to his conflict:** Continuation of the Deposition of Louis Beam, 23.

181 **The arsonist might even have been:** Continuation of the Deposition of Louis Beam, 82.

181 **When Dees was finished:** All quotations in this section are from the Continuation of the Deposition of Louis Beam.

182 **When he returned, he left the car:** Author phone interview with Mike Vahala, August 22, 2019.

183 **"You die . . . you die . . . you die":** AP, "Mental Test Asked for Klan Leader," *Del Rio News-Herald*, May 7, 1981, 7A.

183 **"I didn't say anything about the Vietnamese":** Deposition of David Collins, May 3, 1981, Vietnamese Fishermen's Association v. Knights of the Ku Klux Klan, 30.

183 **Collins once made a trip:** Author phone interview with Carl "Buddy" Richardson, October 22, 2021.

183 **"I haven't wanted to bury any of them":** Deposition of David Collins, 32.

184 **The car careened down the street:** Author phone interview with Mike Vahala, August 22, 2019.

184 **he was wearing body armor:** Author interview with Morris Dees, Montgomery, AL, February 12, 2019.

184 **"He is my enemy and I am his":** AP, "Lawyer Seeking Federal Protection," *Victoria Advocate*, May 7, 1981, 14A.

185 **"By the way," the clerk said:** Affidavit of Morris Dees in Response to Defendants' Motion to Recuse, May 6, 1981, Vietnamese Fishermen's Association v. Knights of the Ku Klux Klan, 2.

185 **Adamo was waiting by the elevator:** The details surrounding the potential ex parte conversation are drawn from the affidavits of Louis Beam (which includes Sam Adamo's version of events), Morris Dees, and Judge McDonald's final memorandum and order on the matter, as well as my own interviews with Dees, Adamo, and McDonald.

185 **Adamo, incensed, asked the clerk:** Memorandum and Order, Vietnamese Fishermen's Association v. Knights of the Ku Klux Klan.

## 27. A SUIT ON THE BRINK

186 **she could hardly allow Klansmen:** Author phone interview with Judge Gabrielle K. McDonald, September 19, 2019.

187 **Louis Beam wasn't there to talk about clerks:** Memorandum and Order, Vietnamese Fishermen's Association v. Knights of the Ku Klux Klan, Civ. A, no. H-81-895, United States District Court for the Southern District of Texas, 543 F. Supp. 198 (S.D. Tex. 1982), 4.

187 **He felt like he was on a roller coaster ride:** Email to author from Sam Adamo Sr., July 3, 2020.

187 **"During my twelve years as a Klansman":** Memorandum and Order, Vietnamese Fishermen's Association v. Knights of the Ku Klux Klan, 4.

187 **"Let me tell you," Judge McDonald declared:** AP, "Black Judge Won't Disqualify Self in Klan Case," *Fort Worth Star-Telegram*, May 8, 1981, 8D.

187 *Isn't it reasonable for the Klan to feel:* Author phone interview with Judge Gabrielle K. McDonald, September 19, 2019.

188 **In 1975, Motley drew a case:** Tomiko Brown-Nagin, "Identity Matters: The Case of Judge Constance Baker Motley," *Columbia Law Review* 117, no. 7.

188 **"If background or sex or race":** Blank v. Sullivan & Cromwell, 418 F. Supp. 1, 4 (S.D. N.Y. 1975).

189 **The current plan was to tail him:** Author phone interview with Nam Văn Nguyễn, Houston, March 28, 2019.

189 **Here, he was accused:** Author interview with Nam Văn Nguyễn, Houston, March 28, 2019.

189 **Whenever he ran out of food:** Author phone interview with Michael Phương Minh Nguyễn, October 20, 2021.

189 **"The elders of our community":** Morris Dees and Steve Fiffer, *A Season for Justice* (Simon & Schuster, 1991), 32.

190 **Their battle with the Klan:** Denise Hensley and Jon McConal, "Shrimpers Pour Oil on Troubled Waters," *Fort Worth Star-Telegram*, May 17, 1981, 10A.

190 **ferocious assault on John Lewis:** David Niven, *The Politics of Injustice: The Kennedys, the Freedom Rides, and the Electoral Consequences of a Moral Compromise* (University of Tennessee Press, 2003), 80.

191 **When the mob descended on the hospital:** John Blake, "Shocking Photo Created a Hero, but Not to His Family," CNN, May 16, 2011.

191 **when Henley came in, he expressed his support:** Millard Fuller, *Love in the Mortar Joints* (New Century, 1980), 47.

191 **Dees, whose fee of $5,000:** Fuller, *Love in the Mortar Joints*.

191 **enjoyed the publicity:** "Marathon Legal Test Indicated," *Montgomery Advertiser*, May 28, 1961, 1.

191 **condemned for representing the Klansman:** Laurence Leamer, *The Lynching* (William Morrow, 2016), 133.

191 **"Sometimes lawyers are called counselors":** Dees and Fiffer, *A Season for Justice*, 33–35.

## 28. "THIS COURT IS THEIR ONLY HOPE"

193 **Kids pranced around in junior Klan robes:** Dan Bradford, "Grand Dragon Beam Offers to Reconcile with Vietnamese," *Galveston Daily News*, May 9, 1981, 2-A.

194 **"The rally is open to white Christians":** AP, "Klan Offers Reconciliation to Viets," *New Braunfels Herald-Zeitung*, May 10, 1981, 3A.

194 **"In a way, you feel":** "Klan Rally Against Vietnamese Fishermen 1981," YouTube video, at 1:06, from KTRK Houston report, May 9, 1981, posted by ABC13 Houston, May 13, 2018, https://www.youtube.com/watch?v=1Jic2kOPPOU.

194 **Unable to torch their cross:** Dan Bradford, "Klan Leader Insists He's Not Man of Hate," *Galveston Daily News*, May 11, 1981, 2A.

195 **On the other side:** Morris Dees and Steve Fiffer, *A Season for Justice* (Simon & Schuster, 1991), 37.

195 **Seated nearby were men:** Morris Dees and Steve Fiffer, *A Lawyer's Journey* (American Bar Association, 2001), 38.

195 **Nor did he know:** Martin Waldron, "2 Bombings Laid to 4 in Houston," *The New York Times*, June 12, 1971, 35.

196 **Berg couldn't avoid the profundity of the moment:** Author phone interview with David Berg, October 22, 2019.

198 **"a helluva lot more violent than Vietnam!":** Vietnamese Fishermen's Association v. Knights of the Ku Klux Klan, 518 F. Supp. 993 (S.D. Tex. 1981).

199 **At one point, when he explained:** UPI, "Vietnamese Fisherman Takes Stand in Suit," *Galveston Daily News*, May 13, 1981, 1.

199 **Her husband worked as a cook:** Dees and Fiffer, *A Season for Justice*, 41.

200 **Another caller warned her:** SAC Houston to Director, April 27, 1981. Federal Bureau of Investigation case files. FOIA.

200 **Khang, bewildered, cleared out:** Statement of Mrs. J. F. Anderwald, May 5, 1981, Vietnamese Fishermen's Association v. Knights of the Ku Klux Klan, Civ. A, no. H-81-895, United States District Court for the Southern District of Texas, 543 F. Supp. 198 (S.D. Tex. 1982). Southern Poverty Law Center case file.

200 **"white-haired with glasses":** Dees and Fiffer, *A Season for Justice*, 41.

202 **"This court is their only hope":** Southern Poverty Law Center case file.

## 29. FREEDOM OF SPEECH AND ASSEMBLY

204 **"Sure was," snapped Fisher:** AP, "Tensions between Ku Klux Klan, Viet Shrimpers High As Deadline Nears," *New Braunfels Herald-Zeitung*, May 12, 1981, 3A.

206 **"I never said no such thing":** "Testimony of Louis Beam," Vietnamese Fishermen's Association v. Knights of the Ku Klux Klan, Civ. A, no. H-81-895, United States District Court for the Southern District of Texas, 543 F. Supp. 198 (S.D. Tex. 1982), 42.

## 30. THE RULING

209 **"are opposed to the refugees coming here"**: Dale Maharidge and Ann Reed, "Viet Refugees Target of Hate Campaign," *The Sacramento Bee*, May 14, 1981, A32.

209 **"Register Jews—not guns"**: AP, "Viets' Lawyers Denied U.S. Marshal Protection," *Victoria Advocate*, May 9, 1981, 10A.

210 **"fighting words"**: Memorandum and Order, Vietnamese Fishermen's Association v. Knights of the Ku Klux Klan, Civ. A, no. H-81-895, United States District Court for the Southern District of Texas, 543 F. Supp. 198 (S.D. Tex. 1982).

210 **"reasonably foreseeable effect of intimidating" them**: Memorandum and Order, Vietnamese Fishermen's Association v. Knights of the Ku Klux Klan.

211 **"to show sympathy for the Vietnamese"**: Leon Daniel, UPI, "Klan, Refugees Battle on Galveston Bay," *Latrobe Bulletin*, June 15, 1981, 9.

212 **To him, McDonald's ruling was**: AP, "Viet Shrimpers Win KKK Harassment Suit," *New Braunfels Herald-Zeitung*, May 15, 1981, 2A.

212 **"I think it was better to fight this dispute in court"**: AP, "Vietnamese Shrimpers Win Court Order," *The Seguin Gazette-Enterprise*, May 15, 1981, 9A.

## 31. FALLOUT

213 **As the sun rose**: Author interview with Morris Dees, Montgomery, AL, February 12, 2019.

213 **"We thank God that the Vietnamese people"**: AP, "Vietnamese Shrimpers Bless Their Fleet," *The Daily Advertiser*, May 16, 1981, 4.

213 **"We have to be especially careful"**: AP, "Vietnam Shrimpers Win Lawsuit," *Odessa American*, May 16, 1981, 2D.

214 **"It's okay for the government to limit"**: Leon Daniel, UPI, "Klan, Refugees Battle on Galveston Bay," *Latrobe Bulletin*, June 15, 1981, 9.

214 **"to get public sympathy"**: UPI, "New U.S.-Vietnamese War Shapes Up in Texas," *The Arizona Republic*, June 13, 1981, D7.

214 **Slapped with an injunction**: Author phone interview with Marilyn Collins, September 4, 2019.

214 **"I doubt if Beam will deal on this"**: Letter from Morris Dees to Sam Adamo, June 15, 1981, Southern Poverty Law Center case file.

215 **he was convicted on separate charges**: AP, "Klan Leader to Appeal Conviction," *Del Rio News-Herald*, July 9, 1981, 14.

215 **When she answered**: AP, "Beam Hunted," *Galveston Daily News*, March 20, 1982, 5-B.

215 **"Adamo knew a doctor"**: Author phone interview with Marilyn Collins, September 4, 2019.

215 **after falling behind on payments on his Oldsmobile**: Author phone interview with David Collins, September 29, 2019.

216 **David and Seabrook firefighters**: "Arson Eyed in Seabrook, Kemah Fires," *Houston Post*, December 11, 1981, 4A.

216 **it would be decades**: Author interview with David Collins, Kemah, TX, August 29, 2019.

216 **Judge McDonald received an envelope**: Letter to Judge Gabrielle K. McDonald, May 21, 1981. Federal Bureau of Investigation case files. FOIA.

216 **When the FBI asked if she wanted to prosecute**: "Notice to Close File. Civil Rights Division," May 19, 1983. Federal Bureau of Investigation case files. FOIA.

217 **"I think the sex appeal":** AP, "Judge Prohibits Ku Klux Klan from Holding Military Training," *Galveston Daily News*, June 4, 1981, 2-A.

217 **They code-named their patrols:** UPI, "Gulf Fishermen, KKK Bring Night Watch of Vietnamese," *Tyler Courier-Times*, May 16, 1982, 14.

218 **He denied their petition:** "Decision on Permit Application Submitted by American Fishermen Association and the Ku Klux Klan," May 24, 1982, provided by R. W. "Bill" Kerber.

218 **Flyers appeared around town:** Flyer provided by R. W. "Bill" Kerber.

218 **"The death of Billy Joe":** UPI, "Klan Obtains Memorial March Approval," *Tyler Morning Telegraph*, June 1, 1982, 9.

218 **"The Vietnam War has never ended":** Pandora Ryan, "Klansmen Get Ready for Rally in Seabrook," *Galveston Daily News*, June 12, 1982, 2A.

218 **The day before the march:** Ryan, "Klansmen Get Ready for Rally in Seabrook."

219 **A black trucker's hat:** Andy Mangan, "Klansmen Find Waters Rough in Quest to Woo Fishermen," *Austin American-Statesman*, June 11, 1982, 1.

219 **"He knows as much about fishing":** Mangan, "Klansmen Find Waters Rough in Quest to Woo Fishermen," A20.

219 **"There are no constitutional rights involved here":** AP, "Seabrook Police to Be Stationed on Klan March," *Galveston Daily News*, June 12, 1982, 6-B.

219 **"Hell," Fisher joked:** Author interview with R. W. "Bill" Kerber, Kemah, TX, May 15, 2019.

220 **At five dollars a pop:** Andy Mangan, "Calm Greets Klan's Vietnamese Protest," *Austin American-Statesman*, June 13, 1982, B2.

220 **"The American Dream Is for Americans FIRST!":** Nancy Smeltzer, "White Supremacy KKK Rally Theme," *Longview News-Journal*, September 26, 1982, 2-A.

220 **There was Glen Hutto:** Seabrook Police, "Vehicles/Registrations KKK Rally and Parade," provided by R. W. "Bill" Kerber.

220 **A young White woman with feathered bangs:** Seabrook Police surveillance photos provided by R. W. "Bill" Kerber.

220 **"I think they are the dumbest Americans we've got":** Mangan, "Calm Greets Klan's Vietnamese Protest."

221 **"to show my appreciation for what the Klan did":** AP, "Klan Carries Coffin in March to Protest Fisherman's Death," *Galveston Daily News*, June 13, 1982, 1.

221 **After an explosion at Union Carbide:** "Explosion, Fire Causes Viewed," *Victoria Advocate*, August 23, 1980, 2A.

221 **The same month Judge McDonald issued her injunction:** Harry Hurt III, "The Cancer Belt," *Texas Monthly*, May 1981.

222 **Liver and brain cancer:** *Texas Gold*, directed by Carolyn M. Scott (2005), Vimeo, https://vimeo.com/64020468.

222 **But her fellow shrimpers:** Don Brown, "Quality of Bay Waters Doubtful Factor," *Victoria Advocate*, July 14, 1981, 4C.

222 **A few years later:** Joe Nick Patoski, "Seadrift Nation," *Texas Observer*, November 4, 2005.

## 32. BILL BAILEY'S NEWSPAPER

227 **Her husband was asleep:** Author phone interview with Diane Wilson, September 10, 2021.

229 **In 1982, for the first time:** "Exploitative Labor Practices in the Global Shrimp Industry," prepared by Accenture for Humanity United, May 2013.

229 **At Mustang Island:** Ron George, "Researcher Observes Tar Reef 300 Feet from Mustang Dunes," *Corpus Christi Caller-Times*, January 12, 1983, 2B.

229 **In 1984, a tanker grounded:** "M/V Alvenus," *IncidentNews*, NOAA, https://incidentnews .noaa.gov/incident/6267.

230 **"Go on, read it":** Diane Wilson, *An Unreasonable Woman: A True Story of Shrimpers, Politicos, Polluters, and the Fight for Seadrift, Texas* (Chelsea Green, 2005), 35.

230 **"EPA: Texas Tops U.S. in Industrial Air Pollution":** AP, "EPA: Texas Tops U.S. in Industrial Air Pollution," *Victoria Advocate*, June 20, 1989, 7B.

230 **And in the county breakdown:** Wilson, *An Unreasonable Woman*, 36.

231 **Galveston Bay to the north:** AP, "EPA: Texas Tops U.S. in Industrial Air Pollution."

231 **"The Texas sky":** AP, "Texas Leads U.S. in Air Pollution," *Tyler Morning Telegraph*, June 20, 1989, 5.

231 **"Going over to city hall!":** Author phone interview with Diane Wilson, September 10, 2021.

232 **"Fern, I need a town meeting!":** Wilson, *An Unreasonable Woman*, 42.

## 33. STIRRING THE POT

234 **copying things from the article:** AP, "Texas Leads U.S. in Air Pollution," *Tyler Morning Telegraph*, June 20, 1989, 5.

235 **"I need you to take the meeting clear outta town!":** Author phone interview with Diane Wilson, September 10, 2021.

236 **As many as three thousand workers:** "Calhoun Group Gets Update on Projects," *Victoria Advocate*, June 4, 1988, 5C.

236 **To boot, the state of Texas:** AP, "Taiwan Polluter Lured by State Officials," *The Monitor*, September 11, 1989, 4A.

236 **An additional $10 million:** Louise Popplewell, "Calhoun Port Construction Project Nears Completion," *Victoria Advocate*, March 28, 1993, 9A.

236 **The dredging would happen:** Diane Wilson, *An Unreasonable Woman: A True Story of Shrimpers, Politicos, Polluters, and the Fight for Seadrift, Texas* (Chelsea Green, 2005), 117.

236 **"Hopefully, the meeting":** Linda Hetsel, "Calhoun Unit Sets Meeting on Emissions," *Victoria Advocate*, July 28, 1989, 9A.

237 **"Well, good. That's good":** Wilson, *An Unreasonable Woman*, 46.

237 **"absolutely no health concerns":** Linda Hetsel, "'No . . . Concerns' in Calhoun," *Victoria Advocate*, June 24, 1989, 5D.

237 **"You've got to go out and get industry":** Robert Cullick, "Texas Lures Firm with Spotty Environmental History," *Houston Chronicle*, September 10, 1989, A1.

238 **"If they can't locate here":** Linda Hetsel, "Formosa's New Plant Discussed," *Victoria Advocate*, September 1, 1989, 8D.

238 **"First meetings are always the hardest":** Wilson, *An Unreasonable Woman*, 67.

238 **"I have forgot the words":** Wilson, *An Unreasonable Woman*, 72.

239 **"We just want a safe place for our children":** Hetsel, "Formosa's New Plant Discussed."

239 **now known as the Cancer Belt:** Wilson, *An Unreasonable Woman*, 75.

## 34. CHAIRMAN WANG COMES TO SEADRIFT

240 **He'd been a wreck:** Author phone interview with Diane Wilson, September 15, 2021.

240 **"Do you *know* what it is you're doing?":** Diane Wilson, *An Unreasonable Woman: A True Story of Shrimpers, Politicos, Polluters, and the Fight for Seadrift, Texas* (Chelsea Green, 2005), 76.

241 **Lynch reminded her:** Wilson, *An Unreasonable Woman*, 108.

241 **For a county struggling with nearly 16 percent unemployment:** Peter Elkind, "The Wooing of Chairman Wang," *Texas Monthly*, February 1989, 124.

241 **By holding meetings about pollution:** Author phone interview with Diane Wilson, September 15, 2021.

241 **"It's either industry or unemployment":** Elkind, "The Wooing of Chairman Wang," 124.

242 **Given that Alcoa was cutting its workforce:** Elkind, "The Wooing of Chairman Wang."

242 **"I thought an environmental group *helped* a community":** Wilson, *An Unreasonable Woman*, 97.

242 **"a serious compliance problem":** Linda Hetsel, "Formosa's New Plant Discussed," *Victoria Advocate*, September 1, 1989, 8D.

242 **They asked why she didn't just call up Formosa:** Author phone interview with Diane Wilson, September 15, 2021.

242 **More than once:** Diane Wilson, "Are You Too Well Behaved," *The Ecologist*, October 2004, 31.

243 **But whenever she asked:** Author phone interview with Diane Wilson, September 10, 2021.

243 **Over a meal of Matagorda Bay gumbo:** Elkind, "The Wooing of Chairman Wang," 126.

243 **The school board was already deliberating:** Wilson, "Are You Too Well Behaved," 31.

243 **"Once we regarded foreigners with suspicion":** Elkind, "The Wooing of Chairman Wang," 124.

244 **Formosa assured the public:** Sam Howe Verhovek, "Shrimpers Voice Fear on Growth of Factory," *The New York Times*, June 20, 1993, 16.

244 **It wasn't until 1969:** Lorraine Boissoneault, "The Cuyahoga River Caught Fire at Least a Dozen Times, but No One Cared Until 1969," *Smithsonian Magazine*, June 19, 2019.

244 **hung a colorful sign:** Elkind, "The Wooing of Chairman Wang," 127.

244 **The subsequent headline:** Greg Bowen, "Formosa Building 'World's Cleanest' Plant," *Victoria Advocate*, October 8, 1989, D1.

## 35. STOP PLANT NO. 6 OR DIE

245 **"An environmental impact statement":** Author phone interview with Diane Wilson, September 10, 2021.

245 **Formosa's executives were unwilling:** Jim Blackburn, *The Book of Texas Bays* (Texas A&M University Press, 2004), 157.

246 **The local paper touted:** "Earth Day Trees," *Victoria Advocate*, April 21, 1990, D1.

246 **"Sure! . . . Howdy's talkin' to big industry":** Diane Wilson, *An Unreasonable Woman: A True Story of Shrimpers, Politicos, Polluters, and the Fight for Seadrift, Texas* (Chelsea Green, 2005), 62.

247 **A third of the rivers were dangerously contaminated:** Michael Scott Feeley, "Reclaiming the Beautiful Island: Taiwan's Emerging Environmental Regulation," *San Diego Law Review* 27, no. 4 (1990), 914.

247 **Toxic water had conferred:** Feeley, "Reclaiming the Beautiful Island," 915.

247 **In 1988, fishermen had waged:** Feeley, "Reclaiming the Beautiful Island," 916.

247 **In 1989, the year of Wilson's awakening:** Feeley, "Reclaiming the Beautiful Island," 917.

247 **One of the activists gave her a banner:** Michael Berryhill, "The Battle for Lavaca Bay," *Houston Press*, May 19, 1994.

248 **He was too poor:** Author phone interview with Diane Wilson, September 15, 2021.

248 **The Keelung struck her:** Berryhill, "The Battle for Lavaca Bay."

248  **Farmers living alongside the lifeless Houchin:** Wilson, *An Unreasonable Woman*, 340.

248  **She watched a Formosa truck:** Wilson, *An Unreasonable Woman*, 344.

249  **"The kids ain't comin' down":** Author phone interview with Diane Wilson, September 15, 2021.

## 36. HUNGER

251  **"Why she has this vendetta":** Greg Bowen, "Formosa Critics Short on Support in Calhoun," *Victoria Advocate*, April 29, 1990, 1.

251  **The college's director of vocational programs:** "Classes Quickly Filled," *Victoria Advocate*, January 9, 1990, 1.

251  **Blackburn hated the idea of a hunger strike:** Jim Blackburn, *The Book of Texas Bays* (Texas A&M University Press, 2004), 158.

251  **Formosa volunteered to submit:** AP, "Formosa Plastics Plans Environmental Study," *Kerrville Times*, January 31, 1991, 2A.

252  **"the strong appearance of a conflict of interest":** Mark Smith, "Bribe-Kickback Claims Tarnish Formosa Project," *Houston Chronicle*, 12A.

252  **The fine was soon reduced:** Smith, "Bribe-Kickback Claims Tarnish Formosa Project."

252  **"Formosa did it":** Author phone interview with Diane Wilson, September 10, 2021.

253  **The construction of the Formosa plant:** Smith, "Bribe-Kickback Claims Tarnish Formosa Project."

253  **When the agent spoke about the lavish birthday party:** Mark Smith, "Contractors Document How Shakedowns Worked," *Houston Chronicle*, June 20, 1993, 1.

253  **Soon after he reported it:** Mark Smith, "Environmentalists Concerned over Pollution Allegations at Plant," *Houston Chronicle*, June 20, 1993, 13.

254  **State health officials:** AP, "Dumping Permit Approved," *Corpus Christi Caller-Times*, August 18, 1993, B4.

254  **millions of pounds of pollutants:** Mark Smith, "Environmental, Safety Fears Grow at Lavaca Bay Facility," *Houston Chronicle*, June 20, 1993, 13A.

254  **"They have taken away our property values":** Smith, "Environmental, Safety Fears Grow at Lavaca Bay Facility," 13A.

254  **the "flushing capacities":** Kevin Daniels, "Bay Faces Uncertain Future If Discharge Permit Is OK'd," *Austin American-Statesman*, February 18, 1993, A17.

255  **By the time her husband emerged:** David Helvarg, *The War Against the Greens: The "Wise-Use" Movement, the New Right, and the Browning of America* (Sierra Club Books, 1994), 262.

255  **She was still on her hunger strike:** Author phone interview with Diane Wilson, September 10, 2021.

256  **Formosa's attorney extended her hand:** Helvarg, *The War Against the Greens*, 261.

256  **"there never was any agreement":** Kate McConnico, "Raw Deals in Point Comfort," *Texas Observer*, September 18, 1992, 17.

256  **She was mostly quiet:** Blackburn, *The Book of Texas Bays*, 160.

257  **"a black pit":** Wilson, *An Unreasonable Woman*, 312.

## 37. LOSING IT

259  **"first time ever":** Linda Hetsel, "Formosa Agrees to Plant Safety Audits," *Victoria Advocate*, August 15, 1992, 12A.

260  **Blackburn stressed that he'd received only $10:** Linda Hetsel, "Calhoun Residents Discuss Formosa Pact, Expansion," *Victoria Advocate*, September 3, 1992, 4C.

260 **Formosa could make tax-deductible contributions:** Greg Harman, "Switch Hitter," *Houston Press*, October 13, 2005.

260 **Blackburn boasted:** Peggy Fikac, AP, "Environmental Groups Protest Formosa Plastics Accord," *Austin American-Statesman*, August 15, 1992, B3.

260 **Formosa was thrilled:** Hetsel, "Formosa Agrees to Plant Safety Audits," 12A.

260 **When a reporter asked:** Fikac, AP, "Environmental Groups Protest Formosa Plastics Accord," B3.

260 **The sound of the *SeaBee*'s engine:** Diane Wilson, *An Unreasonable Woman: A True Story of Shrimpers, Politicos, Polluters, and the Fight for Seadrift, Texas* (Chelsea Green, 2005), 327.

260 **"I was broke":** "Texas Environmental Attorney Paid $200,000 by Formosa Plastics," *Corporate Crime Reporter*, July 14, 2005.

261 **Her sister, whose husband worked at Formosa:** Michael Berryhill, "The Battle for Lavaca Bay," *Houston Press*, May 19, 1994.

261 **Ever since the helicopter descended:** Wilson, *An Unreasonable Woman*, 305.

261 **She knew her marriage was on the brink:** Author phone interview with Diane Wilson, September 10, 2021.

261 **document with forty-four tips:** David Helvarg, *The War Against the Greens: The "Wise-Use" Movement, the New Right, and the Browning of America* (Sierra Club Books, 1994), 263.

262 **She threw the hatch open:** Helvarg, *The War Against the Greens*, 265.

262 **She dug a grave:** Author phone interview with Diane Wilson, September 10, 2021.

262 **One day, she drifted in the *SeaBee*:** Berryhill, "The Battle for Lavaca Bay."

263 **A faulty flange leaked twenty-seven hundred gallons:** Linda Hetsel, "Toxic Spill Cleanup Spawns New Dilemma," *Victoria Advocate*, December 15, 1991, 1D.

263 **Seven hundred gallons of hydrochloric acid:** AP, "Faulty Valves Cited in Coastal Chemical Spill," *Kerrville Times*, July 9, 1991, 2.

263 **The Texas Water Commission:** Linda Hetsel, "TWC Pushes State for Lawsuit," *Victoria Advocate*, February 28, 1992, 7A.

264 **"Support on what?":** Wilson, *An Unreasonable Woman*, 362.

264 **Formosa corporate officers:** Wilson, *An Unreasonable Woman*, 364.

265 **For ten years:** Louise Popplewell, "Formosa Officials Explain Process to Palacios Group," *Victoria Advocate*, July 28, 1993, 3D.

265 **"tell me the truth. I'll do the lying":** "Point Comfort," *Dirty Money*, directed by Margaret Brown (Jigsaw Productions, 2020), Netflix, https://www.netflix.com/watch/81005048?trackId=13752289.

265 **"We know there is this woman":** Wilson, *An Unreasonable Woman*, 366.

265 **"I would rather eat":** Louise Popplewell, "Demonstrators Fail to Daunt Enthusiasm at Formosa Rally," *Victoria Advocate*, July 17, 1993, 7A.

265 **They hauled a coffin:** Steve Ray, "Shrimpers, Environmentalists Protest Formosa Permit," *Corpus Christi Caller-Times*, August 13, 1993, B12.

266 **"I can tell you this":** Berryhill, "The Battle for Lavaca Bay."

266 **"If I repent of anything":** Henry David Thoreau, *Walden*, 1854.

266 **"At some point we must draw a line":** Daniel J. Philippon, *Conserving Words: How American Nature Writers Shaped the Environmental Movement* (University of George Press, 2004), 254.

## 38. THE *SEABEE*

267 **"Oh, hell," muttered Donna Sue:** Diane Wilson, *An Unreasonable Woman: A True Story of Shrimpers, Politicos, Polluters, and the Fight for Seadrift, Texas* (Chelsea Green, 2005), 368.

269  **After a long pause:** Wilson, *An Unreasonable Woman*, 370.

270  **"More than likely":** Wilson, *An Unreasonable Woman*, 376.

270  **He'd had an infamous run-in:** Linda Hetsel, "Seadrift Man Pleads Guilty to Lesser Charges," *Victoria Advocate*, March 23, 1985, 1.

270  **A voice boomed through its loudspeaker:** Wilson, *An Unreasonable Woman*, 377.

272  **"Y'all see me standing here":** Wilson, *An Unreasonable Woman*, 382.

## 39. THE WHISTLEBLOWER

273  **The Wilson-Formosa Zero Discharge Agreement:** Jim Blackburn, *The Book of Texas Bays* (Texas A&M University Press, 2004), 161.

273  **"I believe that's doable":** Diane Wilson, *An Unreasonable Woman: A True Story of Shrimpers, Politicos, Polluters, and the Fight for Seadrift, Texas* (Chelsea Green, 2005), 385.

274  **Wally Morgan called her up:** Author phone interview with Diane Wilson, September 15, 2021.

274  **a "dangerous woman":** Wilson, *An Unreasonable Woman*, 389.

275  **"world's largest crab":** "Rockport, Texas: World's Largest Blue Crab (Gone)," Roadside-America, https://www.roadsideamerica.com/tip/1296.

275  **She laughed and handed it over:** Lily Moore-Eissenberg, "Nurdles All the Way Down," *Texas Monthly*, October 2019.

275  **He had started working:** "Christine Jedlicka Marries Dale Jurasek," *Victoria Advocate*, August 21, 1983, 10C.

276  **When something bad happened at the plant:** "Point Comfort," *Dirty Money*, directed by Margaret Brown (Jigsaw Productions, 2020), Netflix, https://www.netflix.com/watch/81005048?trackId=13752289.

276  **"Go in there, do what you gotta do":** "Point Comfort."

276  **"That's against the law":** "Point Comfort."

276  **"When you start breaking laws":** "Point Comfort."

276  **Students at Point Comfort Elementary School:** Louise Popplewell, "Explosions Rock Formosa Plant," *Victoria Advocate*, October 7, 2005, 1.

277  **Jurasek knew better:** "Point Comfort."

277  **"They have no right!":** "Point Comfort."

278  **"These people need to be dealt with":** "Point Comfort."

278  **Experts believed that the case lost momentum:** "Point Comfort."

278  **"Yeah," he muttered:** "Point Comfort."

278  **He was living in constant fear:** "Point Comfort."

278  **Early research showed that nurdles:** Moore-Eissenberg, "Nurdles All the Way Down."

280  **By 2016, Wilson had filled:** Moore-Eissenberg, "Nurdles All the Way Down."

## 40. JUSTICE

281  **It would take another two years:** Carlos Anchondo, "Environmentalists Take Petrochemical Giant Formosa to Court over Plastics Pollution," *The Texas Tribune*, March 25, 2019.

281  **The weekend before the trial:** Jon Wilcox, "Trial Begins in Activists' Pellet Lawsuit against Formosa Plastics," *Victoria Advocate*, March 25, 2019, 1.

281  **Kenneth Hoyt, the federal judge:** Lily Moore-Eissenberg, "Nurdles All the Way Down," *Texas Monthly*, October 2019.

281 **Lawyers for Formosa:** Jon Wilcox, "Expert Testifies Pellets Poisonous, Numerous," *Victoria Advocate*, March 27, 2019, A3.

282 **Fishing grounds were closed:** Richard C. Paddock, "Toxic Fish in Vietnam Idle a Local Industry and Challenge the State," *The New York Times*, June 8, 2016, 6.

282 **"You have to decide":** Paddock, "Toxic Fish in Vietnam Idle a Local Industry and Challenge the State."

282 **The company finally admitted its responsibility:** Angel L. Martínez Cantera, "'We Are Jobless Because of Fish Poisoning: Vietnamese Fishermen Battle for Justice," *The Guardian*, August 14, 2017.

282 **promising to start adopting:** Jess Macy Yu and Faith Hung, "Exclusive: Broken Rules at $11 Billion Formosa Mill Triggered Vietnam Spill, Report Says," Reuters, November 13, 2016.

282 **Three years later, the bodies of thirty-nine Vietnamese:** Hsiao-Hung Pai, "Vietnamese Migrants Are Not 'Lured' by Traffickers. They Just Want a Better Future," *The Guardian*, October 30, 2019.

283 **He felt bad for them:** Author phone interview with Richard Haight, October 2, 2019.

283 **They didn't seem to recognize him:** Author phone interview with Richard Haight, September 27, 2019.

284 **A year later, he provided sworn testimony:** San Antonio Bay Estuarine Waterkeeper and S. Diane Wilson v. Formosa Plastics Corp., Texas, and Formosa Plastics Corp., U.S.A, Civ. A, no. 6:17-CV-47, U.S. District Court for the Southern District of Texas, Victoria Division (2019), 125.

284 **"Not much chance of that":** Jessica Priest, "Clean Water Act Trial Against Formosa Concludes," *Victoria Advocate*, March 28, 2019, 1.

284 **In approving the agreement:** Kiah Collier, "Retired Texas Shrimper Wins Record-Breaking $50 Million Settlement from Plastics Manufacturing Giant," *The Texas Tribune*, December 3, 2019.

284 **"I know what justice feels like":** Moore-Eissenberg, "Nurdles All the Way Down."

285 **would go toward mitigating:** Collier, "Retired Texas Shrimper Wins Record-Breaking $50 Million."

285 **An executive vice president said:** Collier, "Retired Texas Shrimper Wins Record-Breaking $50 Million."

285 **Facing a loss of tax revenue:** Brian Cuaron, "Students, Staff Say Goodbye to Point Comfort Elementary," *Victoria Advocate*, June 2, 2011.

285 **She still lives on $425 a month:** Author phone interview with Diane Wilson, September 15, 2021.

285 **They are getting a new fish house:** Author phone interview with Diane Wilson, February 9, 2021.

285 **Even though the suit is long over:** Moore-Eissenberg, "Nurdles All the Way Down."

285 **"My children . . . although wealth":** "Point Comfort," *Dirty Money*, directed by Margaret Brown (Jigsaw Productions, 2020), Netflix, https://www.netflix.com/watch/81005048?trackId=13752289.

286 **Upon his death:** George Liao, "Taiwan's Formosa Plastics Scion Wishes to Retrieve, Donate Hidden Assets," *Taiwan News*, July 26, 2020.

286 **"I got a new mugshot":** Aman Azhar, "Many Worry about Dredging Lavaca Bay Superfund Site," *The Daily News*, May 30, 2021.

286 **In June 2021, Formosa vice president:** Chris Ramirez, "Formosa Plastics Wants Calhoun Port Authority New Tax Breaks," *Corpus Christi Caller-Times*, June 29, 2021, A3.

## EPILOGUE

287 **"The Berlin Wall":** *The Thunderbolt,* no. 268 (August 1981), 1, University of Oregon archives.

288 **"guerrilla theater":** Louis R. Beam Jr., *Essays of a Klansman,* 2nd ed. (A.K.I.A. Publications, 1989), 17.

288 **"The heavens do not open":** "Louis Beam Letter," June 1981, Southern Poverty Law Center case file.

288 **"Being sued by the anti-Christ":** *Inter-Klan Newsletter & Survival Alert,* 1983.

289 **"a graph that outlines":** *Inter-Klan Newsletter & Survival Alert,* 1984, 10.

289 **A "true Aryan warrior":** Kevin Flynn and Gary Gerhardt, *The Silent Brotherhood: The Chilling Inside Story of America's Violent, Anti-Government Militia Movement* (Free Press, 1989).

289 **In Mathews's grand vision:** Kathleen Belew, *Bring the War Home: The White Power Movement and Paramilitary America* (Harvard University Press, 2018), 127.

289 **then $3.6 million:** Leonard Zeskind, *Blood and Politics: The History of the White Nationalist Movement from the Margins to the Mainstream* (Farrar, Straus and Giroux, 2009).

289 **He directed $100,000:** Flynn and Gerhardt, *The Silent Brotherhood.*

289 **"It may very well be":** Louis Beam, "Computers and the American Patriot," *Inter-Klan Newsletter & Survival Alert,* 1984, 1.

290 **Beam's bulletin board system:** Chip Berlet, "When Hate Went Online," 2001, 4.

290 **In the "Know Your Enemy" section:** Wayne King, "Computer Network Links Rightist Groups and Offers 'Enemy' List," *The New York Times,* February 15, 1985, 17.

290 **Pressing 8 would pull up:** Mike Williams, "Racist Group Threatens Morris Dees," *The Alabama Journal and Advertiser,* January 1, 1985, 1.

290 **Mathews flung the door:** Kevin Flynn and Gary Gerhardt, *The Silent Brotherhood: the Chilling Inside Story of America's Violent, Anti-Government Militia Movement,* 2016.

290 **"We've gathered good intelligence on him":** Thomas Martinez and John Guinther, *Brotherhood of Murder* (iUniverse, 1999), 168.

290 **In early 1983, he received:** Jesse Kornbluth, "The Woman Who Beat the Klan," *The New York Times Magazine,* November 1, 1987, 26.

291 **After a US attorney concluded:** "Letter from Lawrence Lippe to D. Broward Segrest, First Assistant U.S. Attorney," May 4, 1983, Southern Poverty Law Center case file.

291 **Two twenty-one-year-old men:** Richard E. Meyer, "The Long Crusade: Morris Dees Has Battled the Klan for More Than a Decade. Now His Target Is Tom Metzger and the White Aryan Resistance," *Los Angeles Times Magazine,* December 3, 1989, 20.

291 **they crept inside the center:** Meyer, "The Long Crusade."

291 **"This is the Montgomery Fire Department":** Morris Dees and Steve Fiffer, *A Season for Justice* (Simon & Schuster, 1991), 109.

292 **This was arson:** Rick Harmon, "Klansman a Suspect Hours After Law Center Burned," *Montgomery Advertiser,* February 28, 1985, 1.

292 **He quickly learned:** Dees and Fiffer, *A Season for Justice,* 203.

292 **Of all the posters:** Jerry Thompson, "KKK Suspected in Fire at Suing Law Firm," *The Tennessean,* August 3, 1983, 3-B.

293 **The New York Times ran a story:** "Fire Damages Alabama Center That Battles Klan," *The New York Times,* July 31, 1983, 25.

293 **Before long, the center announced:** May Lamar, "Legal Group Will Build $1 Million Law Center," *Montgomery Advertiser,* June 26, 1984, 1C.

293  A year later, in 1984: Flynn and Gerhardt, *The Silent Brotherhood*.

293  "You're going to have to leave here": Dees and Fiffer, *A Season for Justice*, 234.

294  And then an agent from the FBI: Dees and Fiffer, *A Season for Justice*, 235.

294  Starting at $20,000 a month: Laurence Leamer, *The Lynching* (William Morrow, 2016), 238.

294  On top of other death threats: "Text from Racist Bulletin Board Systems," February 6, 1993, http://www.bbsdocumentary.com/library/CONTROVERSY/EVIL/RACISTBB SES/sampletext.txt.

295  As it turned out: Meyer, "The Long Crusade," 22.

295  Dees told reporters: AP, "Klansmen Indicted in Fire at Law Center," *The Anniston Star*, December 13, 1984, 2D.

295  "Jesus Christ, there's someone": Morris Dees and Steve Fiffer, *A Lawyer's Journey: The Morris Dees Story* (American Bar Association, 2001), 2.

295  "Shoot the motherfucker!": Bill Shaw, "Morris Dees," *People*, July 22, 1991.

296  The officers fanned out: Email to Author from Morris Dees, April 3, 2020.

296  Dees wrote about her sacrifice: Dan Morse and Greg Jaffe, "Critics Question $52 Million Reserve, Tactics of Wealthiest Civil Rights Group," *Montgomery Advertiser*, February 13, 1994, 1.

296  In its early years: Dan Morse and Greg Jaffe, "Klan Focus Triggers Legal Staff Defection," *Montgomery Advertiser*, February 15, 1994, 4A.

297  "Our attention is on the Klan": Morse and Jaffe, "Critics Question $52 Million Reserve," 14A.

297  "The fund-raising letters": Morse and Jaffe, "Klan Focus Triggers Legal Staff Defection," 4A.

297  "I thought we had done": Morse and Jaffe, "Klan Focus Triggers Legal Staff Defection," 4A.

297  A juror married: "Sedition Juror Falls for Defendant," *Spokane Chronicle*, September 12, 1988, A3.

297  Another juror said: AP, "Juror from Supremacist Trial Admires Former Klan Leader," *Springfield News-Leader*, April 27, 1988, 11A.

297  "smash the fascists": Kelly McBride and Theresa Goffredo, "Marchers Make Their Point—Peacefully," *The Spokesman-Review*, April 23, 1989, 1.

297  By the end of the 1980s: Max Baker, "Smaller Klan Remains Large Threat, Foes Say," *Fort Worth Star-Telegram*, February 18, 1990, 22.

298  In 1989, the Southern Poverty Law Center's annual budget: Meyer, "The Long Crusade," 30.

298  Their financial reserves: Dan Morse, "A Complex Man," *Montgomery Advertiser*, February 14, 1994. 5A.

298  By 1994, the endowment: Morse and Jaffe, "Critics Question $52 Million Reserve."

298  The paper quoted Dees: Morse, "A Complex Man."

299  "probably the most discriminated people": Dan Morse, "Equal Treatment? No Blacks in Center's Leadership," *Montgomery Advertiser*, February 16, 1994, 6A.

299  Since selling his half of the company: Dennis Gale, "Jimmy Carter Calls Work 'Gratifying,'" *Rapid City Journal*, July 17, 1994, B1.

299  "Morris has a real flair": Morse and Jaffe, "Klan Focus Triggers Legal Staff Defection."

299  "The market is still wide open": Morse and Jaffe, "Critics Question $52 Million Reserve."

299  "He does not know how to treat people": Morse, "A Complex Man."

299  In the run-up to the *Advertiser's* series: Jim Tharpe, "Panel Discussion: Nonprofit Organizations," May 1999, Nieman Watchdog, http://niemanwatchdog.org/index.cfm

?fuseaction=about.Panel%20Discussion:%20Nonprofit%20Organizations%20May %2099.

300 **"the first lobbying that I know of":** Tharpe, "Panel Discussion."

300 **"That's just the way he deals":** Dan Morse and Greg Jaffe, "Groups Give Law Center Low Marks," *Montgomery Advertiser*, February 18, 1994, 9A.

300 **In 1994, in the wake:** Morse and Jaffe, "Critics Question $52 Million Reserve."

300 **"I want to go back to farming":** Morse, "A Complex Man."

300 **"police state":** Debbie M. Price, "Koresh Watch Draws Some Fools to the Hill," *Fort Worth Star-Telegram*, March 16, 1993, A6.

300 **Many suspected Beam was a co-conspirator:** Kathleen Belew, *Bring the War Home: The White Power Movement and Paramilitary America* (Harvard University Press, 2018), 228.

301 **"I have for 30 years":** "Extremism in America: Louis Beam," Anti-Defamation League, November 30, 1999, https://www.adl.org/news/article/extremism-in-america-louis-beam.

301 **By 2001, the SPLC's endowment:** Jannell McGrew, "Law Center Plans 'Wall of Tolerance,'" *Montgomery Advertiser*, July 5, 2001, 1.

301 **By 2010, the endowment:** Ken Silverstein, "'Hate,' Immigration, and the Southern Poverty Law Center," *Harper's*, March 22, 2010.

301 **By 2014:** Annual Report, Southern Poverty Law Center, 2014, 14.

301 **"No one has ever suggested":** Neena Satija, Wesley Lowery, and Beth Reinhard, "Years of Turmoil and Complaints Led the Southern Poverty Law Center to Fire Its Founder Morris Dees," *The Washington Post*, April 5, 2019.

301 **"Or an anachronism":** Satija, Lowery, and Reinhard, "Years of Turmoil and Complaints."

302 **Cohen resigned shortly thereafter:** Satija, Lowery, and Reinhard, "Years of Turmoil and Complaints."

302 **"I'm not ashamed to say I'm a salesman":** Diana Klebanow and Franklin L. Jonas, *People's Lawyers: Crusaders for Justice in American History* (M. E. Sharpe, 2003), 485.

302 **His old partner:** Chris Bernard, "Fuller Forced Out at Habitat for Humanity," *The NonProfit Times*, January 1, 2005.

302 **"The South is a complex place":** Morse, "A Complex Man."

302 **He said he's considering suing:** Author interview with Morris Dees, Montgomery, AL, August 7, 2019.

303 **"bearded men":** L. R. Beam, "'Clovis First' and the Mysterious Bearded Men of Pre-Columbian America," December 5, 2016.

303 **"falling in love with a Mexican girl":** "Letter from Sam Adamo to Morris Dees," June 23, 1983, Southern Poverty Law Center case file.

303 **"Might've been wrong":** *"Made" in America: Refugee Dreams, Refugee Nightmares*, KUHT Houston, produced by Ginger Casey, January 27, 1988.

304 **When he died:** Author interview with R. W. "Bill" Kerber, Kemah, TX, May 15, 2019.

305 **He keeps the ashes of his parents:** David Kaplan, "Vietnam Refugee a True Success Story," *Houston Chronicle*, April 29, 2005.

305 **"attempting to overthrow":** Eugene Whong, "Recently Released US Citizen Describes Mistreatment in Vietnamese Prison," Radio Free Asia, October 28, 2020.

305 **extensive lobbying:** "Orange County Man Freed from Vietnam Prison," MyNewsLA, October 26, 2020, https://mynewsla.com/crime/2020/10/26/orange-county-man-freed -from-vietnam-prison/.

306 **One Vietnamese family opened a seafood market:** Author interview with Lucy Turoff, Pasadena Historical Society, Pasadena, TX, March 29, 2019.

307 **Officials estimated the initial leak:** Cory McCord, "Ship Collides with Barges, Causing Massive Gas Product Spill in Houston Ship Channel," KPRC, May 11, 2019.

307 **"insurance job":** Author interview with David Collins, Kemah, TX, August 29, 2019.

308 **By the end of the year:** Perla Trevizo, "Hazardous Chemicals Remain in Water Long after ITC Fire," *Houston Chronicle*, November 4, 2019.

310 **the billionaire Taub family:** Author interview with Tom Hults, Kemah, TX, March 28, 2019.

310 **Most of the larger gulf trawlers:** Aaron Nelsen, "Texas Shrimpers Lack Seasonal Foreign Workers As Gulf Season Looms," *Houston Chronicle*, July 4, 2017.

310 **All the restaurants within sight:** Kate Hodal, Chris Kelly, and Felicity Lawrence, "Asian Slave Labour Producing Prawns for Supermarkets in US, UK," *The Guardian*, June 10, 2014.

310 **The most recent National Climate Assessment:** K. Kloesel et al., "2018: Southern Great Plains," in *Impacts, Risks, and Adaptation in the United States: Fourth National Climate Assessment*, vol. 2, ed. D. R. Reidmiller et al. (U.S. Global Change Research Program, Washington, DC), 987–1035, doi: 10.7930/NCA4.2018.CH23.

310 **"getting drowned in freshwater":** Meera Subramanian, "It's 'Going to End with Me': The Fate of Gulf Fisheries in a Warming World," *Inside Climate News*, December 28, 2018.

310 **"It's like I told 'em":** Author interview with Jody Collins, Kemah, TX, May 15, 2019.

# Index